T0326368

THE WINE VALUE CHAIN IN CHINA

ELSEVIER
ASIAN STUDIES SERIES

Series Editor: Professor Chris Rowley,
Cass Business School, City University, London, UK;
Institute of Hallyu Convergence Research, Korea University, Korea
Griffith Business School, Griffith University, Australia
(email: c.rowley@city.ac.uk)

Elsevier is pleased to publish this major Series of books entitled Asian Studies: Contemporary Issues and Trends. The Series Editor is Professor Chris Rowley of Cass Business School, City University, London, UK and Department of International Business and Asian Studies, Griffith University, Australia.

Asia has clearly undergone some major transformations in recent years and books in the Series examine this transformation from a number of perspectives: economic, management, social, political and cultural. We seek authors from a broad range of areas and disciplinary interests covering, for example, business/ management, political science, social science, history, sociology, gender studies, ethnography, economics and international relations, etc.

Importantly, the Series examines both current developments and possible future trends. The Series is aimed at an international market of academics and professionals working in the area. The books have been specially commissioned from leading authors. The objective is to provide the reader with an authoritative view of current thinking.

New authors: we would be delighted to hear from you if you have an idea for a book. We are interested in both shorter, practically orientated publications (45,0001 words) and longer, theoretical monographs (75,000−100,000 words). Our books can be single, joint or multi-author volumes. If you have an idea for a book, please contact the publishers or Professor Chris Rowley, the Series Editor.

Dr Glyn Jones
Email: g.jones.2@elsevier.com

Professor Chris Rowley
Email: c.rowley@city.ac.uk

THE WINE VALUE CHAIN IN CHINA

Consumers, Marketing and the Wider World

Edited by

ROBERTA CAPITELLO

STEVE CHARTERS

DAVID MENIVAL

JINGXUE (JESSICA) YUAN

AMSTERDAM • BOSTON • HEIDELBERG • LONDON
NEW YORK • OXFORD • PARIS • SAN DIEGO
SAN FRANCISCO • SINGAPORE • SYDNEY • TOKYO

Chandos Publishing is an imprint of Elsevier

CHANDOS
PUBLISHING

Working together
to grow libraries in
developing countries

www.elsevier.com • www.bookaid.org

Publisher: Glyn Jones
Acquisition Editor: George Knott
Editorial Project Manager: Tessa de Roo
Production Project Manager: Debasish Ghosh
Designer: Mark Rogers

Typeset by MPS Limited, Chennai, India

CONTENTS

Part II Consumers

Part III Markets and Distribution

Part IV China in the Wider World of Wine

Part V Final Reflections

LIST OF FIGURES

LIST OF TABLES

LIST OF CONTRIBUTORS

L. Agnoli
ESC Dijon/Burgundy School of Business, Dijon, France

T. Atkin
Sonoma State University, Rohnert Park, United States

G. Atwal
University Bourgogne Franche-Comté, Groupe ESC Dijon-CEREN, Dijon, France

D. Begalli
University of Verona, Verona, Italy

T. Bouzdine-Chameeva
KEDGE Business School, Bordeaux, France

R. Capitello
University of Verona, Verona, Italy

S. Charters
ESC Dijon/Burgundy School of Business, Dijon, France

S. Cholette
San Francisco State University, San Francisco, United States

J. Cohen
Ehrenberg-Bass Institute for Marketing Science, Adelaide, Australia

A.M. Corsi
Ehrenberg-Bass Institute for Marketing Science, Adelaide, Australia

N. Cunha
University of Aveiro, Aveiro, Portugal

L. Curran
Université de Toulouse, Toulouse Business School, Toulouse, France

Y. Fang
Northwest A&F University, Yangling, China

J. Fountain
Lincoln University, Lincoln, New Zealand

M.-A. Genand
Interprofessional Committee of the Wines of Champagne, Epernay, France

H. Han
Neoma Business School, Reims, France

J.H. Hanf
Geisenheim University, Geisenheim, Germany

K. Heine
EMLYON Business School, Lyon, France; EMLYON Business School,
Shanghai, China

H. Liu
James Cook University, Townsville, QLD, Australia

L. Lockshin
Ehrenberg-Bass Institute for Marketing Science, Adelaide, Australia

S.M.C. Loureiro
Instituto Universitário de Lisboa (ISCTE-IUL), Business Research Unit
(BRU/UNIDE) and SOCIUS, Lisbon, Portugal

B. Mazzinghi
Journalist and Consultant, Shanghai, China

B. McCarthy
James Cook University, Townsville, QLD, Australia

D. Menival
ESC Dijon/Burgundy School of Business, Dijon, France

V. Seidemann
University of Rostock, Rostock, Germany

G. Szolnoki
Geisenheim University, Geisenheim, Germany

M. Thorpe
Curtin Business School, Curtin University, Perth, Australia

P. Winter
Georg Müller Stiftung, Eltville am Rhein, Germany

H. Yang
Northwest A&F University, Yangling, China

J. Yuan
Texas Tech University, Lubbock, TX, United States

L. Zeng
Geisenheim University, Geisenheim, Germany; University of South Australia,
Adelaide, Australia

W. Zhang
KEDGE Business School, Bordeaux, France

X. Zhang
Northwest A&F University, Yangling, China

M. Zhu
Shenzhen Tourism College of Jinan University, Guangzhou, Guangdong, China

ABOUT THE EDITORS

Roberta Capitello is Associate Professor in Agricultural Economics at the University of Verona (Italy), Department of Business Administration, where she teaches courses on wine economics and food and wine marketing. Her special research interests are in consumer behaviour, marketing and communication in the wine industry. Her recent publications include journal articles and book chapters on the analysis of wine consumer decision-making process, with focus on emerging wine markets, food and wine consumer behaviour, online communication, destination branding and wine tourism. She can be contacted at roberta.capitello@univr.it.

Steve Charters is Director of Research in the School of Wine and Spirits Business, ESC Dijon/Burgundy School of Business in Dijon, France. He was previously Professor of Champagne Management at Reims Management School and before that taught at Edith Cowan University in Perth, Australia. He develops research projects and courses relevant to the wine business generally. His research interests include the relationship of wine to place, drinker perceptions of quality in wine, the mythology surrounding wine consumption, the motivation to drink, and the motivations and experience of the wine tourist. He is a member of the editorial board of the *Journal of Wine Research*, the *British Food Journal* and the *International Journal of Wine Business Research* and is one of only 350 members of the Institute of Masters of Wine in the world. He can be contacted at steve.charters@escdijon.eu.

David Menival is director of the Champagne industry for a regional Bank, Crédit Agricole du Nord Est, and Professor expert for the Burgundy School of Business, France. He obtained a PhD in economics in 2008 from the University of Reims. He focuses both professionally and academically on champagne. His academic research is mainly focused on the quality signals and value creation of wines, the creation and/or improvement of reputation, generational habits and the impact of wine tourism on the future sales of wine. His current publications look at the role and the evolution of territorial brands in wine industry. He can be contacted at david.menival@ca-nord-est.fr.

Jingxue (Jessica) Yuan is Associate Professor of Hospitality Management at Texas Tech University, Lubbock, TX, USA. Her spectrum of research interests includes consumer behaviour in wine tourism, wine tourism marketing and wine festivals and events. Her record of publications includes book chapters on global wine tourism and food/wine festivals/events around the world and numerous scientific articles on analyzing wine tourist behaviour, marketing wineries and wine festivals in the cyber space and investigating consumer perceptions of wine label design. Recently Dr. Yuan has published two articles in top-tier research journals investigating the phenomenon of wine tourism in China and Chinese wine tourist behaviour. She can be contacted at jessica.yuan@ttu.edu.

ABOUT THE CONTRIBUTORS

Lara Agnoli is Associate Professor at the School of Wine and Spirits Business, Burgundy School of Business, Dijon in France. Previously, she has worked as a research fellow at the University of Verona (Italy) for 6 years. She holds a Ph.D. in Wine Economics and Rural Development from the University of Florence in 2010. Her research focuses on wine and food consumer decision-making process and behaviour, choice modelling and demand analysis. She can be contacted at lara.agnoli@escdijon.eu.

Thomas Atkin is Professor of Operations and Supply Chain Management at Sonoma State University where he teaches in the Wine Business Programme. He received his Ph.D. in Supply Chain Management from Michigan State University in 2001 after a 25 year career in management. His research interests include customer−supplier relationships, sustainable business practice, wine consumer preferences, and international wine logistics. He has published in *International Journal of Wine Business Research*, *Negotiation Journal*, *Journal of Business Logistics* and *Journal of International Food and Agribusiness Marketing*. He can be contacted at tom.atkin@sonoma.edu.

Glyn Atwal is Associate Professor of Marketing at Burgundy School of Business, France. His teaching, research and consultancy expertise focuses on luxury marketing and strategy. He is coeditor of *Luxury Brands in Emerging Markets* (Palgrave Macmillan). Prior to academia, Glyn worked for Saatchi & Saatchi, Young & Rubicam and Publicis. He can be contacted at glyn.atwal@escdijon.eu.

Diego Begalli, Ph.D., is Professor in Agricultural Economics at the University of Verona (Italy), Department of Business Administration. He has more than 25 years of academic experience in the field of agribusiness and food and wine marketing. He teaches courses in Wine Business Management and Wine Marketing. His research activity is focused on agro-food business management, consumer behaviour, and wine and food products branding. His recent publications include articles on collective brand strategies in food and wine territorial systems, wine consumers' behaviour, and analysis of impacts of climate change on wine businesses performance. He can be contacted at diego.begalli@univr.it.

Tatiana Bouzdine-Chameeva is Senior Professor of Information and Decision Sciences at KEDGE Business School. She holds a Ph.D. in Applied Mathematics from Moscow University, Russia. She defended the two habilitation thesis — in IS in Russia and in management in France. For several years she was a head of the Wine and Spirits Management Academy research team in Bordeaux. Her research is in wine markets, wine distribution channels, strategic decisions, performance efficiency and sustainability in wine sector. She authored several case studies on wine and spirits (sake) as well as tourism industry. Tatiana is involved in numerous interdisciplinary studies with research teams from US, UK, Australia, New Zealand and Japan. She received honorary membership and awards from the prestigious JSPS (Japan Society for the Promotion of Science). Tatiana publishes in top journal such as *Decision Sciences*, *Operation Research*, *Journal of Retailing* and *Supply Chain Forum*. She can be contacted at tatiana.chameeva@kedgebs.com.

Susan Cholette is a Professor of Decision Sciences in the College of Business at San Francisco State University. Prior to her university appointment, she served as a project manager at Nonstop Solutions (now Manhattan Associates) and as a supply chain consultant for Aspen Technologies. She earned her Ph.D. in Operations Research at Stanford University and her B.S.E. in Electrical Engineering at Princeton University. Her research focuses on supply chain efficiency and sustainability, especially for the food and beverage sectors, and some of her earlier contributions appear in *Interfaces*, *International Journal of Production Research*, *International Journal of Production Economics*, Journal of Cleaner Production, *Informs Transactions on Education*, *Supply Chain Forum: an International Journal*, *Journal of Optimization Theory and Applications*, *Journal of International Journal of Pricing and Revenue Management*, *International Journal of Wine Business Research*, *Journal of Consumer Marketing*, *Journal of Global Marketing*, *International Journal of Wine Marketing* and *Economia Agro-Alimentare*. She can be contacted at cholette@sfsu.edu.

Justin Cohen is a marketer with experience in Asia, Europe and North America developing high level global collaboration with stakeholders. Expertise is in route-to-market decision making, emerging markets (in particular China), retailing, online advertising, luxury brand, wine & food marketing. He can be contacted at justin.cohen@marketingscience. info.

Armando Maria Corsi is Senior Research Associate at the Ehrenberg-Bass Institute for Marketing Science, and the Programme Director for the Master of Marketing at the University of South Australia Business School. His research focuses on wine and other premium and luxury products, and examines consumer behaviour for wine and food products, packaging and retailing. For the past four years Dr Corsi has been chief investigator of some major projects examining the effects of non-price promotions in store, tracking the ever changing Chinese wine market, improving the techniques to describe wines to Asian consumers, and exploring the most effective ways to teach them about wine. Armando has authored more than 40 refereed journal and trade articles on food and wine marketing. He can be contacted at armando.corsi@marketingscience.info.

Louise Curran is Senior Lecturer in International Business in Toulouse Business School (TBS) in France. She received her Ph.D. from Manchester Metropolitan University in 1995. Her research interests include the interactions between government policy and trade and investment flows, EU trade policy making and EU−China trade relations. She has published widely on these issues including in the *Review of International Political Economy*, the *Journal of Business Ethics* and the *Journal of World Trade*. She can be contacted at l.curran@tbs-education.fr.

Yulin Fang, Ph.D., is Professor and the Associate Dean of the College of Oenology at the Northwest Agriculture & Forestry University in Yanglin, Shaanxi Province, China. He is currently serving as the Associate Director of the Wine Grape Association of Shaanxi Province, China. Prof. Fang is the reviewer for an array of internationally-circulated academic journals such as Food Chemistry and Food Research International. His research has been focused on oenology and viticulture. He has been the PI or co-PI of more than 20 research projects sponsored by national or provincial grants. He has published more than 130 research articles, including 22 SCI and EI papers, and edited five textbooks. He has obtained six Invention Patents. He can be contacted at fangyulin@nwsuaf.edu.cn.

Jo Fountain is a Senior Lecturer in Tourism Management at Lincoln University, New Zealand. Her research interest in wine, and wine tourism, dates back more than a decade and encompasses a range of contexts, including New Zealand, Australia, France and China. Her wine tourism research has focused primarily on visitors' expectations and experiences of wine tourism, however more recent projects have explored the perceptions and motivations of the suppliers of the wine tourism experiences. As a member of a number of cross-cultural teams, she has undertaken research on wine consumption and wine socialization experiences, and the consumer perceptions of the image of different wine varieties. She can be contacted at joanna.fountain@lincoln.ac.nz.

Marie-Anne Humbert Genand is graduated in intellectual property law from the Panthéon-Assas University (Paris II) in 2008. She started her career as an in-house lawyer and in private practice. In 2010 she joined the Comité Champagne, responsible for protecting the appellation of origin "Champagne" worldwide. She is now the Head of the legal department of the Comité Champagne. She can be contacted at marie-anne.humbert-genand@civc.fr.

Huaiyuan Han is Associate Professor of International Economics at NEOMA Business School, France. His research interests are in wine market and corporate social responsibility in China. He has written books, cases studies and academic articles concerning Chinese market and economy. He obtained his Ph.D. from the University of Reims Champagne-Ardenne. He can be contacted at huai-yuan.han@neoma-bs.fr.

Jon H. Hanf holds the Chair of International Marketing Management at Geisenheim University, Germany. He is head of all wine economic programs on B.Sc and M.Sc level. Before starting to work at Geisenheim University he has been the head of the Marketing Research Group of Leibniz-Institute of Transition Economics in Halle (Saale), Germany. He received his habilitation as well as doctorate at the Justus-Liebig University Giessen, where he worked as the manager of the institute on cooperative research. He received his diploma in Business Economics at the University of Stuttgart-Hohenheim. Overall, Jon has published more than 100 peer-reviewed articles in Strategic Management, Vertical Coordination, & Cooperation and Internationalization. Additionally, he also worked as a consultant for the World Bank, FAO and GIZ. His first visit to Asia has been in 1978 and since then he returned frequently to numerous countries in Asia (including China) on business purpose but also for vacation. He can be contacted at jon.hanf@hs.gm.de.

Klaus Heine introduced the first luxury marketing course offered at a German university at TU Berlin in 2006. Since his doctoral dissertation he specializes in luxury brand-building and especially in the identity of luxury brands. He conducted the first millionaire survey in Germany about their luxury preferences as well as many other qualitative and quantitative luxury consumer surveys in Europe and China. As a luxury marketing professor at EMLYON business school in Lyon and Shanghai, he combines applied-oriented research with lecturing about luxury brand management and practical projects with a big variety of companies from luxury start-ups to leading luxury brands from France, Germany and China. He can be contacted at heine@em-lyon.com.

Hongbo Liu is a Senior Lecturer in Economics at College of Business, Law & Governance, James Cook University, Australia. She is specializing in resource and environmental economics, health economics and welfare economics, with particular interests in food consumption and its impacts, in tourism and in economic development. Her recent research applies her economics expertise to analyze a few issues in gerontology. She has led and participated projects in both Australia and China. She can be contacted at hongbo.liu@jcu.edu.au.

Larry Lockshin is Professor of Wine Marketing and Head of the School of Marketing at the University of South Australia. He has a Ph.D. from Ohio State University in Marketing and an M.Sc. from Cornell University in Viticulture. He has published over 120 academic articles; over 250 trade articles and has a book on wine marketing, *This Little Pinot Went to Market*. His research interests are consumer choice behaviour for wine including how extrinsic and intrinsic factors interact. He also works on packaging and shopping behaviour for consumer goods. His research extends to measurement issues in understanding consumer behaviour. He is currently working on several consumer wine-related projects in China and instore behaviour in Australia. He can be contacted at larry.lockshin@marketingscience.info.

Sandra Maria Correia Loureiro is Professor at the University Institute of Lisbon and a researcher in the UNIDE and SOCIUS research centres. Her current research interests include consumer-brand relationship, online environment and tourism experience. Her papers were published in a variety of peer reviewed journals, such as International journal of *Hospitality Management, Journal of Travel & Tourism Marketing, Journal of Service Management, Journal of Brand Management* or *Journal of Cleaner Production* and at well reputed international conferences, such as EMAC, ANZMAC, GAMMA-GMC, World Marketing Congress. She also won the Best Paper Premier Award 2012 of the GAMMA-Global Marketing Conference (comprises EMAC, ANZMAC, KSMS and Japan association of marketing) and the Highly Commended paper award at the 7th EuroMed Conference. She can be contacted at sandramloureiro@netcabo.pt.

Bianca Mazzinghi is an Italian journalist and a wine professional and writer. She studied Chinese language and culture at University and, after some years working as a journalist in Italy with magazines and news agency, in 2013 she decided to move to China to continue her professional career. She worked first for a local wine importer, then for the popular wine magazine and Wset school Tastespirit. During the last three years she travelled in more than 20 cities for business reasons, developing a solid knowledge of the country and its expanding wine sector. Wine educator and Wset level 3 holder, she is in her second year of the Wset Diploma. She currently cooperates with different companies, medias and Wset recognized schools in Italy, China and South America. She can be contacted at bianca8809@gmail.com.

Breda McCarthy is a Senior Lecturer in Marketing at James Cook University (Australia), with research interests in sustainable food systems, ethical consumption, wine consumption, cultural enterprises and the strategic marketing activities of small to medium sized enterprises. She has published conference papers, journal articles, book chapters and case studies. She employs quantitative and qualitative research methodologies and has a particular interest in grounded theory and the longitudinal, case-based approach to research. She is committed to developing cases for teaching purposes. She can be contacted at breda.mccarthy@jcu.edu.au.

Namércio Pereira da Cunha is a business consultant and holds Ph.D. in Marketing and Strategy at the University of Aveiro, Portugal. He has published in the Journal of International Food and Agribusiness Marketing and has also participated in scientific conferences such as EMAC, EuroMed Conference and Circle Conference. His research deals with the relationship quality of an exchange business-to-business relationship, particularly in wine industry. He can be contacted at namercio@gmail.com.

Vera Seidemann is a postdoctoral researcher in consumer behaviour at University of Rostock, Germany. She can be contacted at vera.seidemann@uni-rostock.de.

Gergely Szolnoki grew up in Hungary and studied agricultural sciences — specializing in marketing — at the Szent Istvan University in Gödöllö, Hungary. He went to Germany in 2003 and finished his Ph.D. at the Justus Liebig University in Giessen on the topic "Influence of packaging and sensory evaluation of wine on the willingness to buy". He is an associate professor at the Geisenheim University where he focuses on research fields such as consumer behaviour, market analysis, wine sensory, and social media. He teaches both in undergraduate and in M.Sc. programs as well as supervises Ph.D. students. He has published several articles and books in German, English and Hungarian. He can be contacted at gergely.szolnoki@hs-gm.de.

Michael Thorpe is currently an Adjunct Professor with the Curtin Business School in Western Australia. He has researched widely in the areas of international trade, investment and finance, with a focus on China and the East Asian region as well as the economies of the Arabian Gulf. His work has been published widely in numerous books and international refereed journals and he has worked as an academic and consultant in a number of countries, including France, the United Arab Emirates, China, Vietnam, Singapore, Malaysia, Hong Kong, Taiwan and Mongolia. He served as the President of the Economic Society of Australia (WA) for 5 years and has held a number of editorial positions on international academic journals. He can be contacted at michael.thorpe@cbs.curtin.edu.au.

Peter Winter is the owner of Weingut Georg Müller Stiftung, Germany. He bought the estate in 2003. The estate was founder member of the VDP, Association of German Predicate Estates in 1910. Prior to Peter Winter becoming a winegrower he worked for four decades for WIV Wein

International AG, Germany, the last 17 years as President. When Peter Winter left WIV in 2003 it was the 7th largest wine company in the world. He can be contacted at peter.winter@georg-mueller-stiftung.de.

Hecai Yang is an associate professor of marketing at the College of Ecology, the Northwest Agriculture & Forestry University in Yanglin, Shaanxi Province, China. His research interests include economic analysis of wine industry, wine culture and wine marketing. He was the editor-in-chief of *Regulations of Wine Production & Wine Market* and also an editor of four volumes of Enterprise Management. He has conducted more than 10 research projects and published more than 30 research articles. He received two major research awards granted by the provincial government. He can be contacted at hecaiyang@nwsuaf.edu.cn.

Lishi Zeng is a Ph.D. candidate in marketing and research associate at Geisenheim University and Ehrenberg-Bass Institute for Marketing Science at University of South Australia. She works on projects funded by wine authorities all around the world with an emphasis on understanding consumer behaviour in emerging wine markets. Her current research looks into wine adoption among Chinese consumers. She completed her M.Sc. in viticulture and oenology at Montpellier SupAgro and Geisenheim University in 2014. Besides academic research, she also worked in the industry across Europe and China, under different cultural contexts. Her knowledge of wine industry covers from vine to wine, and cellar to consumer's glass. She can be contacted at lishi.zeng@hs-gm.de.

Wenxiao Zhang is currently a Ph.D. student in KEDGE Business School, France. After getting a Master degree in marketing from the University Paris XIII, Wenxiao worked in the "Wine and Spirits' Management Academy" research group with Tatiana Bouzdine-Chameeva. Her thesis focuses on Chinese wine market development and wine distribution channels' structure, and she has published her first article in 2014 in Asian Journal of Management research. For several years Wenxiao was a Vice president of Yan Tai Wu Chao Red Wine Co. Ltd., responsible for importing wines from France, Italy, Spain and selling them to Chinese customers. Then she worked in Hong Kong, and moved afterwards to Ningxia. Wenxiao is a deputy secretary in the International Federation of Vine and Wine of Helan Mountain's East Foothill: the eastern side of the Helan

Mountains in Ningxia has been proven to be a most promising wine producing area! She can be contacted at wenxiao.zhang@kedgebs.com.

Xiaorong Zhang is an associate professor at the Department of Foreign Languages, the Northwest Agriculture & Forestry University. She received her MA degree in linguistics from the Chinese University of Hong Kong. Her research interests include second language acquisition, syntax and studies on public speaking. She is a member of Asia TEFL Association. She hosted several research projects and teaching reform projects, including Inter-Language Study in Second Language acquisition and An Innovation in the Teaching of Advanced English. She has published over 20 papers on key research journals. She is the chief English editor of the official website of the Northwest Agriculture & Forestry University. She can be contacted at zhangxiaorong@nwsuaf.edu.cn.

Mingfang Zhu is an Associate Professor of Tourism Management in Shenzhen Tourism College, Jinan University. Her research interests are mainly on destination marketing, tourist behaviour and wine consumption behaviour. She can be contacted at zhu_mf@sz.jnu.edu.cn.

ACKNOWLEDGMENTS

We would like to thank the reviewers of the book chapters: Nelson Barber, Maureen Benson-Rea, Alessio Cavicchi, Armando Corsi, Huaiyuan Han, Per Jenster, Chris Taylor and Bruna Zolin. Their efforts have greatly contributed to improve the quality of this book through their feedback, corrections and suggestions.

We are grateful to the publisher Elsevier and in particular to George Knott, Acquisitions Editor, Tessa de Roo, Editorial Project Manager and Debasish Ghosh, S&T Book Production Project Manager, for their contribution to the development and publication of this book.

Finally, we must acknowledge the patience and understanding of our families for the time and energy expended in trying to bring this book to fruition.

R. Capitello, S. Charters, D. Menival and J. Yuan

PART I

Context

CHAPTER 1

Introduction

S. Charters[1], J. Yuan[2], R. Capitello[3] and D. Menival[1]
[1]ESC Dijon/Burgundy School of Business, Dijon, France
[2]Texas Tech University, Lubbock, TX, United States
[3]University of Verona, Verona, Italy

THE RISE OF WINE IN CHINA

For almost 20 years now China has been touted as 'the next big thing' in wine; first in consumption and more recently for its production. Its potential impact has become mythologized; that is, it takes on a meaning beyond mere reality to explain otherwise hidden developments and portents. This is partly because it is a large nation and barely known within the key international centres of wine production around the world (a factor magnified by the fact that it is only in the last 30 years that it has been perceived in the West to be 'emerging'). In addition, there is also a dearth of concrete statistical data about wine in the country (which would reduce the reliance on stories) and what does exist seems to be of uncertain accuracy. Yet the narratives that abound seem to underline its strange nature when compared to traditional wine cultures. For example, the mixing of Chateau Petrus with Sprite, the number of bottles of Chateau Lafite sold in the country each year well in excess of local production, or the fact that some of its wine regions are so cold in winter that the vine trunks need to be buried.

We term these stories 'myths' not because they are not true (they probably all are) but because they represent an important representation of the 'otherness' of China for the traditional cultural shapers of wine production and consumption. Consequently it is because of this mythology that we consider the time is ripe for a book that examines the engagement of China and the Chinese with wine. There has already been a growing amount of research into the wine market in China (see below), and rather less about wine production in the country, but these studies need to be moved on further so that academics studying the engagement of the Chinese with wine and practitioners seeking to deal effectively with the country have a clearer view about it and less reliance on stories — however quaint they may seem.[1]

This work focuses on mainland China although Hong Kong, as a major point of entry and a more 'Westernized' market (thus easier for Europeans and Anglo-Saxons to deal with) is inevitably significant and addressed at various stages throughout. The greater Chinese area — including Taiwan and even Singapore — is significant as part of the overall impact of the culture on the changing wine markets of east Asia, but their inclusion would have made an already complex subject even more difficult, and so have been excluded.

WHAT DOES EXISTING RESEARCH TELL US ABOUT CHINA?

Literature (i.e., articles written in English language and published in referred academic journals) based on research studies developed explicitly and empirically to address Chinese wine consumption/consumers began to emerge after 2005, when China became the world's fastest-growing wine market. The rapid development of wine consumption in China can be attributed to many reasons, but is primarily due to ever-increasing household incomes and a change of lifestyle by the middle class. Interestingly, in an effort to preserve national stocks of rice for the production of food rather than alcohol, government policies and campaigns have been promoting wine-drinking, contributing in part to the upsurge of wine sales and wine consumption (Mitry et al., 2009; Moslares and Ubeda, 2010). With media attention to wine spreading on the rise, an increase in wine consumption in general and higher demand for complex and high-quality wine, academic studies on the Chinese wine market built on empirical evidence have been slowly but steadily rising (see Table 1.1).

Currently, wine is still seen as a luxury good and image product in China (Agnoli et al., 2014; Liu and Murphy, 2007; Muhammad et al., 2013; Xu et al., 2014). The symbolic association of wine with an affluent and trendy Western lifestyle, social status and prestige was mentioned in nearly every academic article on Chinese wine consumption. Apparently

[1] In fact their very quaintness or naivety may be one way of trying to give a sense of control over what is, to some from traditional wine countries, a potentially threatening awakening; a wine culture that is not necessarily subject to Western norms and expectations.

Table 1.1 A Summary of Empirical Studies on Chinese Wine Consumers

Author(s)	Date	Methodology	Sample size	Major findings
Balestrini and Gamble	2006	Interviewer-administered (structured) questionnaire in Shanghai, China	100	Quality was ranked most influential, followed by country-of-origin (COO), in wine purchasing decision by Chinese wine consumers. COO is given more credit when wine buyers purchase wine for special occasions rather than private consumption.
Liu and Murphy	2007	In-depth interviews and a semi-structured questionnaire of open-ended questions in Guangzhou, China	15	For Chinese consumers, wine means red wine. Red wine's health aspect and good social image were important attributes by the subjects. Chinese consumers drank red wine on special occasions. Chinese consumers had little wine knowledge and purchased foreign red wine on important occasions.
Heathcote and Barlow	2007	Wine sensory tasting of nine wines and self-completion questionnaire in Shanghai, China and Melbourne, Australia	129	This preliminary investigation into the taste preferences of Chinese wine consumers for red wine, and cross-cultural differences between the wine markets in Shanghai and Melbourne found that Chinese in Shanghai are less likely to consume wine at home with a meal.
Hu, Li, Xie, and Zhou	2008	Questionnaire at shopping malls in Shanghai and Hangzhou, China	148	COO effect is generally important when Chinese consumers evaluate wine. COO is more important than brand as an indicator of wine quality when Chinese consumers evaluate wine for special occasions, gift-giving and in consuming in public.

(*Continued*)

Table 1.1 (Continued)

Author(s)	Date	Methodology	Sample size	Major findings
Lee, Huang, Rozelle, and Sumner	2009	Direct observation and survey in supermarkets in eight Chinese cities	61	Chinese consumers buy more red wine than white wine and have chosen sweet wine or wine with very high alcohol content. A lack of knowledge about premium wine existed in Chinese consumers.
Yu, Sun, Goodman, Chen and Ma	2009	Questionnaire from wine consumers ("now" market) and from university students (market coming "on-line") in Beijing	230 122	Subjects intend to pay a low price for "daily use" wine and higher prices for wine intended for gift-giving. Chinese wines were the top choice in terms of CCO influence. The four most influential wine purchase attributes are to have tasted the wine previously, origin, brand name and a recommendation.
Li, Jia, Taylor, Bruwer and Li	2011	Highly-structured questionnaire from 54 universities in 28 provinces in China	414	Most Chinese young adults lack even the most basic wine knowledge and prefer red wine to white wine. They like to drink wine at home. They drink wine for social communication or for health. Females are more knowledgeable about wine and express more positive interest in future wine-drinking than males.
Somogyi, Li, Johnson, Bruwer and Bastian	2011	Four focus groups with ethnic Chinese wine consumers residing in the Adelaide area, Australia	36	Chinese wine consumers are influenced by face and status. They believed red wine was particularly good for their health. Wine consumers are choosing to drink wine (or mix it with soft drinks) due to its lower alcohol content than other alcoholic beverages.
Camillo	2012	Online survey in over 30 major cities in China	438	Chinese consumers perceive all good wine to be red and when consumed or given or received as a gift, it causes *mianzi* (face). Taste, COO, and quality associated with brand recognition ranked highest. Wine, particularly red wine, is a healthy beverage.

Authors	Year	Data	N	Findings
Williamson, Robichaud and Francis	2012	A set of 14 Australian and international wines assessed for hedonic liking by consumers in Beijing, Shanghai and Guangzhou	310	Two consumer clusters (80% of the consumers) preferred sweeter wines and had low acceptance to wines with strong acidity. The third cluster liked wines with higher purple colour, and had a lower liking score for wines with higher astringency. Years of consumption of wine are linked to preferences.
Muhammad, Leister, McPhail and Chen	2013	Monthly China Customs data on wine imports (quantities, values and prices) from the World Trade Atlas database	Jan. 2002 to Dec. 2011	A greater preference is found for wine from traditional Old World suppliers, Italy and France. Future imports will likely come from the largest and oldest wine-producing counties, France and Italy. The growing consumption of French and Italian wine is likely due to limited wine knowledge.
Lin and Tavoletti	2013	Survey of wine consumers in Beijing, China	779	Respondents drink wine because of social intercourse needs, mental relaxation and improvement of life and taste. Respondents are most likely to drink wine in restaurants, at home, in karaoke and bars. Most participants would choose to buy imported wine as a gift. Respondents receive information about wine via internet, TV and magazines.
Liu, McCarthy, Chen, Guo and Song	2014	Online survey on Chinese wine consumers in various regions of China	407	Three segments are revealed based on benefit segmentation: extrinsic, intrinsic and alcohol level attribute-seeking. In addition, the market can be segmented according to preferred sources of information: the traditional word-of-mouth sourcing, the traditional media information source and the new media/social network information sourcing.

(Continued)

Table 1.1 (Continued)

Author(s)	Date	Methodology	Sample size	Major findings
Xu, Zeng, Song and Lone	2014	Consumption choice data about domestic-made wines and imported wines from France and the USA	540	Price remains the most important factor affecting Chinese wine choices. Chinese wine drinkers tend to favour expensive wines for public occasions and inexpensive wines for their own consumption. COO matters to the Chinese consumer. US wines are found to be a good substitute for Chinese wines but neither US nor Chinese wines are a good substitute for French wines. Chinese consumers admire French wines for consumption as well as for gift purchases. Chinese consumers have a strong preference for branded wine and wines that have a longer age, both for family uses and for gift purchases.
Agnoli, Capitello and Begalli	2014	Monthly data for import quantity and value from Eurostat and the United Nations Commodity Trade Statistics Database	January 2005 to July 2012	Chinese consumers are distinctively (1) characterized by price sensitivity towards nongeographically branded wines and COO wines with low reputation; (2) differentiation-oriented – assessing imported wine as a luxury product; (3) linked to leading European geographical brands.
Yang and Paladino	2015	Online survey from Chinese wine consumers	617	COO and ethnocentrism significantly impacted on the formation of purchase behaviour toward wine as a gift. A negative relationship was found between perceived product image and attitudes/ purchase intention of gift-giving of wine.

Source: Adapted from Ye, H.B., Zhang-Qiu, H., and Yuan, J., 2016. Intentions to participate in wine tourism in an emerging market: theorization and implications. J. Hosp. Tour. Res. Published online 5 March 2014. http://dx.doi.org/10.1177/1096348014525637-O.

wine-drinking is considered a gesture of gracefulness and elegance and reveals classiness and good taste. Wine has even become a so-called "trophy drink" for the newly rich (Hu et al., 2008). Further, Chinese consumers see foreign-made wines as a symbol of exotic food culture, sophistication and fashion (Agnoli et al., 2014; Xu et al., 2014). The volume of wine imports in China has increased by an astonishing 26,000% in the decade from 2000 to 2011, and import demand for expensive wines has consistently increased in particular (Muhammad et al., 2013). Chinese consumers hold French wine in high regard, more than any other source of exports (Lin and Tavoletti, 2013; Muhammad et al., 2013; Yang and Paladino, 2015; Zhang-Qiu et al., 2013).

In addition to the symbolic meanings attached to wine, another underlying motivation for wine-drinking appears to be based in indigenous Chinese culture and has became a fundamental component to the Chinese wine-drinking culture, the existence of which still needs to be substantiated. This motivation is connected with the wine itself as many Chinese people consider red wine solely when they consume the product. Red wine initially gained more popularity than white wine because red is the colour of luck in traditional Chinese culture; hence the perceived connotation of red wine with prosperity and good fortune (Liu and Murphy, 2007; Somogyi et al., 2011; Xu et al., 2014). Red wine is thus more often seen at important occasions such as state or business banquets, celebration of Chinese New Year, and/or eating out with people of significant status. However, there is another intriguing phenomenon in the alleged Chinese wine-drinking culture also related to red wine. The extended beliefs about and attraction of red wine's heart-healthy benefits can be found in every published article discussing the Chinese wine market and wine consumers. This notion of wine consumption for health-related purpose was linked loosely to traditional Chinese medicine, in which distilled spirits containing Chinese herbs are consumed to assist in improving physical health (Somogyi et al., 2011).

To date, the Chinese market remains red wine oriented (90% of total consumption) (Agnoli et al., 2014). However, the trend is gradually changing. White wines have more recently penetrated the market, with a strong preference showcased for German imports from areas specializing in white wine (Agnoli et al., 2014).

A strong wine culture still awaits development in China (Heathcote and Barlow, 2007; Jenster and Cheng, 2008; Moslares and Ubeda, 2010). While the country is proud of its long history of local gastronomic culture, referred to as the "drinking and eating culture," the practice of matching wine with Chinese-style food has been difficult (Ye et al., 2016). As novice and nontraditional wine drinkers, Chinese consumers are not well sophisticated in the area of wine culture and only slowly developing a palate for higher quality wine (Lee et al., 2009; Moslares and Ubeda, 2010).

Interestingly, the overall profile of Chinese wine consumers has undergone little change during the last ten years. Chinese consumers generally have poor knowledge about wine (Li et al., 2011; Liu and Murphy, 2007), despite the fact that some consumers are indeed becoming more knowledgeable and willing to participate in wine-related activities (Camillo, 2012; Liu et al., 2014). Chinese consumption of wine still predominantly takes place at special occasions (Balestrini and Gamble, 2006; Hu et al., 2008; Liu and Murphy, 2007). When purchasing wine, Chinese consumers use European territorial brands or Country of Origin (COO) cues considerably (Agnoli et al., 2014; Balestrini and Gamble, 2006; Williamson et al., 2012; Yu et al., 2009). The prominence of "group conformity" and "normative influence" affect Chinese consumers' wine gift-giving behaviour when they place brand, COO, price and gift packaging on top of the list (Yang and Paladino, 2015). Nevertheless, small groups of loyal wine enthusiasts in major urban areas have become the driving force behind the development of the industry (Lee et al., 2009) and it is possible that a fundamental change in attitudes and demand for wine is developing (Lin and Tavoletti, 2013; Muhammad et al., 2013). The potential of the "Chinese wine market" is enormous.

THE STRUCTURE OF THIS STUDY

We have tried to make this book as broad and as valuable as possible. It is an academic study, but also includes contributions by two nonacademic authors which we have considered valuable for readers of all backgrounds for the insights they offer. It is primarily a book about business, markets and management, but again, in order to give context for the business focus, some of our authors examine other areas such as the impact of the legal processes and regulations on wine businesses and the development of wine production in the country. It is also produced from a multinational perspective. Many of our contributors are of Chinese origin, but Italian, Australian, German, American, British, Portuguese, French, Hungarian,

New Zealand and Russian researchers also feature — allowing for multiple cultural perspectives on a complex emerging wine market.

Part 1 of this book, as well as including this introduction, also provides a context for what follows. Thus Chapter 2, Some Fundamental Facts about the Wine Market in China (by Lishi Zeng and Gergely Szolnoki), gives some basic and essential insights to the operation of the Chinese wine market, including its size and distribution and the historical development and (crucially) the recent social framework which have started to reshape it. This is followed by a short explanation of the legal framework within which the wine industry operates in China, kindly provided by Marie-Anne Genand who is Head of the Legal Department of the Interprofessional Committee of the Wines of Champagne.

Part 2 'Consumers' deals with the Chinese wine market. Gifting remains a key part of Chinese culture and a cement for social relations, so that even with the recent crackdown on corruption it remains a significant area for study, as Vera Seidemann, Glyn Atwal and Klaus Heine demonstrate. Joanna Fountain and Zhu Mingfang then offer specific insights into young Chinese consumers who (as the book demonstrates repeatedly) are the key generational drivers of wine consumption in the country. This is followed by three chapters that consider different cues to wine choice: an analysis of store image perception provided by Armando Maria Corsi, Justin Cohen and Larry Lockshin; the significance of location with a study on regional differences in perceptions of territorial (regional) brands by David Menival and Huaiyuan Han; and an investigation of wine purchasing behaviour with a focus on young and wealthy wine drinkers by Hongbo Liu and Breda McCarthy.

Part 3 is more widely about markets and distribution. Jon Hanf and Peter Winter contribute a chapter on the market entry strategies of small and medium sized wine estates, specifically using the case study of a producer in the Rheingau which is quite small but has been in the market for over a decade. There is then an analysis of wine distribution channels in the country (Tatiana Bouzdine-Chameeva, Jon Hanf and Wenxiao Zhang) and a consideration of relationship management in distribution channels, focusing particularly on Portuguese wine producers and their Chinese distributors, by Sandra Maria Correia Loureiro and Namércio Cunha. Finally, Susan Cholette and Tom Atkin consider some specific problems around the shipping of wine to China and how they could be overcome.

China in the wider world of wine, which is the topic for Part 4, is potentially a huge topic, which we only have space to touch on generally. However, it is important to show that China is now significant, not just because of domestic consumption but because the Chinese are now moving into the wider world, both as tourists (Roberta Capitello, Lara Agnoli, Steve Charters and Diego Begalli) and as investors — as Louise Curran and Michael Thorpe demonstrate in a comparative study of Bordeaux and Western Australia.

We conclude with some final reflections on China and wine generally. We have sought a nonacademic and specifically practitioner-focused viewpoint on the issues around being in the market, to balance the more scholarly approach, and this is given by Bianca Mazzinghi, who spent some years working in distribution in the country. This piece was a snapshot from early 2016. It will date — but it still underlines how variable the market is and how much subject to rapid changes. It is focused on those seeking to export there, but has insights for academics and those interested in other aspects of the market and wine's growing role in the country. This part also includes an invited piece from an academic who works outside the field of wine business. Professor Yulin Fang from Northwest A&F University is one of the country's most noted wine scientists. From his technical stance he observed the growth of wine in China for over 20 years now, and so together with two colleagues (Hecaui Yang and Xiaorong Zhang) there is an overview of the development of the Chinese wine industry. Although China is primarily viewed internationally as a consuming country, the fact that it is now one of the top ten wine-producing countries in the world with, from 2014, the second largest vineyard area of any nation, means that its wines are going to be significant internationally at some point in the future. This is therefore an appropriate point at which to offer practitioners an insight into how production has been developing and where it might be going in the future. After this, the final chapter is our conclusion, as editors, on what this book has achieved, and the key points which can be taken from it.

REFERENCES

Agnoli, L., Capitello, R., Begalli, D., 2014. Geographical brand and country-of-origin effects in the Chinese wine import market. J. Brand Manag. 21 (7/8), 541—558.

Balestrini, P., Gamble, P., 2006. Country-of origin effects on Chinese wine consumers. Br. Food J. 108 (5), 396—412.

Camillo, A.A., 2012. A strategic investigation of the determinants of wine consumption in China. Int. J. Wine Bus. Res. 24 (1), 68−92.

Heathcote, E.N., Barlow, E.W.R., 2007. China's emerging wine market − a cross-cultural analysis of consumer taste preferences. Aust. N. Z. Wine Industry J. 22 (3), 86−90.

Hu, X., Li, L., Xie, C., Zhou, J., 2008. The effect of country-of-origin on Chinese consumers' wine purchasing behavior. J. Technol. Manag. 3 (3), 292−306.

Jenster, P., Cheng, Y., 2008. Dragon wine: developments in the Chinese wine industry. Int. J. Wine Bus. Res. 20 (3), 244−259.

Lee, H., Huang, J., Rozelle, S., Sumner, D., 2009. Wine markets in China: assessing the potential with supermarket survey data. J. Wine Econ. 4 (1), 94−113.

Li, J.-G., Jia, J.-R., Taylor, D., Bruwer, J., Li, E., 2011. The wine drinking behavior of young adults: an exploratory study in China. Br. Food J. 113 (10), 1305−1317.

Lin, H., Tavoletti, E., 2013. The marketing of Italian wine brands in China: the "mainstreaming" approach. Transit. Stud. Rev. 20, 221−237.

Liu, F., Murphy, J., 2007. A qualitative study of Chinese wine consumption and purchasing: implications for Australian wines. Int. J. Wine Bus. Res. 19 (2), 98−113.

Liu, H.B., McCarthy, B., Chen, T., Guo, S., Song, X., 2014. The Chinese wine market: a market segmentation study. Asia Pac. J. Mark. Logistics 26 (3), 450−471.

Mitry, D.J., Smith, D.E., Jenster, P.V., 2009. China's role in global competition in the wine industry: a new contestant and future trends. Int. J. Wine Res. 1, 19−25.

Moslares, C., Ubeda, R., 2010. China's wine market: strategic considerations for Western exporters. Int. J. Chin. Cult. Manag. 3 (1), 69−84.

Muhammad, A., Leister, A.M., McPhail, L., Chen, W., 2013. The evolution of foreign wine demand in China. Aust. J. Agric. Resour. Econ. 58, 392−408.

Somogyi, S., Li, E., Johnson, T., Bruwer, J., Bastian, S., 2011. The underlying motivations of Chinese wine consumer behavior. Asia Pac. J. Mark. Logistics 23 (4), 473−485.

Williamson, P.O., Robichaud, J., Francis, I.L., 2012. Comparison of Chinese and Australian consumers' liking responses for red wines. Aust. J. Grape Wine Res. 18, 256−267.

Xu, P., Zeng, Y.C., Song, S., Lone, T., 2014. Willingness to pay for red wines in China. J. Wine Res. 25 (4), 265−280.

Yang, Y., Paladino, A., 2015. The case of wine: understanding Chinese gift-giving behavior. Mark. Lett. 26, 335−361.

Ye, H.B., Zhang-Qiu, H., Yuan, J., 2016. Intentions to participate in wine tourism in an emerging market: theorization and implications. J. Hosp. Tourism Res. Published online 5 March 2014. <http://dx.doi.org/10.1177/1096348014525637-O>.

Yu, Y., Sun, H., Goodman, S., Chen, S., Ma, H., 2009. Chinese choices: a survey of wine consumers in Beijing. Int. J. Wine Bus. Res. 21 (2), 155−168.

Zhang-Qiu, H., Yuan, J., Ye, B.H., Hung, K., 2013. Wine tourism phenomena in China: an emerging market. Int. J. Contemp. Hosp. Manag. 25 (7), 1115−1134.

CHAPTER 2

Some Fundamental Facts about the Wine Market in China

L. Zeng[1,2] and G. Szolnoki[1]
[1]Geisenheim University, Geisenheim, Germany
[2]University of South Australia, Adelaide, Australia

INTRODUCTION

According to the Organization Internationale de la Vigne et du Vin (OIV) in 2014 (Aurand, 2016), world wine production reached 28 billion litres, with global wine consumption estimated at 24 billion litres. In the Old World, traditional wine producing countries like France produced 4.7 billion litres, whilst French consumers drank 2.8 billion litres. Within the same period, Germany produced 0.9 billion litres and imported 1.5 billion litres, but consumed 2 billion litres. In the New World, Australia produced 1.2 billion litres, whilst consumption was a mere 0.5 billion litres. Many other countries that have a relatively long history in wine making, and drinking, are facing a similar situation: supply (production and import) exceeds demand. In established markets, the wine category remained stable, while in emerging markets, the category grew by both volume and value sales. Fig. 2.1 illustrates that emerging markets, where consumers drink much less wine per capita than their established counterparts, are the main force to drive the global wine market growth. Therefore, reaching these consumers is likely to contribute positively to the global wine category.

When it comes to emerging markets on a global scale, China is a good example. According to Euromonitor International (2015b), China has experienced double-digit growth for nearly a decade. However in 2013, the Chinese import wine market experienced its first decline of 4% by volume and 3% by value, shrunk to 377 million litres, which is worth 9.6 billion renminbi (approx. 1.5 billion USD). In 2014, *Wine Intelligence* (Su, 2014) reported that there were 38 million import wine drinkers who consumed import wine at least twice a year. This figure had doubled from the 2011 report, and by 2015, the trade data from General

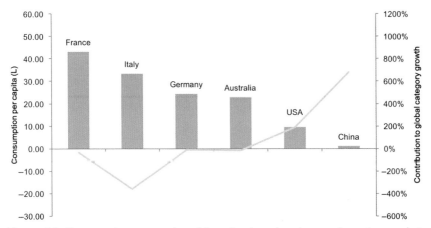

Figure 2.1 Consumption per capita of key developed and emerging wine markets and their contribution to global wine market growth in 2014. *Source: OIV 2016,* © *Euromonitor International 2016, elaborated by the authors.*

Administration of Custom (GAC) witnessed the recovery of the import wine sector with 43% growth in import volume. The import wine industry was saved by the increasing number of import wine consumers.

However, the power of the rapid growth and the frangibility behind the sharp decline still remains unclear.

Therefore, this chapter aims to take a macro view of the Chinese import wine market within a longer timeframe to understand its past and present, and foresee its future opportunities and challenges. It starts with a macro assessment of the political, economic, social and technological factors; discusses the alcoholic drink market and further explores the wine market; and finishes with a snapshot about the import wine sector, based on secondary research. Specific wine consumer behaviour will not be covered in detail.

THE MACRO ENVIRONMENTAL CONTEXT IN CHINA

Political and Legislative Factors

The following political and legislative factors focus on the degree to which the Chinese government has influenced the wine industry. Some of them are part of the government's strategic plans for the industry, such as the Four Changes, which affect the long-term direction of industrial development. Some others are not part of the industrial policies but have affected the wine industry indirectly for a shorter term, such as the anti-corruption campaign.

The 'Four Changes' Strategy

Drinking alcohol has been part of Chinese culture for thousands of years. Long before the wine industry took off at the beginning of the 20th century, the Chinese had formed their habit of drinking grain spirit and grain wine (Cochrane et al., 2003). The Chinese government considered preserving grain produce as a food source rather than an alcohol source, and concerned about the health and social problems aroused by high-strength alcoholic drinks. In 1987, the National Winemaking Conference proposed the Four Changes strategy for the alcoholic beverage industry, which was the change from high-strength alcohol to low-strength alcohol, from distilled wine to fermented wine, from low-end wine to high-end wine, from grain wine to fruit wine. Grape wine belongs to fermented fruit wine, therefore the development of the grape wine industry benefited from the support of the national strategy (Li et al., 2009). In 2002, the State Economic and Trade Committee also announced their focus on the development of grape wine and other fruit wine. This pushed the development of low-strength rice wine, keeping the development of beer industry stable, and controlling the total production of high-strength rice spirits (Yang and Fang, 2008). Later in this chapter a figure presents the alcoholic drink market structure which will further demonstrate the positive influence of national strategy on the development of the grape wine industry. Thus, the nation accelerated the development of the grape wine industry.

New National Wine Standard

On the 1st January 2003, the State Economic and Trade Committee implemented the new Chinese Wine Technical Specifications. At the same time, the old industrial standard of half base wine (QB/T 1980−94) expired, and all the half base wine was required to be taken off shelves before 30th June 2004 and be removed from the grape wine category. The half base wine contained at least 50% grape fermented base wine and other ingredients, usually sugar or juice. Consequently, half base wine was sweet and cheap. Most of the consumers from older generations, particularly around the traditional wine growing regions in the north, were accustomed to half base wine and took it as a reference for wine. In 2006, according to the Chinese Wine Technical Specifications and OIV's definition of wine, the new national standard of wine (GB 1503-2006), replacing the old one (GB/T 15037-94), defined wine as being made by a complete or partial alcoholic fermentation of fresh grapes or grape juice. Consequently, China's wine standards were brought into line with international ones.

Anticorruption Campaign

Wine facilitates social exchange and creates a sophisticated and serious atmosphere. It is commonly served at Chinese business banquets especially when women attend. The more valuable food and drink the host offers, the greater the respect is shown. This may lead to lavish spending of public or corporate funds on business-related entertainment and gifting. As early as April 2012, a government campaign against such phenomena in the public sector was initiated. One year later, the new Chinese president Mr. Xi Jinping made anticorruption and modest living his political platform, which was followed by arresting a series of corrupt officials. These actions had a ripple effect on hotels and restaurants where this kind of state-related business entertainment usually took place, as well as the luxury goods sector like fine wines which were preferred gifts instead of cash bribes. The country was under the atmosphere of antiostentatiousness. Before one of the two main wine sales peaks, the Mid-Autumn Festival in September 2013, officials were too scared to receive gifts, such as moon cakes and alcoholic beverages. In some government institutions, the reception offices were filled with unclaimed gifts, as reported by a local newspaper one day before Mid-Autumn Festival in 2013 (Lu, 2013). Anticorruption has been making noise for a long time, but the increasing awareness of citizenship of the people and the explosive growth of social media has made public surveillance possible and popular, according to John Watkins, CEO of the leading importer ASC Fine Wines (Mustacich, 2013). He notes, "The last thing a mayor wants to do is to be seen with a real-estate developer at a restaurant, have his picture taken and have it gone on the Chinese version of Twitter". Inevitably, the anticorruption movement has not only had an effect on fine wines, but also most of the category (Mustacich, 2013).

Economic Factors

Macroeconomic Situation

In the early 21st century, China had a remarkable economic development, with the annual Gross Domestic Product (GDP) growth rate above 10%, even reaching 14% in 2007 (Fig. 2.2). Economic growth was the focus of that era, at the price of the sustainability of many other aspects, including the environment. However, such production-fuelled and investment-driven growth reached its ceiling. The figure is expected to drop further, but the growth will be more sustainable, balancing development in all aspects. China is stepping onto a new stage of growth, which is called *the New Normal* by President Xi Jinping.

Meanwhile, China's Consumer Price Index (CPI) has been fluctuating. The inflation level has cooled in recent years, as Fig. 2.3 outlines.

Chinese currency appreciated (Fig. 2.4), the exchange rate of USD to renminbi fell, especially between 2007 and 2008 with a drop of 9%. By March 2016, the exchange rate slightly rose up to 6.5 renminbi for 1 USD. The value of the Chinese currency has direct effects on the cost of insurance and freight (CIF) of imported wine. The appreciation of currency has partially compensated for the rise of price due to domestic inflation.

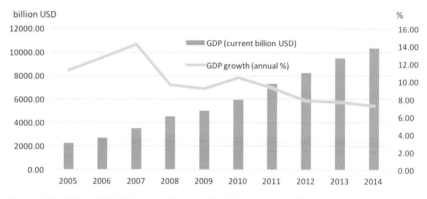

Figure 2.2 China GDP 2005—14. *Source: World Bank 2016, elaborated by the authors.*

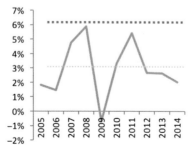

Figure 2.3 China Consumer Price Index growth rate 2005—14. *Source: World Bank 2016, elaborated by the authors.*

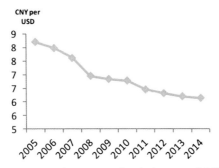

Figure 2.4 Chinese currency exchange rate (period average) 2005−14. *Source: World Bank 2016, elaborated by the authors.*

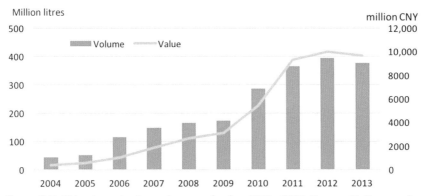

Figure 2.5 China import wine volume and value 2004−2013. *Source: © Euromonitor International 2016, elaborated by the authors.*

Reduction of Import Tax and Free Trade Agreement

Since January 1st 2006, the tariff of import bottled wine decreased from 43% to 14% (total tax rate from 85.9% to 48.2%, including value-added tax and consumption tax), and bulk wine decreased from 43% down to 20% (total tax rate from 85.9% to 56%).

As shown by Fig. 2.5, the volume and value of import wine hit a turning point in 2006 and entered a period of dramatic growth. The lower cost of import wine became more and more competitive with domestic wine in terms of the price/quality ratio, evidenced by the increasing share of imported wine of the whole wine market, from 4% in 2006 and then 21% in 2010.

Of course, such rises were credited to Free Trade Agreements (FTAs). In 2016, a total of three FTAs have been signed that are relevant to wine trade between China and Chile, New Zealand and Australia. Early in 2005, China signed the first wine-related FTA with Chile. Import tax of bottled wine from Chile reduced from 14% to 0 in the following 10 years. In 2016, bottled wine from Chile is free of import tax. In 2008, wines from New Zealand became the second beneficiary of FTA with China. Import tax of New Zealand wine decreased to 0 in 2012. The third one is with Australia. From 2016 to 2019, Australian wine entering into China will gradually become tax free. Thus, the reduction of import tax and FTAs boosted the import wine sector and changed the composition of import country of origin (COO), as our detailed discussion will present.

With the double benefits of Chinese currency appreciation and reduction of import tax, imported wine has become more competitive than domestic wine.

Social Factors

World Bank data in 2016 shows that in the past decade, China's population remained relatively stable between 1.3 and 1.4 billion. But the demographic profile, such as age distribution and the urban/rural population percentage varied. Between 2010 and 2011, the urban population exceeded the rural population. In a report from McKinsey (Barton et al., 2013), the urban consumers who have annual household incomes from 106,000 to 229,000 renminbi are defined as upper-middle class. This segment accounted for 20% of urban households in 2002 and is expected to increase to 56% in 2022. The difference of this transformation is dwarfed by the mass middle class who have an annual household income from 60,000 to 106,000 renminbi. The middle class of sophisticated consumers who seek quality will soon emerge as the dominant force. Such prediction of consumption upgrade has been reported in a recent report from Nielsen on mobile devices (Nielsen, 2016). Besides, the geographic presence of this upper-middle class will move from Tier 1 to Tier 3 cities, from coastal regions to inland areas.

More consumers are able to afford wines.

Technological Factors
Wine Education

In 1985, Northwest Agriculture and Forestry University started to enrol students for viticulture and oenology study. In 2011, China Agricultural University and four more universities joined the crew, providing bachelor programs in viticulture and oenology or wine science. Some of these universities also offer postgraduate wine programs (Tao et al., 2012). A certain amount of students will look for further wine study overseas when they graduate. Also there are increasing academic communication and exchanges between domestic universities and foreign academic institutions, which provide human capital for the development of wine industry in China. Within the universities and institutions, grape and wine research commonly focuses on wine region classification, grape breeding, viticulture mode selection and oenological techniques (Li et al., 2009).

In 2005, Escent Wine, a leading company in wine education and market research based in Beijing, first introduced the Wine and Spirits Education Trust (WSET) into mainland China. It became the first Approved Programme Provider (APP) of the WSET in mainland China. From here, the WSET has made efforts to penetrate into the market by customizing its course into the local language.

Besides the WSET, other wine professional certificates are becoming more and more popular in China, such as Master of Sommelier, ISG and Australia A$^+$. Due to the popularity of wine, certificated wine drinkers are becoming the opinion leaders in industry.

Technical Innovations

The buying behaviour of Chinese consumers is changing with the adoption of new technologies, namely those based on IT innovations. Progress on e-commerce and social media provides a new route to marketing. According to Kuo et al. (2015), e-commerce stimulates new consumption by increasing product variety and availability, and will account for 45% of total consumption in the next 5 years. According to a report by Nielsen, the online market size of the wine category grew 71%, approaching the share of hypermarket sales in 2015 (Nielsen, 2015). Wine sales channels are the most digitalized among all the alcoholic categories.

E-commerce, coupled with social media tools, simplifies the process of reaching, engaging and interacting with end users for business. This emerging trend is particularly essential to wine industry with the target of mass consumers.

However, rather than overtaking the attention of physical retailers, the integration of on-line and off-line is intended to create a seamless experience for consumers (Van Bommel et al., 2014). For example, you see an interesting bottle advertised on TV, try it in the nearest retail shop, do more research to find the best deal online, place an order with a digital payment system, have it delivered to your home the next day, and share the consumption experience on social media or in person.

Summary

This section focuses on the analysis of the macro environment of China. The influence of these macro factors on the wine market is inevitable but also out of marketers' control. In the reviewed decade the anticorruption campaign and threats aroused by economic slowdown has threatened the Chinese wine industry and forced it to fight for survival in a challenging market reality. The trade is getting less dependent on the old model of earning a high margin from traditional sales channel built on *guanxi* (a Chinese term loosely referring to interpersonal connections) (Fan, 2002), and concentrating on developing a new growth strategy based on reaching more new wine consumers. What is more, such transformation sails with the wind of the growing upper-middle class which has gained stronger purchasing power, and with the internet innovations. The Chinese wine market is expected to grow in a more sustainable way as the national economy does. The environmental context seems to be providing fertile soil for the cultivation of a new wine market − the detail of which we will now explore further.

ALCOHOLIC BEVERAGE MARKET IN CHINA
Market Size

According to Euromonitor International (2015a), the alcoholic drinks market in China doubled its size from 30 billion litres in 2002 to 60 billion litres in 2012. In 2006, the market reached a growth peak at 12% but then slowed down after 2008. It settled at a stable growth rate of 6% for a few years and was then followed by a further slow-down to 1% growth in 2013. The market size, both in volume and value, has remained stable since then. In 2014, the market worth 61 billion litres and 1200 trillion renminbi was the biggest alcoholic drinks market in the world.

Market Composition

In terms of the structure of the alcoholic beverage market, beer is the predominant category, followed by spirits, nongrape wine, and grape wine (Fig. 2.6).

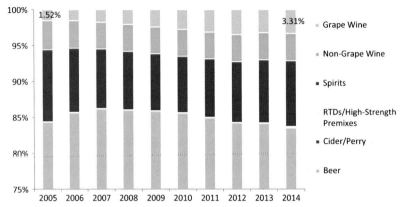

Figure 2.6 Alcoholic beverages market share by categories 2005–14.
Note: The categories "RTDs/High-strength Premixes" and "Cider/Perry" account for very little market share so that they are not shown in the figure. *Source: © Euromonitor International 2016, elaborated by the authors.*

In the past decade, the share of the beer category has gone through ups and downs. The growth of the beer category size has continuously slowed, from the peak of 14% in 2005 to 0 in 2014. The spirit category has been impacted by the anticorruption campaign and the economic growth slowdown too. The main players in the spirit category launched affordable new products targeting the mass consumers as an immediate reaction, and the category has started to grow slowly again since 2007. The share of the nongrape wine category remains stable. It has grown along with the general alcoholic drink market. The most noteworthy categories are ready to drink (RTD)/high-strength premixes and grape wine. The market size of RTD/high-strength premixes category, as a newly emerged category, has kept flying with a double-digit growth rate, and exploded to 140% from 2013 to 2014. Credit for this goes to the substantial investment in advertising by big brands to increase the penetration of the category into entertaining occasions among young consumers. Such explosive growth is also related to the way that Chinese people adopt foreign spirits. Blending favourable sweet green tea into whisky is a simple, direct, and effective way to mask the bitter flavour and to dilute the burning sensation from high volume alcohol. Such methods have also been applied in the grape wine category or anything that is not taste-friendly. The RTD/high-strength premixes even further simplified this need.

Grape wine is another category with double-digit growth. Its weight in the alcoholic drinks market increased from 1.5% in 2005 to 3.3% in 2014.

It is hard to estimate the ceiling of the category share according to other established markets in Asia because the alcohol market structure varies in different markets; such variance exists among different regions in China as well.

Regional Markets

China is a country covering 9.6 million square kilometres of land divided into 33 administrative divisions with a population of 1.4 billion. A simplified view that considers China as one market may lose the internal dynamic of the market reality.

The East, North and Northwest and Middle China are the top three regional markets, followed by the South, Southeast and Northwest. Generally speaking, people in the North drink more alcoholic beverages than those in the South.

The evolution of regional markets follows the mainstream of the grand national market, but at the same time, regional markets retain their own market structure (Fig. 2.7). For instance, as shown in Fig. 2.7, people drink more beer in the South, the North and Northeast than in other regions, because there are big local breweries within the region such as Tsing Tao Beer and Harbin Beer in the Northeast, and Zhujiang Beer in the South. Spirits makes up the highest share in the Southwest due to the allocation of the capital of Chinese high-strength grain spirits, Guizhou, within the region. In the Northwest, people are used to drinking spirits

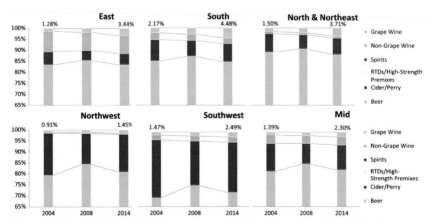

Figure 2.7 Regional alcoholic beverage market share by categories 2004—14. Note: the percentage number on top of the column indicates the share of grape wine category out of the overall alcoholic drink category. *Source: © Euromonitor International 2016, elaborated by the authors.*

from grain to keep warm in response to the cruel climate. In the eastern plains, low-strength rice/grain wine is part of the tradition. Generally speaking, inland consumers prefer spirits and high-strength alcoholic drinks like rice/grain spirits; coastal residents favour milder alcoholic beverages such as beer and wine.

In the eastern coastal developed regions (top 3 in Fig. 2.7), the share of the grape wine category has doubled in the past decade. It has grown faster than those in the western inland developing area (bottom 3 in Fig. 2.7). As the geographic centre of the emerging upper-middle class shifts towards inland regions and with the assistance of e-commerce, the share of the grape wine category in the western inland developing area should be expected to have bigger space for growth than their developed counterparts on the eastern coast. The alcoholic drinks market in the Middle China region is bigger than in the South, but Middle China only drinks half of the grape wine volume of that consumed in the South. This part of growth may further contribute to the nation-wide grape wine category growth.

PROFILE OF THE OVERALL WINE MARKET IN CHINA

Market Size

From 2005 to 2014, China's wine market size has quadrupled in volume, from 547 million litres to 2 billion litres. Its value size grew even faster after 2007, reaching 134 billion renminbi in 2014. Chinese consumers are drinking more expensive wine than previous years (Fig. 2.8).

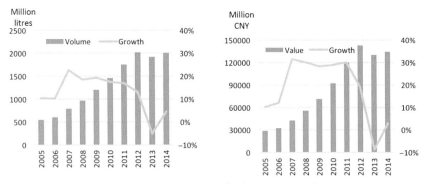

Figure 2.8 China market sales by volume and value 2005−14. *Source:* © *Euromonitor International 2016, elaborated by the authors.*

In 2014, the North and Northeast market contributed the most volume, reported to be at 625 million litres. The East market recorded 0.4 million litres less but earned the most value, documented at 47 billion renminbi, followed by the North and Northeast at 39 billion renminbi. The sales from the South were 394 million litres and 28 billion renminbi. The rest of the country only had a mere 373 million litres in volume and 21 billion renminbi. The Northwest market is the smallest market unsurprisingly, with 42 million litres and 2 billion renminbi, as it is the most rural area with the least population.

Distribution Channels

Wine sales channels changed dramatically in 2013. According to the statistics by Euromonitor International (2016) (Fig. 2.9), the share of on-trade channels slumped 10% between 2013 and 2014. The sharp change may have been influenced by the anticorruption campaign. Sales through off-trade channels continued to grow with the increasing interest of at-home consumption because of the rise of the affluent upper–middle class and the adoption of e-commerce.

When breaking down the data into regional markets, variations exist. The share of the on–premises channel is higher in eastern and southern coastal markets than in inland regions. Therefore, understanding of local dining habits in these areas is important.

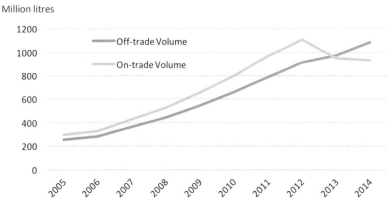

Figure 2.9 Wine sales volume: on-trade vs. off-trade. *Source:* © *Euromonitor International 2016, elaborated by the authors.*

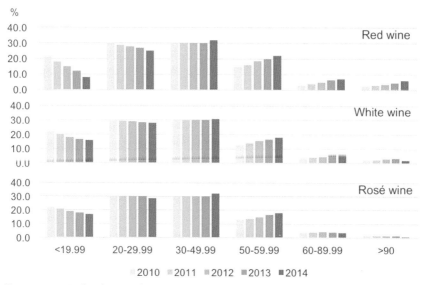

Figure 2.10 Red, white and rosé wine sales by price segments, off-trade 2010–14. *Source: © Euromonitor International 2016, elaborated by the authors.*

Price Segments

The mainstream retail price is between 20 and 50 renminbi. Fig. 2.10 outlines a trend where the share of wine sold below 30 renminbi is decreasing while the segment over 50 renminbi increased. Chinese consumers favour wines priced higher than 50 renminbi, which may explain why value growth of the wine market has increased compared to volume growth.

Fig. 2.10 shows that the willingness to pay more for better quality red wine, which may not be applied to white and rosé wine. In 2014, the segment of white wine over 90 renminbi and those over 60 renminbi for rose wine decreased.

Wine Types

Red still wine dominates the Chinese wine market, accounting for 72% of the total market in 2014 (Fig. 2.11). Since 2012, red still wine sales have decreased while sales of sparkling wine, still white and rosé wine have continually increased. The decreasing share of red wine may be impacted by the government constraints on extravagant expenditure of public funds on business entertainment where premium red wine was usually served.

Notably, sparkling wine reached a market volume of 12 million litres, which is over 10 times of the size of the subcategory only a decade ago.

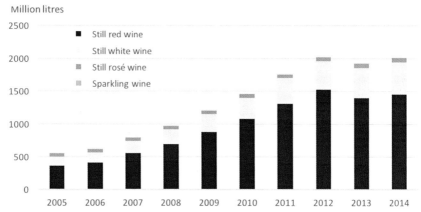

Figure 2.11 China wine sales by wine type 2005−14. *Source:* © *Euromonitor International 2016, elaborated by the authors.*

It has been increasing at a growth rate of between 45% and 55% since 2010. This may be due to an increase of foreign sparkling wine in the market; also because the image of sparkling wine fits on the auspicious occasions where Chinese people like to celebrate and entertain with alcohol. White still wine reached the sales volume of 491 million litres in 2014, with a slow growth of 7%. Rosé wine has maintained a slow annual growth rate between 2% and 4% for the past decade.

Regional markets share the same patterns as the national market, only differing slightly in terms of the share of rosé wine. Rosé wine has not penetrated into the Mid and Northwest market as yet.

Grape Varieties

In the Chinese market, the main red varieties are Cabernet Sauvignon, a blend of Cabernet Sauvignon and Syrah, Merlot and Muscat *Hambury*. The white grapes are Chardonnay, Dragon Eye and Riesling (Fig. 2.12). Merlot and Riesling have become popular in the past 5 years.

Domestic Wine Production

According to data from OIV (Aurand, 2016), China produced 1.2 billion litres of grape wine, making it the fifth biggest wine producing country in the world with a total vine growing surface of 799 thousand hectares. The volume of wine production increased by 2.4% in 2012, followed by a decline of 12.8% in 2013 and 1.6% in 2014. Production may have the potential to grow with the increasing yield from new vineyards.

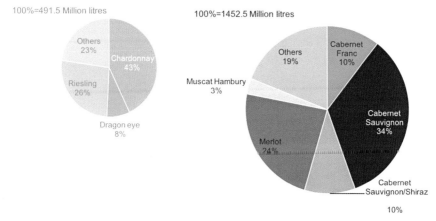

Figure 2.12 China wine sales by grape varieties 2014. *Source:* © *Euromonitor International 2016, elaborated by the authors.*

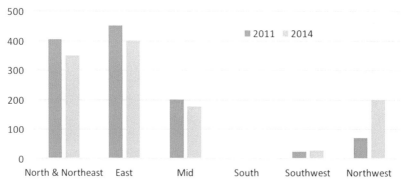

Figure 2.13 Regional wine production in volume 2012 and 2014. *Source: AskCIData 2014, elaborated by the authors.*

Wine production regions in China spread across the north of the country from the eastern coast to the western desert. According to data from AskCIData, in 2014 the humid east coast, where the biggest player Changyu is located, contributed the greatest wine production for China with a volume of 400 million litres (Fig. 2.13). The North and Northeast region produced 350 million litres. This region includes big commercial players like The Great Wall as well as boutique wineries such as Grace Vineyard. Due to its high latitude, it is very cold in winter so the vines have to be buried into the soil to survive for the winter. In subregions like Liaoning, the temperature is low enough to produce ice wine. The Ningxia wine region, which is situated further inland within the

Northwest area, rose as a new superstar with worldwide recognition. Its potential for high quality Chinese wine has attracted investment into the region. Its production tripled over a three-year period. This region benefits from abundant sun light and heat but also suffers from extreme climatic conditions. In addition to the rising fame of the Ningxia region, the Xinjiang region has also started to prove its potential for better quality wines within the region. Down south in Yunnan, which is located at a high altitude with a distinctive meso-climate, is one of the rare wine growing areas in the Southwest.

Often it is commented that China's terroir causes difficulties in viticulture practice and high costs in wine production. This makes it not an ideal place for wine making. However, the increasing quality of Chinese wine has been proved in international challenges thanks to the improvement of viticulture and oenology techniques, industrial standards, increased financial investment, the devotion and passion of young professionals, as well as healthy competition with import wine. All these factors inject new blood into China's domestic wine industry.

Main Players

In 2014, the three major players in the Chinese wine market were Yantai Changyu Group Co., Ltd, COFCO Ltd. and Citic Guoan Group, which make up 3.2%, 2.8% and 1% of total market share by volume, respectively. These three companies represent the brands Changyu, Great Wall and Suntime, together accounting for 7% brand share of the wine category. Both the company and brand share of Changyu and COFCO have decreased in the past five years, while Citic Guoan took over the third position from Yantai Weilong Grape Wine Co Ltd (Euromonitor International, 2015b).

These top three players produce wine from their own vineyards, contract grape growers, or bulk wine from Chile, Australia, South Africa and so on. They act as importers for bottled wine at the same time. They also invest in vineyards and wineries overseas. However, the wine market is becoming increasingly competitive with more new entries, thus the shares of these main players is in decline.

EXPLORATION OF THE IMPORT WINE MARKET
Market Size

The import wine sector has experienced high speed growth since 2009 with annual growth of 65% between 2009 and 2010, and 28% between

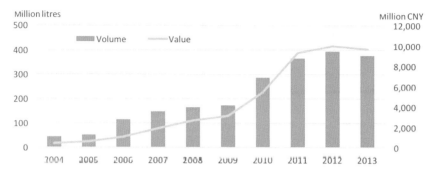

Figure 2.14 China import wine market size by volume and value 2004−2013. NB: The statistics by GAC for 2014 and 2015 are not included in this graph because they are international trade data but sales data. *Source:* © *Euromonitor International 2016, elaborated by the authors.*

2010 and 2011 (Fig. 2.14). In 2013, both import volume and value decreased. According to the latest statistics released by the GAC of China, 583 million litres of wine was imported in 2015, which represented a 43% increase compared to 2014. Wines from most of the COOs had a double-digit growth, especially Australia which has started to benefit from the FTA with China.

The market share of import wine has been increasing for the past years, from 2% in 2002 to 25% in 2011. Regarding the reduced domestic wine yield and the strong recovery of trade volume, the share of import wine sales is expected to grow in the near future.

Country of Origin

The French wine industry has made a strong marketing effort to gain penetration with a wide portfolio, and has become the leading player in the Chinese imported wine sector since 2010. The share of COO is highly susceptible to FTA. A jump in volume and value as well as share growth for Chile and Australia were evident in the first year when the FTAs were implemented. As shown in Fig. 2.15, before 2005, Chile dominated the import wine market with bulk wine import in volume. In 2007, one year after the reduction of import wine tax due to the bilateral FTA between Chile and China, the market share of Chilean wine doubled but has since cooled. Meanwhile, Chile, Australia and Spain have continued to fight for their market positions. According to GAC trade statistics, Australian wine recorded 56.46% growth in import volume and 77.74% increase of import value in 2015, the first year when the

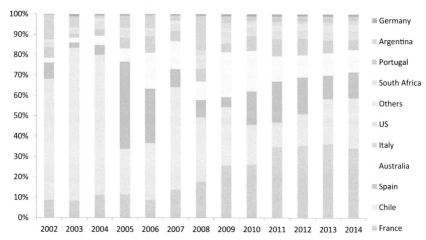

Figure 2.15 China import wine market share by countries of origin in volume 2002–14. *Source: © Euromonitor International 2016, elaborated by the authors.*

Table 2.1 Wine supply balance sheet by volume (billion litres) in China 2008–12

	2008	2009	2010	2011	2012
Production	1.26	1.28	1.30	1.32	1.35
Import	0.16	0.17	0.29	0.37	0.39
Export	0.01	0.00	0.00	0.00	0.00
Consumption	1.40	1.45	1.52	1.63	1.71
Pro. + Imp. − Exp. − Con.	0.01	0.00	0.07	0.05	0.03

Source: OIV 2014, elaborated by the authors.

China—Australia FTA was executed. The export of premium Australian wine benefited greatly from the FTA.

Since 2010, the COO distribution has become more even and less of a monopoly. Current consumers are more rational and open to trying wines from countries other than France.

Wine Supply Balance

According to OIV statistics (Aurand, 2016) (Table 2.1) the supply volume of domestic production and import satisfied the demand of consumption and export in the past 5 years. There is overstock in the market that needs to be consumed.

However, the market needs to increase the number of wine drinkers to consume the increasing production and import.

LIMITATIONS OF THE SECONDARY DATA

Market decline by transition is obviously threatening news, but from a long-term perspective regarding the market transition, it may not be a pure defect. With the removal of sales from conspicuous state funds on business entertainment, the figures better reflect the reality of the mass market and unveil the purchase behaviour by real consumers. For a long time, what was available in the market to a large extent determined what consumers drank and shaped their preference. Availability and preference interacted with each other by the reinforcement of repeat consumption. Let's take COO as an example. French bottled wine was the most available, and well known, besides domestic wines so consumers were more likely to choose it. After a period of repeat exposure to French wine, consumers adapted to its style and it became the reference for wine. They habitually continued to consume French wine, which drove up the demand for French wine. Thus, more French wine was imported to meet the demand, and this added back to its availability.

One of the limitations of this analysis is that the secondary statistics provided here are descriptive, describing the patterns in the past and predictions for the future. The reason why the patterns look like this shows the need for more in-depth market research on primary data, which is not the purpose of this chapter. Obviously in a market where economic growth is consumption-driven, consumer studies are indispensable.

The other constraint of emerging market analysis based on secondary data is its precision and timeliness. It is easy to obtain reliable macroeconomic statistics from the National Bureau of Statistics, but it is hard to obtain reliable industrial data in China, particularly for a relatively new industry like wine. The statistics of production and trade are not well documented, which might be the reason why some foreign businessmen regard the Chinese market as 'mysterious'. In this chapter, statistical deviation of the same figures provided by different data sources can be up to 30%. Even from the same source, such as the customs office, websites of three different departments provide different numbers for the same indicator. Furthermore, the statistics that databases provide are usually not up to date. The latest data provided by commercial database providers, such as Euromonitor International and IWSR, or industrial authorities like OIV, are delayed by one or two years. A transitioning market like China may undergo dramatic changes within two years. Therefore, the most beneficial use of secondary data is to gain an overall impression of the market from the patterns and trends, rather than investigate precise figures. A comprehensive description of the market requires the use of primary data.

CONCLUSION

Summary of the China Wine Market

Having impressed the global market for roughly a decade, the Chinese wine market has been influenced by the national economic transformation in recent years. The market has struggled mainly in the following three aspects:

- sales of on-trade channels in decline due to the anticorruption campaign;
- sales of the red wine category dropped;
- production and sales of domestic wine decreased.

However, the market started to recover more recently led by the following drivers:

- the rise of the affluent and sophisticated upper-middle class which pushed consumption upgrade/premiumisation;
- increased penetration of e-commerce elevated inland market growth potential;
- improved domestic wine quality met the quality-driven demands of the upper-middle class;
- beneficial trade agreements increased the import of wine;
- sparkling wine appreciation.

Practical Implications

Impacted by the political and economic inhibitors, the wine industry in China may take a few years to recover. The phase of easy rapid growth is gone. However, China is still contributing to the overall growth of the global wine industry. In the longer term, the social and technological factors will drive the industry into a healthier and more understandable growth track. However, as a relatively new alcoholic drink in China, wine is not the only choice for Chinese consumers. Therefore, it is more important than ever to strategically identify and reach new wine consumers among the emerging upper-middle class, and be present in the communication and sales channels that they prefer.

ACKNOWLEDGMENTS

The authors would like to thank Dr Roberta Capitello and Mr Demei Li for their supervision, Mr Kai Yu and Ms Kirsten Victory for their valuable comments on the chapter.

REFERENCES

Aurand, J.-M., 2016. Conjoncture Vitivinicole Mondiale 2015. Organisation Internationale de la Vigne et du Vin, Paris.

Barton, D., Chen, Y., Jin, A., 2013. Mapping China's middle class [Online]. McKinsey & Company. Available at: <http://www.mckinsey.com/industries/retail/our-insights/mapping-chinas-middle-class> (accessed 8.08.2013).

Cochrane, J., Chen, H., Conigrave, K.M., Hao, W., 2003. Alcohol use in China. Alcohol. 38, 537−542.

Euromonitor International, 2015a. Alcoholic Drinks in China. Euromonitor International.

Euromonitor International, 2015b. Wine in China. Euromonitor International.

Fan, Y., 2002. Questioning guanxi: definition, classification and implications. Int. Bus. Rev. 11, 543−561.

Kuo, Y., Walters, J., Gao, H., Wang, A., Yang, V., Yang, J., et al., 2015. The new China playbook [Online]. 2016 The Boston Consulting Group. Available at: <https://www.bcgperspectives.com/content/articles/globalization-growth-new-china-playbook-young-affluent-e-savvy-consumers/?utm_source=201602Globalization&utm_medium=Email&utm_campaign=otr> (accessed 5.04.2016).

Li, H., Li, J., Yang, H., 2009. Review of Grape and Wine Industry Development in Recent 30 Years of China's Reforming and Opening-up. Mod. Food Sci. Technol. 25, 341−347.

Lu, Y., 2013. Mooncakes piled up at the reception without being claimed for weeks. Guangzhou Daily, 18 September.

Mustacich, S., 2013. China cuts back on big-buck Bordeaux. A government campaign against lavish spending has led wine drinkers to spend less. Wine Spectator. Available at: <http://www.winespectator.com/webfeature/show/id/48299> (accessed 13.06.2013).

Nielsen, 2015. This is the real big data for alcoholic drink market - Nielsen teaches you how to sell baijiu. Available at: <https://mp.weixin.qq.com/s?__biz=MzA4NjA2NTQwOQ==&mid=206764177&idx=1&sn=72c9e43b403785e9d5b2c094d5cd1b42&uin=MjUxMzIwNjA2MQ%3D%3D&key=710a5d99946419d94 17994667aaf81b7efeeaf0b1be7d7e4596714cc7cbfdc102ca0a3e06cca8d98cef18d60f4b5-e285&devicetype=iMac+MacBookPro9%2C1+OSX+OSX+10.10.5+build (14F27)&version=11020201&lang=en&pass_ticket=VXYArRYE8EoAyvvEbbiSYK% 2FXMzqVGBDw8q3P5ZTXrVuKlVR70l38RE3TM1qDeb3Z> (accessed 8.04.2016).

Nielsen, 2016. Consumption upgrading − a battle yet to win for Chinese manufacturers. Available at: <http://www.nielsen.com/cn/en/insights/news/2016/nielsen-consumption-upgrading-a-battle-yet-to-win-for-chinese-manufacturers.html>. (accessed 8.04.2016).

Su, R., 2014. The new Chinese wine drinker. Wine Intelligence. Available at: <http://www.wineintelligence.com/the-new-chinese-wine-drinker/> (accessed 4.06.2016).

Tao, Y., Yang, H., Lan, Y., 2012. Explore the strategy of professional wine education in China from an international perspective. China Brewing 31, 190−192.

Van Bommel, E., Edelman, D., Ungerman, K., 2014. Digitizing the consumer decision journey [Online]. McKinsey & Company. Available at: <http://www.mckinsey.com/business-functions/marketing-and-sales/our-insights/digitizing-the-consumer-decision-journey> (accessed 12.04.2016).

Yang, H., Fang, Y., 2008. Study on the driver, risk and strategy for the development of Chinese wine industry. Inquiry Econ. Issues, 30−33.

CHAPTER 3

The Regulatory Environment for Wine in China

M.-A. Genand
Interprofessional Committee of the Wines of Champagne, Epernay, France

THE DEVELOPMENT OF A WINE MARKET
The Implementation of a Regulatory System

Trade liberalization achieved through several national economic reforms launched from the end of the 1970s resulted in China joining the World Trade Organization (WTO) on December 11, 2001. Its accession has led to reduced duties on foreign alcohol and an increase in imports. Additionally, China's economic growth was accompanied by a rise of consumption and a change in consumer habits in favour of a Western lifestyle. Foreign brands have always been reputed for their image of prestige and their quality, particularly in the case of wines and spirits. As a consequence, China is now the fifth-highest wine consuming country in the world and French wines account for more than one third (in volume) of the total imports of wine. It is also now the second in the world in terms of its vineyard surface area.[1] Despite a recent slowdown in import growth, foreign brands remain highly prized. Consequently, in the field of wine, China has set up various regulations concerning classification, terminology, additives, labelling, etc.

There is, however, a downside to such success. Cases of counterfeiting of alcohol brands have increased; their success helped by the fact that Chinese consumers have little knowledge of the products. Most of them buy a wine because its name is famous or because of the place of origin. Bordeaux, Burgundy, or Champagne are indeed well-known geographic places for wines and they are all concerned about the phenomena of counterfeiting.

In view of the strengthening of the protection of intellectual property rights — before its accession to the WTO — China has taken into

---

[1] OIV report on the world vitivinicultural situation, 6 July 2015.

account the need for foreign investors to secure their rights and thus acceded to several international treaties covering different aspects of the intellectual property.[2] The accession of China to such legal treaties was an important step in leveraging the protection for right-holders and strengthening the prerogatives given to the authorities in charge of the registration and the implementation of the intellectual property rights.

China's accession to the WTO included also acceptance of complying with the Trade-Related Intellectual Property Rights (TRIPS) Agreement. The key principle of national treatment[3] was included as part of the Chinese intellectual property laws, as well as the reference to geographical indications (GIs) as defined in Article 22[4] of the Agreement ('Protection of Geographical Indications'). In order for China to comply with this Agreement, the Trademark Law was amended in 2001. For the first time, a trademark was legally defined as any visible sign that can serve to distinguish the goods of a natural person, legal person, or other organization from those of another, including any word, design, letter of the alphabet, numeral, three-dimensional symbol and colour combination, or any combination of the above. Apart from giving a protection to three-dimensional trademarks, this reform has also established a system of protection for GIs by the means of the registration of collective and certification trademarks. In addition, two others reforms have been implemented in China to specifically protect GIs, namely the Provisions for the Protection of Products of Geographical Indication (in 2005) by the General Administration of Quality Supervision, Inspection and Quarantine (AQSIQ) and the Measures for the Administration of Geographical Indications of Agricultural Products (in 2007) by the Ministry of Agriculture.

---

[2] China joined the World Intellectual Property Organization (in 1980) and acceded to the Paris Convention for the Protection of Industrial Property (in 1985), the Madrid Agreement Concerning the International Registration of Marks (in 1989), the Berne Convention for the Protection of Literary and Artistic Works (in 1992), the Patent Cooperation Treaty (in 1994), the Protocol Relating to the Madrid Agreement Concerning the International Registration of Marks (in 1995), the WIPO Copyright Treaty (in 2007).

[3] 'Each Member shall accord to the nationals of other Members treatment no less favourable than that it accords to its own nationals with regard to the protection of intellectual property' (TRIPS Agreement, Article 3.1).

[4] 'Indications which identify a good as originating in the territory of a Member, or a region or locality in that territory, where a given quality, reputation or other characteristic of the good is essentially attributable to its geographical origin' (TRIPS Agreement, Article 22).

The Requirements for the Labelling of Wines

Several mandatory requirements must be respected for the export of wines to China. The labelling in particular is regulated by the General Standard for the Labelling of Pre-packaged Foods (GB 7718-2011, as well as GB 2758-12 and GB 2757-12). Besides the front label, a back label written in Chinese is compulsory and must be approved by authorities before the arrival of bottles. Information required shall include the following: brand name in Chinese, place of production, type of wine (according to the Chinese classification), date of bottling, appellation, list of additives, the mention of 'contains sulphites', content of alcohol, volume, name and address of the distributor, agent or importer and country of origin.

Other standards have to be met, in addition to the gathering of a number of shipping documents, such as the sanitary certificate, production permission and analysis of the wine. However, it is notable that Chinese standards are not in line with relevant international and European standards with regard to at least two points. While in Europe, the reference to the category of the wine may be omitted for wines whose labels include the name of a protected designation of origin (PDO) or a protected geographical indication (PGI), Chinese standards do not allow a derogation from the obligation to designate the type of wine. With regard to the second point, Chinese standards set specific requirements for the date of bottling. The date indeed must be indicated with the year (2 or 4 numbers), the month (2 numbers) and the day (2 numbers). Such compulsory particulars are not included in European legislation.

In addition to the rules that strictly apply to labelling, several analyses are required for products being imported to China. They consist of 14 parameters: pressure (at 20°C), density (at 20°C), alcoholic strength (at 15°C), glucose—fructose, volatile acidity, sulphur dioxide, copper, iron, lead, dry extract, citric acid, antiseptic compounds, methanol and phthalates. However, China finally recently confirmed that a test report for phthalates was no longer required to accompany imported wines and spirits. Instead, it has adopted a risk-based sampling at China's border. Many wine producing countries have recognized the definitions and methods of analysis adopted by the International Organization of Vine and Wine (OIV) and introduced them into their own legislation. However, China is not an OIV Member State but it collaborates with this intergovernmental organization with the status of observer.

As the Chinese government attaches more and more importance to food safety, the supervision of imported goods is becoming increasingly stricter.

TOWARDS A CONVERGENCE WITH THE INTERNATIONAL STANDARDS OF LAW FOR THE WINE SECTOR

A Dual System Built on Trademarks and *sui generis* Appellations of Origin

China has the peculiarity of having two distinct administrations in charge of the protection of GIs. Therefore, their registration can be achieved through two systems: a certification mark or collective mark with the SAIC and a *sui generis* protection for GIs with the General Administration of Quality Supervision, Inspection and Quarantine (AQSIQ).

The SAIC sits under the authority of the State Council with several divisions in charge of legislation and the enforcement of the laws in the field of industry and commerce. As the SAIC has authority both over trademark registration and enforcement, it has the power to investigate and order cessation of the sale of infringing goods, comprising the confiscation and/or the destruction of the goods and implementation of fines. The China Trade Mark Office, part of the SAIC, acts for the registration of all trademarks including those comprising a geographical name and GIs. In view of their nature, GIs are not registered as private trademarks which would give their holder a monopoly to use the name freely, but as certification or collective marks as defined by Article 3 of the Trademark Law.[5] In any case, both marks provide the same level of protection as for any other name registered as a trademark.

Although the protection given by the Chinese Trademark Law applies to GIs, whether national or foreign, registered or unregistered in China,[6]

---

[5] Article 3: 'For the purposes of this law, a collective mark is a mark registered in the name of a group, association, or any other organization and used by its members to indicate membership. For the purposes of this law, a certification mark is a mark which is owned by an organization that exercises supervision over a particular product or service and which is used to indicate that third-party goods or services meet certain standards pertaining to place of origin, raw materials, mode of manufacture, quality, or other characteristics.'

[6] It was recently confirmed by the Beijing Court of First Instance which recognized that the geographical indication 'Champagne' and '香槟' (Champagne in Chinese) should be protected even though it was not registered in China, Beijing No. 1 Intermediate People's Court, Comité Interprofessionnel du Vin de Champagne v. Beijing Sheng Yan YI Mei Trading Co., Ltd., February 10, 2015.

their registration is strongly recommended to fight efficiently against misuse of their names and counterfeit goods.

The newly revised Trademark Law[7] did not affect the level of protection for GIs. According to Article 16, 'Where a trademark includes a geographical sign that does not describe the location or the origin of the goods in question, the term causes confusion among members of the public and shall be refused registration. Its use as a trademark also shall be prohibited'. Such protection given by the Trademark Law in China does comply with the TRIPS Agreement which aims to protect the consumer against any misleading conduct as to the geographical origin of the good and any use which constitutes an act of unfair competition.

Under the authority of the State Council of the People's Republic of China, the AQSIQ manages the quality and food safety of products in China. It has also been given the power to register and protect national and foreign GIs. Such protection is not of the same nature as to the trademark regime but a *sui generis* protection which is very similar to the European system of promotion and protection of the PDO and PGI. For example, Cognac (2009), Champagne (2013) and Bordeaux (2016) were successfully registered as GIs at the AQSIQ. With the newly published regulation, Measures on Protection of Foreign Geographical Indication Products (2016), it is expected that foreign GIs will enjoy a more comprehensive protection.

An Absolute Need to Protect Intellectual Property Rights

It is essential to protect and register intellectual property rights swiftly, including GIs, when undertaking business in China. It is also recommended to engage in a constructive discussion on this matter before selling in the Chinese market. China indeed uses the 'first to file' system for trademark registration, therefore one may not apply for a trademark if a similar or identical trademark has already been registered in China. Such precaution must also be taken before participating in trade fairs or entering into commercial discussions to avoid any risk of bad faith registration, even if the products have not been imported into China yet.

---

[7] Trademark Law of the People's Republic of China (as amended up to Decision of August 30, 2013, of the Standing Committee of National People's Congress on Amendments to the Trademark Law of the People's Republic of China).

In the light of this, it should be recommended for any person or company intending to trade with China to take advice from professionals, and particularly intellectual property rights experts, to determine how best to protect and defend their intellectual property rights, even in Chinese translation. It is not uncommon to see distributors or third parties register trademarks which have not been registered yet by the wine producers. This widespread conduct is growing with the development of wine business in China and may involve important costs and years of proceedings to have the trademark reassigned even though the brand is well-known.

It is equally useful to consider the question of a Chinese translation as domestic consumers will not necessarily understand the brand if it is written in characters others than Chinese. A translation of the brand — which should be chosen with the assistance of a skilled translator — can therefore help consumers to identify and recognize a product and, ultimately, avoid the multiplicity of unofficial translations. Several options can be considered. On the one hand, the brand may be translated phonetically in order to be as close as possible from the original brand name (Hennessy is translated 'Xuan Ni Shi'). On the other hand, a translation may be chosen to give a similar meaning to the original mark or a particular signification and create a brand image. For example, Rémy Martin's emblem is a centaur. Their name has consequently been translated into 'ren-taô-ma' which is a symbol of virility, wealth, and long life. Chateau d'Yquem (Di Jin) refers to 'the golden drop' in reference to the colour of the wine and its price, and Penfold (Ben Fu) means 'towards prosperity'.

Trademarks can be filed directly with the China Trademark Office via a local trademark attorney or through international registration as China is a member of the Madrid system for the international registration of marks. This system aims to facilitate the registration of trademarks in multiple countries by providing a cost-effective protection in multiple jurisdictions with the filing of a single application with the World Intellectual Property Organization.

The Chinese Trademark law does also allow the registration of three-dimensional trademarks provided that the design does not 'merely indicate the shape inherent in the nature of the goods concerned' and is not 'only dictated by the need to achieve technical effects or the need to give the goods substantive value'.[8] Such registration is particularly useful for getting a strong protection for packaging shapes.

---

[8] Articles 12 and 59 of the Trademark Law.

Guaranteeing the Origin of the Wines

In view of the growth of fake and counterfeit wine and spirits products, China became aware of the importance of guaranteeing the origin of these products and putting in place a computer system to secure the exportation of French wines and spirits to China. After years of discussion with the French Customs authorities, the Chinese authorities (AQSIQ) have agreed to implement in 2015 — first in Shenzhen and Shanghai — the computer system called 'Aubette' which will ensure the traceability and the authentication of the products imported into the country.

The Aubette database for wine and spirits exports to China does allow the AQSIQ to access some logistics and administrative information (electronic administrative documents) and other documents, such as the certificate of origin from Champagne or Cognac which are also used as evidence of the origin of the goods. In the end, it shall both reduce counterfeiting and facilitate export of goods produced in France and exported from France to mainland China. This procedure outlines the commitment of the Chinese administration to secure French wine industry exports to China as well as to international trade generally.

For example, the Champagne certificate of origin is an obligation for any export of Champagne wines, deriving from a French Decree of 5 October 1945. It is delivered by the Comité Champagne which certifies that the exported wines meet all conditions required to benefit from the Champagne appellation of origin. Leveraging its expertise in the delivery of such document, the Comité Champagne has decided to implement an electronic version for all countries of the world to speed up delivery, strengthening the protection of the Champagne appellation by facilitating the controls carried out by the customs authorities both in France and in the country of destination, as well as preserving the environment. This electronic document should be made available in China in late 2016.

THE NEW CHALLENGES OF CHINA

In recent years, the e-commerce market has boomed with new actors offering new opportunities to sell products directly to Chinese consumers online. This significant growth can be explained through various factors — cultural and technological — and the efforts promoted by the Chinese government to make the country a global e-commerce leader. The 'Internet Plus' programme introduced on March 2015 sought to promote e-commerce. The thirteenth 5-year plan approved by the Central Committee of the Chinese Communist Party for the period 2016–20 seeks to promote innovation and online economic activity. In line with this plan, the Chinese Customs authorities have begun to experiment with a system to retrieve the shortfall caused by the sales made on foreign platforms shipping to China. It consists of establishing warehouses under customs authority that can sell online imported goods that have not yet been released. Some big companies have already created such platforms but their success remains to be demonstrated.

China's e-commerce laws are also being improved. A new law shall include several aspects of the protection of the intellectual property rights, the protection of the consumers, the transfrontier e-business and a dispute resolution mechanism. As e-business is a major component of the economy, the SAIC has created a Department for the Regulation on Online Commodity Transaction in charge of regulation and supervision of the business for online goods and services. In 2015, several regional AICs have created locally-based sections to supervise this new economy.

While e-commerce is full of opportunities, it also brings the challenge of counterfeit goods. Sales can be anonymous and go beyond the frontiers, hence increasing the sense of immunity on the part of some sellers and their awareness that they can violate intellectual property rights. In order to cope with that increase it became necessary for the actors of e-commerce to put in place mechanisms to ensure that goods are genuine and respectful of the rights of their owners, and to initiate a dialogue with the authorities. The new law on the e-business will be of great importance in dealing with this specific issue.

However, although China has acquired legislative and regulatory laws in a short time and made substantial revisions that have brought the country closer to international practices, the challenge remains today that law enforcement and judicial practice need to be aligned with the laws.

PART II

Consumers

CHAPTER 4

Gift Culture in China: Consequences for the Fine Wine Sector

V. Seidemann[1], G. Atwal[2] and K. Heine[3,4]
[1]University of Rostock, Rostock, Germany
[2]University Bourgogne Franche-Comté, Groupe ESC Dijon-CEREN, Dijon, France
[3]EMLYON Business School, Lyon, France
[4]EMLYON Business School, Shanghai, China

INTRODUCTION

The Chinese gift economy is a significant market worth about 770 billion renminbi (122 billion US$) per year. The individual demand accounts for about two thirds (506 billion renminbi/80 billion US$) and the demand of organizations for about one third (263 billion renminbi/42 billion US$). In addition, three quarters of all gifts are directly connected to business purposes (China Daily, 2012).

As a result of several prominent corruption scandals, the Chinese president Xi Jinping introduced an official ban of luxury gift-giving in the public sector that coincided with calls for more austerity and restraint. This ban, as part of an over-reaching anticorruption campaign, forbids civil servants from spending public money on opulent banquets, pretentious company cars or making or accepting expensive (luxury) gifts. Moreover, this ban involves the prohibition of advertisements that encourage extravagant gift-giving (BBC, 2013).

Considering the significant size of the luxury market of Mainland China and as personal and business gifts account for approximately 25% of that market, gift-giving has been a reliable source of revenue for luxury brands (CNBC, 2013; Wen, 2012).

However, the demand for products typically given as gifts has declined sharply as a result of Xi Jinping's anticorruption campaign. For example, champagne imports to China were about 1.6 million bottles (75 cl.) in 2014 compared with two million bottles in 2012 (CIVC, 2014). This trend is also evident within the fine still wine sector. According to

Bloomberg, wine sales by leading world auction houses declined in 2013. Sales by Acker Merrall & Condit Co., Christie's International, Sotheby's, Zachys Wine & Liquor Inc. and Hart Davis Hart Wine Co. decreased 15% to US$278 million in 2013 (Collins, 2014). Facing these developments, the fine wine sector in China will certainly become more challenging as a result of new regulations and shifting consumer preferences.

Although there lacks a consensus of defining the fine wine category, it is generally acknowledged that luxury wine products and brands have to meet the general luxury criteria: a high level of price, quality aesthetics, rarity, extraordinariness and a higher degree of nonfunctional associations (Heine, 2013). The notion of 'high price' is however a matter of interpretation. For example, Swindell (2015) asserts that the fine wine business is defined by bottles that cost US$20 or more. Although we acknowledge that the democratization of luxury is evident within the wine sector, we are inclined to follow the price classification of Greene et al. (1999) of the iconic segment as exceeding at least US$50. However, Reyneke et al. (2011) provide an alternative typology of luxury brands and argue that luxury wines have an objective (material), a subjective (individual), and a collective (social) component.

The overall objective of this chapter is to develop a comprehensive understanding of the Chinese luxury gift-giving culture and provide a discussion of strategies that can help stakeholders within the fine wine sector to adapt to a changing environment.

THE CHINESE CULTURE AND ITS AFFECTION TOWARDS LUXURY PRODUCTS

Cultural Dimensions

It is acknowledged that culture has a significant impact on consumer behaviour (De Mooij, 1998). Cultural boundaries often act as criteria for market segmentation while research often focuses on culture as an underlying determinant of consumer behaviour. In general, culture can be defined as an "evolving system of concepts, values and symbols inherent in a society" (Yau et al., 1999, p. 98). To understand a culture and the behaviour of its members, one has to understand the underlying values. Cultural values refer to conceptions of the desirable, of the good and true, the bad and false. They act as guiding principles in life within the specific society (Schwartz, 1999).

The most established concepts to compare national cultures originate from Hofstede and Bond (1984), Hofstede (2011) and Hall (1976). Hall (1976) differentiates between high-context and low-context cultures. A key element in his theory is the context in which communication in a certain culture takes place. In high-context cultures such as China, many things are left unsaid as a few words in combination with gestures or objects can communicate a complex message very effectively (Kim et al., 1998). In low-context cultures such as the United States, communication is more explicit and the context has minimal importance.

Hofstede's (2011) framework of national culture has been applied in a wide and diverse range of consumer marketing and strategic marketing contexts. In Fig. 4.1, Hofstede's (2011) six cultural dimensions are defined. Although a number of researchers has criticized the validity of Hofstede's cultural instrument (e.g., Blodgett et al., 2008; Brewer and Venaik, 2012; McSweeney, 2002; Shenkar, 2001; Smith et al., 2002), the framework is widely recognized as one of the most important applications of national culture types. Fig. 4.2 compares the Chinese value-structure with the most typical representative of Western culture, the US-American value-structure. As the sixth dimension "Indulgence and Restraint" lacks empirical data, this will not be compared.

While there are minor differences between China and the US regarding the dimensions MAS and UAI, there are significant differences regarding IDV, PDI und LTO (Hofstede, 2013). The US represents a typical individualistic

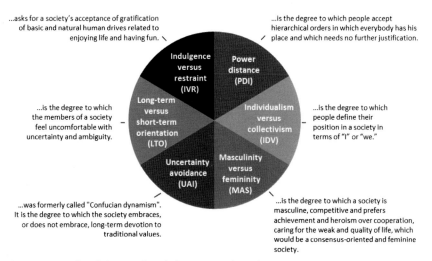

Figure 4.1 Hofstede's six cultural dimensions (2011).

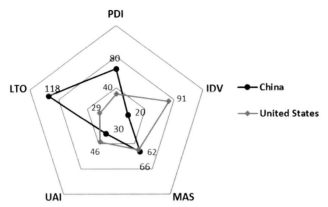

Figure 4.2 Comparison of Chinese and US-American value structures. *Hofstede, G., 2013. The Hofstede Centre. Available from: http://geert-hofstede.com/dimensions.html.*

and low-context culture; China is a typical collectivistic and high-context culture (Hall, 1976; Hofstede and Bond, 1984).

Confucianism has shaped Chinese culture and society for centuries and favours the collective well-being of a society and virtues such as courtesy, selflessness, respect, communal obligation and social harmony — as compared to individual self-fulfilment or individual rights. In such collectivistic cultures, people live in networks and groups. They are deeply involved with each other and have closer and more intimate relationships than people in individualistic societies. These relationships are structured within a strong social hierarchy, which is also reflected by China's very high score on the PDI dimension. A person's identity is deeply embedded in familial, cultural, professional and social relationships (Wong and Ahuvia, 1998). Inner feelings are kept under strong self-control, even when the individual's desires are conflicting with the group's goals. There should be no (explicit) differences between the goals of the individual and the group and the desire for conformity and harmony within a group is of paramount importance.

In individualistic cultures like the US, the notion of nonconformity is often regarded positively as being authentic (Kim et al., 1998). It is a person's inner self including his or her preferences, tastes, and personal values that regulates one's behaviour as opposed to the social hierarchy within the group. In contrast, an individual's social status in collectivistic cultures depends very much on the social position of the groups he or she belongs to (Wong and Ahuvia, 1998). It also influences the extent to which group members identify with their task group's goals (Chatman et al., 2015).

In a similar vein, Triandis (1995) argues that high-context and collectivistic societies emphasize social norms and duty defined by the group.

It can be summarized that China's specific cultural values, including high levels of collectivism, power distance and masculinity, make it a true luxury (addicted) culture. It can also be deduced that social influence is an important determinant of luxury consumption as reported by Zhan and He (2012) in a study of Chinese middle class consumers. The specific combination of cultural values explains why several consumer surveys show especially positive attitudes towards luxury in China (KPMG, 2013).

Major Cultural Concepts in China

Chinese cultural values manifest themselves in two major concepts, Guanxi and Face, which have a strong impact on social and business life in China and particularly within the context of gift-giving.

Guanxi is the most important social and business resource. The word is composed of the Chinese characters *"guan"* and *"xi"*, which means "gate" and "connection". A Chinese person is born into a Guanxi network, but not every relationship has Guanxi from the beginning. Somehow comparable to business networks in the Western world, but far important and salient in everyday life, Guanxi can be understood as a set of rules, social norms and moral principles. Transactions within the Guanxi are based on trust, long-term use and primarily related relationships, referred to by Child (1994, p. 30) as 'the quality of a personal relationship outside an individual's immediate family'. Chinese people commit considerable energy, creativity and sophistication in order to develop Guanxi (Qian et al., 2007). Gift-giving plays a significant central role in building Guanxi that reflects both long-term relationships and short-term benefits (Steidlmeier, 1997) as noted by Yang (1994, p. 6), 'Guanxi involves the exchange of gifts, favours and banquets; the cultivation of personal relationships and networks of mutual dependence and manufacturing of obligation and indebtedness'.

Face can be compared to a mixture of several constructs like prestige, dignity, power, and the degree of respectability and deference a person can claim for himself/herself from others. Confucianism stresses that a person's worth is determined by his or her public actions. The Chinese constantly strive to maintain and improve their own face and also that of other people (Goffman, 1955). The complex face construct can be divided into two intertwined dimensions: Lien and Mien-tzu.

Lien refers to the moral integrity of an individual's character, 'the basic confidence of a society in the integrity of the organization's (or person's) moral character, the loss of which makes it impossible to function within the community' (Dowing, 2001, p. 19). Mien-tzu, on the other hand, stands for reputation and social status. It is gained by personal success (skills and achievements) and by nonpersonal characteristics such as wealth and power, which are reflected by material values or by social connections (Guanxi) (Ho, 1976). It may be lost when group expectations or basic requirements corresponding to one's social position are not satisfactorily fulfilled (Qian et al., 2007).

In doing "facework" (activities to improve and maintain one's face), Mien-tzu can be increased by obtaining favourable comments from the group members, through exemplary behaviour or superior performance. Mien-tzu is essentially impression management — a process by which people aim to control the impressions others have of them. In turn, these impressions and perceptions influence their self- and social-esteem (Leary and Kowalski, 1990). The more people feel that other people's evaluations of their actions are essential for attaining their own goals, the more they engage in impression management. As Mien-tzu relies on other peoples' impressions, a person can only have Mien-tzu if he or she is also able to demonstrate his or her success.

As a result, the specific symbolic meaning of products, such as Château Lafite Rothschild, is used in interaction with others to communicate certain attributes about the owner such as affluence, success or sophistication as failure to do so, 'would jeopardize his/her standing in society, cause him/her to lose mient-tzu and cast into doubt his/her moral integrity in the eyes of society (lien)' (Schütte and Ciarlante, 1998).

LUXURY GIFT-GIVING IN CHINA
The Chinese Gift-Giving Culture

Confucius was quoted as saying: 'we are not a gentleman if we don't take revenge; we are not a man if we don't return a favour.' This therefore implies that doing favours often results in "indebtedness" of the other which prompts the need for returning the favour, e.g., by gift-giving (Yau et al., 1999). A 'need' or a 'duty' for gift-giving is contrary to the classic and idealized Western understanding of gift-giving, i.e., behaviour is driven by altruistic motives and attempts to please the gift recipient without any hidden agenda. Instead, most gifts carry an accompanying behaviour that stems from self-interest or the feeling of obligation of the giver. Such 'egoistic' givers attempt to maximize their own personal satisfaction (Sherry, 1983). They are aware of the fact that receiving a gift (without reciprocating) leads to an unbalanced relationship status between the giver and the receiver. Although the receiver may be pleased about receiving a case of fine wine, this imbalance still results in an uncomfortable tension the receiver feels — and this can be solved by reciprocating with an equivalent or even more valuable gift or with some other favour (Poe, 1977). The gift can be therefore interpreted as a strategic vehicle for the giver to improve his or her social status, to ensure the receivers' commitment or to make use of the receivers' resources (Segev et al., 2012).

Furthermore, self-concept theory states that the selected gift is often more a reflection of the donor's (ideal) self-concept than of the recipient's preferences (Belk, 1984). This implies that the object given as a gift can be considered a "container" for the donor's ideal self-concept that is given in part to the receiver (Sherry, 1983). As a result, by gifting a case of fine wine (if it was not the receiver's explicit wish), the donor does not only communicate appreciation and respect towards the receiver, but also says something about his or her own wealth and power, fine taste and aspiration level.

In Chinese culture, gift-giving is a historically central tradition (Qian et al., 2007). Gifts are given or exchanged specified by the cultural calendar but also spontaneously. There are numerous official occasions such as Chinese New Year, Qingming festival (Tomb Sweeping Day), the moon cake festival (Mid-autumn Festival), Chinese National Day and also numerous other official and private occasions such as birthdays, weddings, after the birth and after the first month of a newborn, and bereavements. These occasions were extended by 'imported' Western occasions such as Valentine's Day, Father's and Mother's Day and Christmas. Besides all the numerous official and private events, gifts are exchanged at business meetings — for instance, at the first meeting, at business lunches or successful contract formations (Qian et al., 2007).

Gift-Giving as a "face act"

The claim 'courtesy calls for reciprocity' is strongly embedded in Chinese life philosophy (Liu et al., 2010). The principle of reciprocity serves as the main base of Guanxi — and at the same time it is quite close to the

Western understanding of corruption and bribery. Gifts are seen as social investments and lead to the desired continuity of Guanxi (D'Souza, 2003). Roughly comparable to double-entry bookkeeping, Guanxi is a constant continuation of mutual favours between the parties involved. A person will only be regarded as a "gentleman" (or "grande dame") when the repayment for a favour is of greater value than what was received before (Yau et al., 1999). This results in a helix of increasingly expensive gifts and favors. Once the principle of reciprocity is broken, Guanxi cannot be maintained (Qian et al., 2007).

As already mentioned above, gifts are a reflection of the donor's ideal self and play a crucial role in symbolic interaction. But gift-giving in collectivistic cultures helps to reinforce group-affiliated self-concept rather than a personal, characteristic-based self-concept, which is predominant in individualistic cultures (Belk, 1976, 1984).

Gift-giving can therefore be considered as a "face act" as it offers the chance to improve face by gaining or improving relationships and by using the often highly visible gift-giving act as a vehicle to improve one's own and also the receiver's Mien-tzu (Segev et al., 2012; Yau et al., 1999). According to Schütte and Ciarlante (1998, p. 45), 'In a business or social context, the elaborate norms involved in gift-giving provide a crucial opportunity to gain − or lose − face. Inappropriate gifts, in terms of content or cost, can cause an embarrassing loss of face for both the donor and the recipient'. Yu et al. (2009) found that Beijing participants tend to pay low prices for daily consumption, but higher prices for wines purchased for gift purposes. As Camillo (2012) notes, consumers are motivated to purchase highly reputable wines in order to improve face. This phenomenon is stressed by a representative of a high-end Hong Kong importer, 'Lafite has become a unit of business, and it is not being stored, but drunk. ... The buyers aren't thinking about the price of the wine, but about the value of the relationship or obligation you establish by serving it' (Lewis and Bremner, 2010).

On the one hand, an expensive gift such as fine wine demonstrates the wealth, success and generosity of the giver who can spend lots of money on a gift. On the other hand, the gift also communicates the respect, impression and appreciation the giver has of the receiver who is expected to understand the value of receiving a bottle with the label that says Château Lafite Rothschild.

As it is a Chinese custom that gifts are not opened as long as the donor is present, opulent wrapping and packaging play a crucial role in gift-giving. This is of particular relevance when the gift is presented in the presence of a group gathering to enhance the 'public' impression of the gift's value (Wooten, 2000). For example, Château Mouton Rothschild introduced special bottle packaging for its 2008 label in order to enhance its prestigious appeal within a local Chinese context. The label designed by Chinese painter Xu Lei incorporated a red Chinese character for the number eight, and the year 2008 embossed on the bottle.

RECENT DEVELOPMENTS AND RECOMMENDATIONS

Recent Developments: "The Watch-Wearing Brother"

Radically changing dynamics in China in the last decade such as urbanization, privatization and the influence of Western companies with their fundamentally different business practices have influenced ways to maintain and to improve Guanxi and Mien-tzu. There is evidence to suggest that bribing often tends to replace the traditional idea of Guanxi gift-giving, while the maintenance and improvement of Mien-tzu is focused very much on making use of the symbolic meaning of luxury products. These developments have caused a vicious circle resulting in greater extravagance.

As a consequence, the Chinese public and consequently the Communist party are increasingly suspicious of certain visible signals of corruption and lavishness. Due to a series of recent corruption scandals, Xi Jinping declared a fight against corruption, opulence and extravagance in the public sector and the fostering of frugality (BBC, 2013).

Known as the "Watch-Wearing Brother", the civil servant became the embodied face of corruption and bribery among civil servants. In a high-profile online campaign launched by Sina Weibo, the biggest Chinese micro-blogging platform, images of the "Watch-Wearing Brother" were posted. The images showed the civil servant wearing numerous ultra-expensive watches which ultimately aroused public interest (The Wall Street Journal, 2012). The case set a precedent as the civil servant was officially ousted from his post for the possession of expensive watches and other violations of discipline. Moreover, several other public servants wearing expensive watches and other luxury products that they could never afford with their official salary were subject to intense scrutiny by the media and online communities (The Wall Street Journal, 2012). As a result, many luxury products are no longer on public display (Euromonitor, 2013).

The media attention and public condemnation of signals of extravagance and corruption, supported by the Communist Government, has led to new challenges for luxury gift-giving that also includes fine wines (BBC, 2013). Moreover, changing business practices due to regulatory procedures and Western influences is changing the cultural emphasis of guanxi in corporate China (Chua, 2012). This is underlined by Wilson and Brennan (2010) who reported a diminishing importance of guanxi in a study of UK−Chinese joint ventures. In turn, Chinese consumers find themselves in a dilemma: How to maintain face without using the established instruments? And how to be frugal while being ostentatious?

Recommendations

There is evidence to suggest that the sale of fine wines that were typically bought for gift-giving reasons has declined. Despite these developments, the striving for Mien-tzu and the practice of gift-giving within Guanxi — both deeply rooted in the fabric of Chinese culture — will remain. Stakeholders within the fine wine sector will however need to consider how to adapt strategies to address a changing market environment. The following recommendations should be considered to ensure that the fine wine sector enjoys sustainable growth in this potentially high-growth emerging market.

First, the development of more understated and subtle signals of Mien-tzu. For example, the mid-range brand Baijiu has replaced the luxury-alcohol Maotai at many banquets (Euromonitor, 2013). A shift towards a more understated design to meet these new needs might require new product lines or even subbrands. For example, Pernod Ricard introduced less expensive lines associated with its more high-end names to the Chinese market, such as Ballantine's Finest and Martell Distinction. Although this strategy may undermine the luxury positioning of the original brand, it could enable fine wine producers to bridge the gap between exclusivity and accessibility. For example, Le Petit Mouton de Mouton Rothschild is the second wine of Château Mouton Rothschild that could essentially provide a less ostentatious alternative for gift-giving occasions. Likewise, a deliberate strategy to develop less conspicuous packaging could help to create a more discreet image of the brand, 'with only small design cues to indicate the brand, which can only be picked up by consumers who are aware of what to look for' (Cavender et al., 2014, p. 152). This, however, creates a dilemma for many fine wine marketers as packaging not only plays an important role in determining appropriate gifts, but many elements of the packaging are indeed standardized. A promising business model in this context is the combination of local flavour and global savvy. This may be difficult to implement within the fine wine sector, but examples within other categories demonstrate that this could be a feasible proposition. LVMH launched Chandon China in 2014 which, according to its corporate website, 'is a reflection of its roots: it subtly blends Chinese audacity and modernity with age-old French savoir-faire' (LVMH, 2015). Similarly, Hermès launched Shang Xia in 2010, a homeware label inspired by local crafts; BMW will produce cars with the Zhinuo badge while Daimler will launch new car brand Denza (The Economist, 2013).

Second, marketers need to consider how to position fine wines beyond the advancement of status or self-image. Interestingly, Yang and Paladino (2015) found that consumer attitudes have changed in respect to Chinese gift-giving behaviour in the case of wine. Survey results revealed that product image and gift packaging had significant moderating effects on relationships that were previously assumed to be robust. This is indeed coherent with a shift in attitudes in China in which knowledge ("in the know") and personal enjoyment ("experience") are becoming increasingly relevant drivers of luxury consumption that reflects the significance of the wine consumer cluster in China, 'the intrinsic attribute-seeking customers' (Liu et al., 2014).

Education campaigns can help to inform and educate consumers of the salient attributes of fine wines in order to demonstrate the quality standards such as vintage, quality, variety, region and winemaker. This category of consumer is consistent with the group labelled 'Connoisseurs', defined as possessing strong cultural capital (Bourdieu, 1986) which encompasses an array of linguistic competencies, manners, preferences and orientations. 'Connoisseurs are initiated into the secrets of elaborate rituals that accompany the purchase and consumption of luxury winee' (Heine et al. 2015, p. 240). For example, Wine Residence Beijing (owned by ASC Fine Wines) offers a retail shop, private members club, education centre and an event venue that attempts to deliver an emotional wine appreciation experience. Consequently, consumers are motivated to send subtle signals to other peer members that can only be recognized by those 'in the know' (HBR, 2015).

This should also help to establish new drinking occasions that transcend the gift-giving ritual that is often associated with the acquisition of fine wines. Moreover, promotional campaigns that convey a deeper meaning can be effective to create associations that are not related to gift-giving practices. For example, the champagne brand Ruinart was an official partner of Art Basel Hong Kong, which helps to evoke brand impressions associated with creativity, originality, individuality, sophistication and taste.

Finally, fine wine marketers need to consider targeting customer segment groups who are more likely to be accustomed to new gift-giving practices following the recent introduction of anticorruption legislation. Interestingly, the average age of a Chinese millionaire is 38, with more than half aged between 31 and 45 (GroupM, 2013). This is a generation of luxury consumers who have gained greater exposure to Western cultural practices and will be more familiar with buying luxury products such as fine wines for themselves rather than for others. Fine wine marketers therefore will need to consider which marketing techniques are the most effective to support the acquisition of fine wines for private consumption amongst this segment. For instance, the integration of social media outlets on WeChat or Weibo as part of an overall communications strategy can be an important vehicle to enhance involvement and engagement as consumers seek advice from critics that they respect. In a similar vein, the ability to purchase a wider selection of fine wines via e-commerce sites should help to broaden (democratize) the appeal of fine wines.

CONCLUSION AND FUTURE TRENDS

Gift-giving in China has entered a 'new normal'. As noted by Godart and Zhao (2014, p. 121), gift-giving remains a strong cultural norm in China: 'The habit of giving expensive gifts, especially for special occasions and during festivals, is an integral part of social scripts and business codes'. However, the ongoing government campaign to curtail official corruption and extravagance in China will continue to impact luxury consumption patterns. Moreover, changes in corporate governance in China will continue to play a key role in changing the culture of gift-giving as observed by Cavender et al. (2014, p. 151): 'Firms and government offices are becoming increasingly value-driven, and seek to obtain the best possible deals, rather than simply collaborate with close friends or relations. The practice of following an open bidding process has led to greater transparency in which gifts play a less prominent role'.

Although passion investment will remain an important purchasing motive within the fine wines category, the decline in gift-giving has created a marketing challenge in a fast-changing market environment. A change in consumer sentiment is redefining the social acceptance of the gift-giving ritual in which conspicuous gifts such as fine wines are being replaced with less status-driven alternatives. Fine wine marketers need to consider how to leverage the still important gift-giving purchase occasion but with a less conspicuous brand offering. Likewise, fine wine marketers need to consider leveraging new growth opportunities, whether by creating and promoting new purchase occasions or by targeting new target segments.

The difference between success and failure will be determined by the ability of fine wine marketers to adapt to new regulatory conditions, but also to a changing Chinese consumer sentiment.

REFERENCES

BBC, 2013. China bans luxury gift adverts in austerity push. <http://www.bbc.co.uk/news/world-asia-china-21349722>.

Belk, R., 1976. It's the thought that counts: a signed digraph analysis of gift-giving. J. Consum. Res. 3 (3), 155–162.

Belk, R., 1984. Cultural and historical differences in concepts of self and their effects on attitudes toward having and giving. Adv. Consum. Res. 11, 291–297.

Blodgett, J.G., Bakir, A., Rose, G.M., 2008. A test of the validity of Hofstede's cultural framework. J. Consum. Mark. 25 (6), 339–349.

Bourdieu, P., 1986. The forms of capital. In: Richardson, J.G. (Ed.), Handbook of Theory and Research for the Sociology of Education. Greenwood Press, Westport CT.

Brewer, P., Venaik, S., 2012. On the misuse of national culture dimensions. Int. Mark. Rev. 29 (6), 673–683.

Camillo, A.A., 2012. A strategic investigation of the determinants of wine consumption in China. Int. J. Wine Bus. Res. 24 (1), 68–92.

Cavender, B., Der Arslanian, K., Chan, C., 2014. Luxury in China. The end of bling in luxury brands. In: Atwal, G., Bryson, D. (Eds.), Luxury Brands in Emerging Markets. Palgrave Macmillan, Basingstoke.

Chatman, J.A., Sherman, E.L., Doerr, B.M., 2015. Making the most of diversity: how collectivism mutes the disruptive effects of demographic heterogeneity on group performance. IRLE Working Paper No. 106–115. Available at: <http://irle.berkeley.edu/workingpapers/106-15.pdf>.

Child, J., 1994. Management in China during the Age of Reform. Cambridge University Press, Cambridge.

China Daily, 2012. Chinese spend $122b a year on gifts. Available at: <http://www.chinadaily.com.cn/china/2012-02/10/content_14578717.htm>.

Chua, R.Y., 2012. Building effective business relationships in China. MIT Sloan Manag. Review 53 (4), 27–33.

CIVC, 2014. Les Expéditions de Vins de Champagne en 2014. Available at: <http://www.champagne.fr/assets/files/economie/bulletin_expeditions_vins_champagne2014.pdf>.

CNBC, 2013. Gift-giving crackdown hits China luxury retailers. Available at: <http://www.cnbc.com/id/100445071>.

Collins, G., 2014. Wine sales drop for second year as Bordeaux Demand Wanes. Available from: <http://www.bloomberg.com/news/articles/2014-01-29/wine-sales-drop-for-second-year-as-bordeaux-demand-wanes>.

D'Souza, C., 2003. An inference of gift-giving within Asian business culture. Asia Pac. J. Mark. Logistics 15 (1), 27−38.

De Mooij, M., 1998. Global Marketing and Advertising. Understanding Cultural Paradoxes. SAGE Publications, Thousand Oaks.

Dowing, G., 2001. Creating Corporate Reputations: Identity, Image, and Performance: Identity, Image and Performance. Oxford University Press, Oxford.

Euromonitor, 2013. China's luxury gift culture: dead or alive? Available at: <http://blog.euromonitor.com/2013/04/chinas-luxury-gift-culture-dead-or-alive.html>.

Godart, F., Zhao, Y., 2014. Drivers of China's Desire for Luxury and Consequences for Luxury Brands. In: Atwal, G., Bryson, D. (Eds.), Luxury Brands in Emerging Markets. Palgrave Macmillan, Basingstoke.

Goffman, E., 1955. On face-work: an analysis of ritual elements in social interaction. J. Study Interpers. Processes 18, 213−231.

Greene, A., Heijbroek, A., Lagerwerf, H.A., Wazir, R., 1999. The World Wine Business. Rabobank International, Utrecht.

GroupM, 2013. The Chinese Millionaire Wealth Report 2013. Available at: <http://up.hurun.net/Humaz/201312/20131218145315550.pdf>.

Hall, E.T., 1976. Beyond Culture. Anchor Press−Doubleday, New York.

Harvard Business Review, 2015. Luxury branding below the Radar. Harvard Bus. Rev September, 26−27.

Heine, K., 2013. The concept of luxury brands. Available at: <www.conceptofluxury-brands.com>.

Heine, K., Atwal, G., Ates, Z., 2015. Luxury wine marketing. In: Charters, S., Gallo, J. (Eds.), Wine Business Management. Pearson France, Paris.

Ho, D., 1976. On the concept of face. Am. J. Sociol. 81 (4), 867−884.

Hofstede, G., 2011. Dimensionalizing cultures: the Hofstede model in context. Online Read. Psychol. Cult. 2, 1−26.

Hofstede, G., 2013. The Hofstede Centre. Available from: <http://geert-hofstede.com/dimensions.html>.

Hofstede, G., Bond, M.H., 1984. Hofstede's culture dimensions: an independent validation using rokeach's value survey. J. Cross-Cultural Psychol. 15 (4), 417−433.

Kim, D., Pan, Y., Park, H., 1998. High- versus low-context culture: a comparison of Chinese, Korean, and American cultures. Psychol. Mark. 15, 507−521.

KPMG, 2013. Global reach of China luxury. Available at: <https://www.kpmg.com/FR/fr/IssuesAndInsights/ArticlesPublications/Documents/global-reach-china-luxury.pdf>.

Leary, M., Kowalski, R., 1990. Impression management: a literature review and two-component model. Psychological Bulletin 107 (1), 34−47.

Lewis, L., Bremner, C., 2010. Grand cru becomes a vintage obsession for Beijing's elite. The Times 11 December, 53.

Liu, H.B., McCarthy, B., Chen, T., Guo, S., Song, X., 2014. The Chinese wine market: a market segmentation study. Asia Pac. J. Mark. Logistics 26 (3), 450−471.

Liu, S., Lu, Y., Liang, Q., Wei, E., 2010. Moderating effect of cultural values on decision making of gift-giving from a perspective of self-congruity theory: an empirical study from Chinese context. J. Consum. Mark. 27 (7), 604−614.

LVMH, 2015. Chandon China. Available at: <http://www.lvmh.com/houses/wines-spirits/chandon-china/>.

McSweeney, B., 2002. Hofstede's model of national cultural differences and their consequences: a triumph of faith — a failure of analysis. Hum. Relat. 55, 89—118.

Poe, D.B., 1977. The giving of gifts: anthropological data and social psychological theory. Cornell J. Soc. Relat. 12 (1), 47—63.

Qian, W., Razzaqu, M.A., Keng, K.A., 2007. Chinese cultural values and gift-giving behaviour. J. Consum. Mark. 24 (4), 214—228.

Reyneke, M., Berthon, P.R., Pitt, L.F., Parent, M., 2011. Luxury wine brands as gifts: ontological and aesthetic perspectives. Int. J. Wine Bus. Res. 23 (3), 258—270.

Schütte, H., Ciarlante, D., 1998. Consumer Behaviour in Asia. Palgrave Macmillan, Basingstoke.

Schwartz, S.H., 1999. A theory of cultural values and some implications for work. Appl. Psychol. 48 (1), 23—47.

Segev, R., Shoham, A., Ruvio, A., 2012. What does this gift say about me, you, and us? The role of adolescents' gift giving in managing their impressions among their peers. Psychol. Mark. 29, 752—764.

Shenkar, O., 2001. Cultural distance revisited: toward a more rigorous conceptualization and measurement of cultural differences. J. Int. Bus. Stud. 32 (3), 519—536.

Sherry, J., 1983. Gift giving in anthropological perspective. J. Consum. Res. 10 (2), 157—168.

Smith, P.B., Peterson, M.F., Schwartz, S.H., 2002. Cultural values, sources of guidance, and their relevance to managerial behaviour: a 47-nation study. J. Cross-cultural Psychol. 33 (2), 188—208.

Steidlmeier, P., 1997. Business ethics and politics in China. Bus. Ethics Q 7, 131—143.

Swindell, B., 2015. Survey: Fine wine prices expected to rise. Available at: <http://www.pressdemocrat.com/business/3411787-181/wine-prices-expected-to-rise>.

The Economist, 2013. Beyond bling. Available at: <http://www.economist.com/news/business/21579015-life-getting-harder-purveyors-luxury-china-growth-prospects-are-still>.

The Wall Street Journal, 2012. Time Runs Out for Watch-Wearing Brother. Available at: <http://blogs.wsj.com/chinarealtime/2012/09/22/time-runs-out-for-watch-wearing-brother/>.

Triandis, H.C., 1995. Individualism and Collectivism. Westview Press, Boulder, CO.

Wen, W., 2012. Sales of luxury brands in China slow. Available at: <http://www.chinadaily.com.cn/china/2012-07/20/content_15601795.htm>.

Wilson, J., Brennan, R., 2010. Doing business in China: is the importance of guanxi diminishing? Eur. Bus. Rev. 22 (6), 652—665.

Wong, N.Y., Ahuvia, A.C., 1998. Personal taste and family face: luxury consumption in Confucian and western societies. Psychol. Mark. 15 (5), 423—441.

Wooten, D., 2000. Qualitative steps toward an expanded model of anxiety in gift giving. J. Consum. Res. 27 (1), 84—95.

Yang, M., 1994. Gifts, Favours, and Banquets: The Art of Social Relationships in China. Cornell University Press, Ithaca.

Yang, Y., Paladino, A., 2015. The case of wine: understanding Chinese gift-giving behaviour. Mark. Lett. 26 (3), 335—361.

Yau, O.H.M., Chan, T.S., Lau, K.F., 1999. Influence of Chinese cultural values on consumer behaviour. J. Int. Consum. Mark. 11 (1), 97—116.

Yu, Y., Sun, H., Goodman, S., Chen, S., Ma, H., 2009. Chinese choices: a survey of wine consumers in Beijing. Int. J. Wine Bus. Res. 21 (2), 155—168.

Zhan, L., He, Y., 2012. Understanding luxury consumption in China: consumer perceptions of best-known brands. J. Bus. Res. 65 (10), 1452—1460.

CHAPTER 5

Young Chinese Consumers' Wine Socialization, Current Wine Behavior and Perceptions of Wine

J. Fountain[1] and M. Zhu[2]
[1]Lincoln University, Lincoln, New Zealand
[2]Shenzhen Tourism College of Jinan University, Guangzhou, Guangdong, China

INTRODUCTION

It is now widely recognized that China is an important wine market and its wine consumption is growing at a strong rate (Anderson and Wittwer, 2013; Camillo, 2012; Noppe, 2012). There is recognition also of the need for research to understand this market of relatively new wine consumers. The past few years has witnessed a proliferation of academic studies and market research exploring the consumption behaviour, purchasing cues and perception of wine amongst Chinese consumers. The general consensus from this research has been that wine is an increasingly fashionable drink for the wealthy elite and Generation X, who aspire to a Western lifestyle (Balestrini and Gamble, 2006; Camillo, 2012; Jenster and Cheng, 2008; Liu and Murphy, 2007; Noppe, 2012; Yu et al., 2009). In this market, red wine, and in particular French red wine, has acquired a very important symbolic role in gift giving, and is a status symbol to impress guests and gain *mianzi* (face) with friends and business partners (Camillo, 2012; Guinard, 2005; Li et al., 2011; Noppe, 2012). The perceived health benefits of red wine for Chinese people have been reported extensively also (Liu and Murphy, 2007; Pettigrew and Charters, 2010; Somogyi et al., 2011).

Most studies indicate that Chinese consumers' wine knowledge remains relatively limited, despite the growing range and availability of foreign wine in this market (Hu et al., 2008; Li et al., 2011; Zhang et al., 2013). Consumers reduce risk in wine purchasing by relying on extrinsic cues, such as country of origin, brand name or price, rather than intrinsic cues such as wine style or grape variety (Balestrini and Gamble, 2006; Liu and Murphy, 2007; Liu et al., 2014). Some Chinese consumers are beginning to develop more mature palates and to learn more about wine, either through informal or formal wine education courses, which are increasing in popularity (Balestrini and Gamble, 2006; Pettigrew and Charters, 2010). The growth of the wine trade throughout China partly accounts for the increase in wine education courses, as attendees are able to demonstrate a level of wine competency, thereby positioning themselves at a distinct advantage in the job market for wine or hospitality employment (Taylor, 2009; Taylor et al., 2008). The number of consumers from outside the wine industry now willing to improve their wine knowledge and general wine tasting ability has increased also (Pettigrew and Charters, 2010; Zhang et al., 2013). It has been said that in this context an increase in wine knowledge, coupled with austerity measures enforced amongst officials, may be resulting in a slow transition towards drinking, rather than gifting or investing in, wine (Marquis and Yang, 2014).

To date, relatively few studies have looked specifically at the experiences and perceptions of the youngest cohort of wine consumers in China; those Chinese who constitute Generation Y. This is due in part to their current lack of purchasing power; however, this is an important segment, as it offers a glimpse of the future of the Chinese wine market (Li et al., 2011). Globally, much has been written about this generation as it assumes fundamental importance in the consumption of a range of products and services, including wine (Charters and Mueller, 2011; Lancaster and Stillman, 2002; Thach and Olsen, 2006), and understanding their perceptions and experiences of wine is crucial for the wine industry. Generation Y is not a homogeneous cohort. In particular, there are significant cultural differences between and within countries regarding young people's engagement with wine, based on different norms and values, which are perhaps greater than age-related similarities (Charters and Mueller, 2011; Silva et al., 2014). For example, in less traditional wine drinking markets, evidence suggests that consumption of wine by younger consumers is increasing (e.g., Fountain and Lamb, 2011; Thach and Olsen, 2006), while wine consumption trends in most European countries, including France and Italy, indicate lowering levels of wine consumption amongst younger consumers (e.g., Macle, 2008; Parkinson, 2011).

The studies that have explored the characteristics and behaviours of young Chinese wine consumers have returned mixed results. For example,

Camillo (2012) reports that three-quarters of all wine purchased in his sample was by 19- to 35-year-olds, who were becoming increasingly knowledgeable about wine. By contrast, Li et al. (2011) found that Chinese young adults have only very basic wine knowledge and drink wine infrequently, however females were more knowledgeable about wine and expressed more interest in continuing wine drinking in the future, reversing the previously reported perception of wine in the Chinese market as more masculine (Liu and Murphy, 2007). Camillo (2012) and Li et al. (2011) both report that their young respondents mirrored the Chinese market as a whole in their preference for red wine and in their perception that red wine has health benefits. A study by Yu et al. (2009) compared the characteristics of typical wine consumers with university students and found some evidence that wine is becoming an everyday drink for young consumers, rather than a 'special occasion' drink, suggesting a democratization of wine. In this study, the younger consumers were more confident in their self-assessment of wine knowledge, although an explanation for these findings was not investigated. Camillo (2012) found that participation in wine related activities amongst young Chinese had a significant impact on patterns and levels of wine consumption.

An issue which has not been examined in the Chinese context is the wine socialization process. In other cultural contexts, while studies examined the contexts and reference groups that influence wine consumption patterns (see Charters and Pettigrew, 2003; Ritchie, 2011; Thach and Olsen, 2006), there has been limited work on wine socialization (although see Olsen et al., 2007; Velikova and Fountain, 2011; Velikova et al., 2013). The research that has been conducted has identified the strong influence of other people in the decision to drink wine amongst Generation Y in both Old World and New World contexts, but differences in the situation in which wine is first consumed between cultures, the age of consumption, and the wine style consumed. For example, Velikova et al. (2013) report that both Old and New World wine consumers are far more likely to first consume with friends than with parents, a finding echoing that from Olsen et al. (2007). While most Old World consumers first tried wine in an everyday context accompanying a regular meal, the first wine experiences of New World participants generally occurred at a special occasion. Red was the first wine consumed by two-thirds of Old World respondents, compared to only one third of New World respondents, who were most likely to try white wine. No study of this type has been conducted in a Chinese context.

The current research investigates the early wine experiences of young Chinese university students, their current wine consumption behaviour and perception of wine, and expectations of future wine consumption. The research has been undertaken jointly by an English-speaking researcher and a Chinese researcher, aided by a local research assistant. The research has been based on focus groups, offering the distinction of a qualitative study providing in depth insights into a cohort of consumers who are likely to represent an important source of wine consumers in coming decades.

METHODOLOGY

Much of the research on young Chinese wine consumers to date has been based on quantitative methodologies, particularly online surveys, although some qualitative research has been undertaken (Liu and Murphy, 2007; Pettigrew and Charters, 2010). Given the exploratory nature of this research, it was felt that a qualitative approach offered the best opportunity to explore issues in depth. The choice of focus groups was based on the fact that a similar approach has been used with success to investigate young people's engagement with wine elsewhere (e.g., Charters et al., 2011; Ritchie, 2011; Silva et al., 2014), and a study of Chinese consumers (albeit based in Australia) has been undertaken using focus groups (Somogyi et al., 2011).

Four focus groups of 5−7 students (24 participants in total) were recruited by the research assistant to take part this study. The students were recruited from within the hospitality and tourism programs of Shenzhen Tourism College, in Guangdong Province. While it is acknowledged that this sample will not be representative of all young Chinese people, specifically targeting university students engaged in the hospitality and tourism industries is likely to capture a higher proportion of those who might represent future wine consumers for a number of reasons. First, current wine consumers are generally highly educated, so university graduates are likely to form an important segment of future wine demand (Li et al., 2011; Yu et al., 2009). Secondly, many of these students have completed internships as part of their studies in hotels, restaurants and bars, giving them greater exposure to wine. Finally, many students from these programs enrol in an elective course offered at the college which teaches wine education and appreciation, so the impact of formal wine education on wine knowledge and consumption behaviour could be explored.

A snowball sampling technique was used whereby the focus groups were recruited through student networks by the research assistant, a student herself. This is a popular approach in many Chinese studies, in part due to the cultural importance of relationships, or *guanxi* (Li et al., 2011; Liu and Murphy, 2007). An effort was made to ensure a good gender balance, and a range of levels of wine involvement, including regular and infrequent wine drinkers. There was no pressure to participate in the study, and no incentives for involvement, although students were informed that at the end of the focus group they would be able to taste a couple of wines from New Zealand which may have been an attraction for some participants. The local Chinese researcher on this project is a lecturer of these students and teaches wine appreciation to many of them, so to avoid any conflicts of interest she was not involved in the recruitment process or present during the focus groups, and did not see the transcripts of the focus groups until names and identifying details had been changed.

The focus groups were held on the campus of Shenzhen Tourism College and took from 60 to 90 minutes to complete. Each focus group was facilitated by a non-Chinese speaker, accompanied and supported by the Chinese research assistant, who is knowledgeable about wine. Most of the participants had relatively competent English skills, however to capture the nuances of meaning all questions were translated into Chinese, and participants were free to respond in the language of their choice. The first focus group was conducted almost entirely in English, while two were almost entirely in Chinese, and the final group contained participants who responded in a mix of English and Chinese.

The focus groups commenced with the participants completing a short demographic survey. Each group then engaged in a short exercise involving a display of six bottles of New Zealand wine that participants were asked to rank in order of preference for tasting using any criteria they wanted. The exercise was repeated then with participants ranking the attractiveness of the wine labels, which ranged from very traditional to contemporary designs. In discussing their responses to this exercise, participants also shared their preferences for various wine styles and their perception of different wines. Following this, participants were asked about their early experiences of wine, more specific questions about their current wine consumption preferences and perception of wine and wine behaviour, and finally, their views about their future consumption of wine. All focus groups were audio recorded, with the permission of the participants, and were transcribed, then translated into English. The transcripts were then analyzed for key themes, framed around the key research questions.

FINDINGS AND DISCUSSION

Characteristics of the Sample

As the sample was made up of university students it is unsurprising that all participants were aged 20–22 years. There was a dominance of females (58%) over males (42%). The majority of the students (71%) were studying hotel management degrees at the college, with seven students (29%) completing tourism management degrees and one student studying golf management. Slightly more than half of the respondents (13 students) came from southern China, with 38% coming from Guangdong Province. The remaining students came from throughout the country from as far north as Heilongjiang, although none of the respondents came from Beijing or Shanghai.

Early Experiences with Wine

The situations in which most respondents first tried wine were generally similar, and suggest the importance of special occasions in the wine socialization experience in emerging wine markets (Velikova et al., 2013). All but two respondents spoke of their first experience of wine being in a family setting, and the majority of these occasions were in the context of a celebration, in particular Chinese New Year or a family occasion such as a wedding or birthday. A number of respondents mentioned that they first tried wine during the celebration of a life event of their own, such as a 16th birthday, considered an auspicious milestone, or at their graduation from high school. However, it is noticeable how young these participants were when they first tried wine, with over half of all respondents trying wine before the age of 16 years. Nine respondents (37.5%) were primary school aged (12 years or younger), and four were between 6 and 8 years of age. This is markedly different from previous studies in a Western context where first exposure to wine occurs much later (Olsen et al., 2007; Velikova et al., 2013).

Previous studies have reported that friends have an important role in early experiences with wine (Olsen et al., 2007; Velikova et al., 2013). In the case of these young people, however, the suggestion to consume wine came from a parent or other adult relative. In some cases there seems to have been quite considerable pressure placed on the child to try the wine, often explained in terms of the need to join in a celebration, but parents also stressed the health properties of wine:

> My father is pushing me 'come on, you can drink!' [He] thinks red wine is good for my health (first wine 12–13 years).

> I was in the fifth grade in primary school. I drank red wine mixed with Sprite at home. My dad told me it is good for skin (first wine 10–11 years).

> [I drank] for happiness, my parents suggested me to drink for fun. My mum also told it is good for skin (first wine 13 years).

In only a couple of cases did respondents feel they had made their own decision to try wine. The following participant was unusual in the fact that she was not with her family when she tried wine, and was also in a restaurant setting:

> The first time I drank wine is on my 16th birthday with my friend. We have very close birthdays so we celebrated together. We were in a Western restaurant and we ordered steak with wine. It was Chinese wine, not expensive, because we brought in the restaurant and we were still students. I tried a little at that time. It was bitter. I didn't have a good first impression about wine at that time. Later until I started to drink wine with my family, I began to feel it is tasty (first wine 16 years).

As in this case, the majority of respondents indicated that the first wine they tried was not of high quality. Respondents spoke of it being home-made, or cheap, with perhaps dubious origins. As one young male noted, '*I guess it is faked, maybe only 20RMB and it was not bought in the supermarket, it was outside the supermarket*'. Only a few respondents indicated that they were encouraged to try the wine because of some aspect of the wine itself, rather than the situation. For example, one female explained, '*I remember that I first drink the red wine at a family party. My father told me it is from France, and it was so expensive, so I had the opportunity to have a try*'.

For the large majority of respondents their first experience of wine was not a positive one. For example, one young woman recounted how, after having her first mouthful of wine '*Soon later I vomited in the restroom*'. Other respondents spoke of not liking the taste, describing it as 'bitter', and of a range of negative physical reactions, for example:

> My first time to drink wine maybe is my tenth year birthday. In the dinner my father brought a bottle of red wine.…. I just drank a little, but not more than 10 minutes, I am asleep… I even haven't eaten my dinner. (first wine 10 years).

The first time I drank, it was red wine, in my uncle's wedding... with my relatives and friends. Why did I drink it? Because we were all happy and people all drank it. So I have no choice I drank it too. About half an hour later, I felt a little dizzy. (first wine 16-17 years).

Current Wine Experiences and Wine Knowledge

Two-thirds of respondents (16 students) had completed the wine education course offered at the college as part of their tertiary studies. Despite this, the majority of the respondents described their wine knowledge as 'basic' (described as knowing the names of wine styles but unable to distinguish between them), while seven respondents indicated they had no wine knowledge, including three of those who had taken the wine education course. Only one respondent described her wine knowledge as at an intermediate level (that is, she knows different wine styles and can identify them). Subsequent discussions, however, revealed that a number of the respondents had been quite modest in their assessments, and had considerable knowledge not only about wine styles, but specific varietals and the characteristics of wines from different countries and regions around the world. It maybe, however, that this knowledge is primarily based on education from books and teachers, rather than from personal experience of the wines.

Excluding tasting in a formal education setting, most respondents consumed wine infrequently, with 18 respondents reporting they consumed wine less than once a month. Six respondents reported consuming wine more often, with four respondents consuming wine monthly and two respondents consuming wine weekly. Four of these six respondents described themselves as 'regular wine drinkers'. It was generally these more regular drinkers who expressed the highest levels of wine knowledge, and all six had completed the wine education course.

The most common situation in which wine is currently consumed amongst these participants is on special occasions, including Chinese New Year. This was particularly the case with the most infrequent wine drinkers, who indicated they might consume wine only once or twice a year and only on these types of occasions. Most participants reported also that they consumed wine more frequently in the presence of their family in their home town; a finding reported elsewhere (Liu and Murphy, 2007; Yu et al., 2009). More frequent drinkers consumed wine in a broader range of settings, but still consumed most wine when they went home. As one young male reported: *'[I consume wine] about once a month.*

I will drink more frequently when I go back home, during Chinese New Year I drink almost every day'.

There were other respondents who consumed wine in less formal settings, such as at a party or bar with friends, again often in the context of some sort of celebration. In this situation, wine was described as a drink for friendship, as this female participant explains:

> In my daily life, the most occasions I will consume some wine is my friend's birthday, in my dormitory. It is a day for my friend, and maybe we will have bottles of wine. We could have some things to eat and at the same time we can talk about our life… I think it is a good thing, when I graduate from school, several years later, I will remember this friendship.

The social aspect of wine was important to most respondents, however the association with sharing time with friends appealed to females more than males. One young man suggested he was more likely to *'drink beer when I meet friends. Wine is too formal for us'*. Another male reflected, *'When it comes to drinks, I would think of beer firstly instead of wine. Usually wine is drunk in high-end restaurants in the evening, not in the daytime'*.

Despite quite a strong association between wine and social occasions, a few respondents suggested that their wine consumption might occur on their own, as a source of relaxation, or for health benefits or an aid to sleep. As one young female explained, *'Sometimes at night, when I lose sleep, drink wine can help me to sleep or improve my skin'*. Another female imagined her future, when she had more money for wine: *'For me, I would drink wine as a way to relax myself after work. For example I always like to drink [red] wine in the bath'*. This use of wine perhaps reflects the more utilitarian view of the purposes of wine consumption as a health aid (cf. Charters, 2006).

There was relatively limited discussion of the consumption of wine in relation to a meal, with only two respondents indicating that this is the main setting when wine consumption occurred; a finding at odds with research with young people in other cultures (e.g., Ritchie, 2011; Thach and Olsen, 2006). Comments about the relationship between food and wine were primarily made by respondents who were more experienced with wine. For example, one male who described himself as a regular wine consumer stated, *'I prefer to choose [wine] due to occasion. If I eat seafood, I would choose white wine accordingly. If is it meat, I will choose red'*.

Amongst the participants of these focus groups there was a very strong preference for white wine, which was described as 'sweet', 'smooth', 'simple' and 'not bitter'. By contrast, red wine was described as 'bitter', 'too complex' and 'too strong'. In many cases, this preference for white wine was due to the belief that *all* white wine is sweet wine, which suggests that experiential wine knowledge is limited. Twenty-one of the 24 respondents expressed a preference for white wine over red, including all the males in the focus groups. While males explained they preferred the taste of white wine over red, there were additional reasons for their preferences, including the fact that it was perceived as more thirst quenching, and easier to drink quickly. Only three respondents stated a preference for red wine, and all of these respondents were females who consumed wine less than once a month. These three respondents seemed to have better access to foreign red wine than other respondents, through family or friends, and it was foreign red wine they generally consumed.

While white wine was preferred over red wine, a number of respondents named rosé wine, and especially white zinfandel, as their first choice of wine. This was primarily, but not exclusively, the case for females. When asked why rosé was a favourite, the primary appeal seemed to be the appearance of the wine in the glass, particularly the pink colour, rather than just the sweetness. As one female explained: '*I know most young ladies may like the rosé wine, just such as zinfandel. . .because it is elegant*'. Another female outlined the appeal in this way:

> I think the colour is beautiful, and it tastes good . . .. When you are dating or something like that, you can have a bottle of that kind of wine.

Similarly, sparkling wine was mentioned as a favourite by a couple of female respondents, with the comment made that '*the complex feeling in your mouth will make you feel happy*', reflecting other international research of young people's sparkling wine consumption and perceptions (Charters et al., 2011). It should be noted, however, that the perception of white wine as sweet was echoed in discussion of sparkling wine, with both champagne and cava described by a number of respondents as sweet wines.

A noticeable finding in this research is that brand seemed unimportant to these consumers; in the course of four focus groups no brand names were mentioned, although country of origin, or particular regions were discussed. In fact, unlike previous research, which suggests that extrinsic cues, including brand, are more important to inexperienced wine consumers (e.g., Balestrini and Gamble, 2006; Yu et al., 2009), these respondents primarily spoke about their wine choices in terms of intrinsic characteristics of the wine, in particular taste, as was explained by one female:

> I prefer red wine and my father and brother too. Before party we would discuss about which wine to buy. I don't pay attention to the brand, I focus on the taste.

The Image of Wine

The image of wine for these respondents generally reflected the situations in which they had consumed wine. First, wine was a drink for celebration; whether it be important national holidays, such as Chinese New Year, or family or personal milestones. This social aspect of wine continued in the association of wine with romance, and romantic relationships. This seems to have been perpetuated through a number of Chinese television shows with a romantic theme that shows wine being served in a range of romantic settings. Champagne also had a romantic image for female respondents:

> I had an internship in a bar last year. We had many wines there, in the very romantic occasions you can see a [champagne fountain]. I think it is very beautiful and romantic. I think one day when I get married, I will choose champagne as the first in my mind.

As stated above, the association of wine with health, so often reported in the context of the Chinese market, was particularly strong and unquestioned in this study. The relationship between wine and Western culture was mentioned by a couple of respondents, often in association with the food that would match with wine.

What was particularly apparent in discussions, however, was a clear distinction which emerged between the image of red wine and white wine amongst most respondents. Some respondents talked about wine as suitable only for formal occasions, and talked about it almost exclusively in terms of business and work situations. These respondents associated wine with people of status and money; the comment from this young man typical: '*When you talk about wine, you will think somebody is rich and has high status*'. However, there was a sense also that the formal and serious image of wine was beginning to change, with one regular wine consumer indicating that '*it was more for formal occasion in the past but now it is getting more and more popular*'. This may suggest a democratization of wine, at least amongst some young wine consumers. Further discussions revealed that this more relaxed, fun, wine image largely related to white wine, which was described as better to drink with friends, easier to match with food and more suited to younger people. A female respondent articulates this position:

> Red wine makes me think of social occasions where people gather together and celebrate. It is formal occasions. White wine is more for Western food or buffet with friends.

For most of these young students white wine was viewed more favourably than red wine; not only did they prefer the taste (associating it with a sweeter taste), but they had more favourable impressions of the wine. They acknowledged the continuing status of red wine amongst people of their parents' generation; as a regular wine consumer explained:

> In China, most young people like white wine because they have some knowledge of wine. But as for the older generation, before the days when wine first came into the Chinese market, most people just know the red wine not the white wine. For example, my parents, even my grandparents, they will still like the red wine more than the white wine. In my opinion, the older people they may know little about white wine because the white wine came to the market later than the red wine.

As alluded to above, amongst some of the respondents there was a sense in which a focus on red wine was evidence of a lack of understanding and knowledge about wine; as one young male stated: *'In China, people don't have good knowledge of wine. When it comes to wine, they just think of red wine, they have no idea of white wine'*. In fact, for another young male, preferring white wine was seen as *evidence* of wine knowledge:

> I like white wine. First there are more and more people in China drinking red wines, so it is becoming too common. So if you drink white wine, other people may think you are high level people… if you drink white, I would even think you are more knowledgeable.

This higher knowledge of wine seemed to be leading to a questioning of the traditional beliefs about the superiority of 'Old World' wines, particularly amongst the more regular consumers with higher wine knowledge. In this reassessment, the role of formal wine education classes is clear:

> I think from what I have learnt from the wine lessons, before I think France is the symbol of wine, but nowadays I know the knowledge about it again. I think every country, no matter where in the world, has its features. Every type is different from others. So I think my preference maybe the wine of the New World, such as Australia, New Zealand and America, because the new technologies, methods, and that makes more different types of taste… I think in the Old World, especially the red wine, may be too conventional.

Interestingly this perception carried over to their impressions of wine labels and wine bottles. The wine label which elicited the most negative comments was what might be considered traditionally appealing in a Chinese context. This was a Cabernet Merlot blend in a bordeaux bottle with a label predominantly gold, with a red chevron on it. A comment from a young male typified the response of a sizeable minority when he said: '[That label] looks quite old fashion... usually if we go to buy wine, young people don't want to buy this ... because this wine is not suitable for younger drinkers'.

It should be acknowledged that this dismissal of the 'traditional' was not universal; there were respondents who admired the classic and traditional in both their wine labels and wine choices. So a female respondent commented favourably on the same label:

> I think it has something to do with wealth, maybe I can imagine the picture, maybe some very successful people, they have a lot of money and wonderful family. Maybe they would choose that kind of wine because golden is a mark for success. So I choose that one.

The distinction appeared to be between consumers who had had more exposure to wine, especially in a family context or through wine education classes, and those for whom wine was still a novelty. For example, the respondent who made the previous comment was the oldest of the sample when she first tasted wine (at 20 years of age) and came from a family that did not consume wine at all.

Future Wine Consumption Intentions

At present these respondents have restricted financial resources to choose and buy wines. Whilst respondents spoke about their preferred wine styles, they also acknowledged that as students they currently had limited abilities to purchase the wines they preferred, having to settle for cheaper wine, or wine provided by other people. As one regular wine consumer acknowledged:

> Nowadays the main customers with the purchasing power are mainly middle age people. So those customers may choose the red wine more than the white wine.... [So] now young generation know more about white wine, but they don't have the purchasing power to buy. So most people in China still consume red wine, not white wine.

For this reason, as a final question these students were asked to imagine a time when they have completed their degrees and have well-paying jobs. In this situation, they were asked to consider whether they would continue to drink wine, or drink wine more frequently, and if so, what wine they would drink. Responses to this question fell into three main categories. First, a sizeable proportion of respondents said they would not drink wine more frequently, and would continue to consume wine only on special occasions. This contradicts the findings of Li et al. (2011) who suggested almost all university students aspired to drink more wine. The reasons given by these respondents included that they didn't like the taste of wine, or felt they were allergic to wine. One young male summarized this perspective:

> After I graduate, I will not continue to drink wine because I am allergic to wine. I also don't like to drink wine because I don't like its taste. I heard that people can get addicted to wine very easily. I also know that drinking wine is good for health, but I will try other ways to strengthen my health instead of drinking wine.

A second set of responses suggested that, given the high status and reputation of red wine in particular, wine consumption was something to aspire to and admire. These respondents tended to be less knowledgeable and inexperienced wine consumers, and reflected the traditional view of wine in China. A number of these participants, both males and females, felt that as they aged they would appreciate red wine more as their palates developed. Some explained that they would actively attempt to learn to like red wine by trying it more often, as was the case with this female respondent:

> I think I am not very young anymore. I think I have to learn to try some more graceful variety. I think pinot noir will be a good choice for our girls. It is more graceful. I have to learn how to enjoy that kind of wine.

For this group, appreciating red wine symbolized maturity and adulthood. It was viewed also to be a prerequisite of business. For example, a male respondent explained that in a business environment it would be 'inevitable to drink, particularly red wine'. Similarly, a female participant suggested: 'After I graduate, maybe I would go to work, so it will be quite essential to drink red wine for that'. Another young male felt that the industry for which he was training required wine knowledge and consumption:

> I think I will drink wine in the future, because it is a way to socialize and communicate with others. My major is part of the services industry, I have to know some knowledge and skills of wine … Maybe at a certain age I will choose the wine not because I like it, or I don't have the right to pick up the wine I like. At that time I may drink red wine.

The third set of responses reflected a relative disregard for the traditional view of wine outlined above, with respondents suggesting that they would drink what they liked, and what suited the situation. So, for example, they acknowledged they might need to drink red wine in certain business situations, but in other situations they would enjoy what they liked the taste of, or what suited the food they were eating. It should be acknowledged that the members of this third group were generally those who expressed more self-confidence about their wine knowledge and consumed wine more often. As one male explained. '*When I grow up, I will drink more, because I like the taste and want to try more tastes*'. Another male summarized the sense of these responses:

> When I grow up, the future is difficult to say; I don't know if I will choose the red or the white. But I want to choose what I like, the taste, . . . I want to taste and decide which wine I will buy.

CONCLUSIONS AND IMPLICATIONS

This study has revealed the perceptions and experiences of a small cohort of university students in the southern Chinese city of Shenzhen. It is acknowledged that this sample is not representative of the general population of young people in China, however as university students who are engaged in the study of tourism and hospitality, they may perhaps well represent the future market for wine in China. Findings reveal that these Chinese students were generally exposed to wine at a young age, but did not find the experience enjoyable. Exposure to wine in a range of contexts, including through hospitality internships, socializing with friends and through wine education classes, has resulted in a more positive attitude to wine for many of these students. Perhaps the most interesting finding in this study is the strong preference for white wine and rosé over red wine, despite the respondents' recognition of the status of red wine. Another key finding is the way in which exposure to wine, particularly through wine education classes, may have given these young Chinese wine consumers the confidence to continue to drink white wine, rather than red wine, in the future. At the same time, however, there are a group of young consumers who maintain the traditional perception of red wine as a high status wine, and something to which to aspire. In general, those holding this perspective have either not studied wine education formally, or have had limited exposure to wine outside a formal class setting.

There are a number of implications of this study for wine marketers and wine educators. First, it appears that demand for white wine, and perhaps rosé wine, in China will increase as these young, educated and more knowledgeable wine consumers move into the paid workforce and have the financial capacity to purchase the wines of their choice. Secondly, this study has identified the role of wine education in opening the minds (and hearts) of young Chinese consumers to the world of wine available to them, and strongly suggests the value of wine education in broadening the wine market in China.

REFERENCES

Anderson, K., Wittwer, G., 2013. Modelling global wine markets to 2018: exchange rates, taste changes, and China's import growth. J. Wine Econ. 8 (2), 131−158.

Balestrini, P., Gamble, P., 2006. Country-of-origin effects on Chinese wine consumers. Br. Food J. 108 (5), 396−412.

Camillo, A.A., 2012. A strategic investigation of the determinants of wine consumption in China. Int. J. Wine Bus. Res. 24 (1), 68−92.

Charters, S., 2006. Wine and Society: The Social and Cultural Context of a Drink. Butterworth-Heinemann, Oxford.

Charters, S., Mueller, S., 2011. Guest editorial. Int. J. Wine Bus. Res. 23 (2), 104−106.

Charters, S., Pettigrew, S., 2003. I like it but how do I know if it's any good? Quality and preference in wine consumption. J. Res. Consum. 5, 1021−1027.

Charters, S., Velikova, N., Ritchie, C., Fountain, J., Thach, L., Dodd, T., et al., 2011. Generation Y and sparkling wines: a cross-cultural perspective. Int. J. Wine Bus. Res. 23 (2), 161−175.

Fountain, J., Lamb, C., 2011. Generation Y as young wine consumers in New Zealand: how do they differ from Generation X? Int. J. Wine Bus. Res. 23 (2), 107−124.

Guinard, L., 2005. The Chinese taste for wine. Wines and Vines December, 42−44

Hu, X., Li, L., Xie, C., Zhou, J., 2008. The effects of country-of-origin on Chinese consumers' wine purchasing behaviour. J. Technol. Manag. China 3 (3), 292−306.

Jenster, P., Cheng, Y., 2008. Dragon wine: developments in the Chinese wine industry. Int. J. Wine Bus. Res. 20, 244−259.

Lancaster, L.C., Stillman, D., 2002. When Generations Collide: Who they are, Why they Clash, How to Solve the Generational Puzzle at Work. Harper Business, New York.

Li, J.G., Jia, J.R., Taylor, D., Bruwer, J., Li, E., 2011. The wine drinking behaviour of young adults: an exploratory study in China. Br. Food J. 113 (10), 1305−1317.

Liu, F., Murphy, J., 2007. A qualitative study of Chinese wine consumption and purchasing: implications for Australian wines. Int. J. Wine Bus. Res. 19 (2), 98−113.

Liu, H.B., McCarthy, B., Chen, T., Guo, S., Song, X., 2014. The Chinese wine market: a market segmentation study. Asia Pac. J. Mark. Logistics 26 (3), 450−471.

Macle, D., 2008. Young France isn't drinking wine: the "French Paradox" is becoming a thing of the past. Wine Spectator. Available at: <http://www.winespectator.com/webfeature/show/id/Young-France-Isnt-Drinking-Wine_4162>.

Marquis, C., Yang, Z., 2014. The Chinese wine market: vanguard of a consumption society. Available at: <http://www.ecommons.cornell.edu/bitstream/1813/36861/2/Wine_CPR_FINAL.pdf>.

Noppe, R.P., 2012. Rise of the dragon: the Chinese wine market. Dissertation submitted to the Cape Wine Academy, Cape Town, South Africa.

Olsen, J.E., Thach, E.C., Nowak, L.I., 2007. Wine for my generation: exploring how US wine consumers are socialized to wine. J. Wine Res. 18 (1), 1−18.

Parkinson, J., 2011. Young Italians 'drink less wine than ever'. Decanter. Available at: <http://www.decanter.com/news/wine-news/522786/young-italians-drink-less-wine-than-ever>.

Pettigrew, S., Charters, S., 2010. Alcohol consumption motivations and behaviours in Hong Kong. Asia Pac. J. Market. Logistics 22 (2), 210−221.

Ritchie, C., 2011. Young adult interaction with wine in the UK. Int. J. Contemp. Hospitality Manag. 23 (1), 99−114.

Silva, A.P.C., Figueiredo, I., Hogg, T., Sottomayor, M., 2014. Young adults and wine consumption a qualitative application of the theory of planned behaviour. Br. Food J. 116 (5), 832−848.

Somogyi, S., Li, E., Johnson, T., Bruwer, J., Bastian, S., 2011. The underlying motivations of Chinese wine consumer behaviour. Asia Pac. J. Market. Logistics 23 (4), 473−485.

Taylor, D.C., 2009. Identifying the motivation to attend wine education courses. J. Hospitality Tourism Educ. 21 (4), 65−71.

Taylor, D.C., Dodd, T.H., Barber, N., 2008. Impact of wine education on developing knowledge and preferences: an exploratory study. J. Wine Res. 19 (3), 193−207.

Thach, E.C., Olsen, J.E., 2006. Market segment analysis to target young adult wine drinkers. Agribusiness 22 (3), 307−322.

Velikova, N., Fountain, J., 2011. How young people are socialised to wine: the experiences of the Generation Y cohort in the US and Australasia. Paper presented at the The 6th Academy of Wine Business Research International Conference Bordeaux, France.

Velikova, N., Fountain, J., de Magistris, T., Seccia, A., Wilson, D., 2013. My first glass of wine: a comparison of Gen Y early wine experiences and socialisation in New and Old Worlds markets. Refereed paper. 7th Academy of Wine Business Research (AWBR) Conference. 12-15 June, 2013. Brock University, St Catharines, Ontario.

Yu, Y., Sun, H., Goodman, S., Chen, S., Ma, H., 2009. Chinese choices: a survey of wine consumers in Beijing. Int. J. Wine Bus. Res. 21 (2), 155−168.

Zhang, Q.H., Yuan, J., Haobin, Y.B., Hung, K., 2013. Wine tourism phenomena in China: an emerging market. Int. J. Contemp. Hospitality Manag. 25 (7), 1115−1134.

CHAPTER 6

Store Image Perception of Retail Outlets for Wine in China

A.M. Corsi, J. Cohen and L. Lockshin
Ehrenberg-Bass Institute for Marketing Science, Adelaide, Australia

INTRODUCTION

It has been widely noted that the wine market in China is expanding rapidly (Lockshin, 2014). In order to be part of this expansion, wine producers must place their wine on shelves or online to make sales. Understanding the perception consumers have for different traditional retail and online outlets is important, because wineries can strategically think about the chains where their products could be distributed. Typically, wine exporters do not think about the actual chains where their wines will be sold. They often leave this to the distributor or importer. However, different retailers may suit different brand growth plans, so understanding consumer perceptions of retailers can be useful in long term market planning.

The literature uses store image (SI) to assess how consumers view different retail offerings. SI is typically measured using several dimensions (product range, pricing, staff, image and location) (e.g. Burt and Carralero-Encinas, 2000; Lockshin and Kahrimanis, 1998). By dividing the perception of retailers into different dimensions, researchers and marketers can better understand not only the overall view of consumers, but what factors go into creating that view.

Despite the number of papers published on the concept of SI, there is not much published on Chinese retail and online outlets, probably because major retailers are rather new in the Chinese marketplace. On top of this, there are very few SI studies of wine retailers worldwide. This study aims to rectify both of these issues. The chapter is organized as follows: first, a short description of how wine is sold in China is presented. This is based mainly on the authors' visits and data collection in China.

Next, a formal literature review of SI research is presented. This review provides the basis for the SI measures used in the survey. The subsequent section clearly describes the sample and the actual data collection instrument. This is followed by the analysis and presentation of the results. The results are placed into the context of how wine brands might use SI to help develop their retail marketing strategy in China. Finally, some of the issues with the current research and future research directions are discussed.

STATE-OF-THE-ART ON WINE RETAILING IN CHINA

Not long ago, there was little hard data available on the Chinese wine market. The main sources of market data currently emanate from global secondary providers such as Datamonitor and Euromonitor. Their statistics indicate that China is a very attractive market. Datamonitor International (2015) reports that the Chinese retail wine market will grow by 112% in value and 103% in volume over the next five years. This follows a very positive trend, which has characterized both the off-premise and on-premise sectors for the past five years, with the first growing by 45% by volume and 87% by value, and the second growing by 32% and 53% respectively (Euromonitor International, 2015). However, Euromonitor International (2015) reports that the on-premise market suffered in 2014 due to the austerity measures and a reduction of consumption of wine in public settings by government officials, suggesting that this will have a positive impact on the retail market.[1]

Another key source of data is export market statistics that are tracked by the exporting governments and also Chinese Customs. Through numerous discussions with both brands and distributors active in China and comparing their figures with that of Customs, it may surprise many to hear that this data is actually quite accurate. Yes, there are stories of Custom officials taking a 'personal tax' here and there, but this only has an impact on business in the ultra-premium market of wines and cognac where, for example, there may only be four cases of Louis XIII entering the entire Chinese market. Therefore, accessing Chinese Customs data can provide a good indicator of what wine lands in China. However,

[1] For more details on the attitudes, perceptions and behaviour of Chinese consumers in the on-premise sector, we invite the readers to consult Corsi et al. (2015).

there is very little data available on what is actually sold, where, and through what channel.

Most of the discussion amongst those interested in the Chinese wine market revolves around questions regarding the country of origin most preferred and their perceptions by Chinese wine drinkers. Cohen et al. (2014a,b) using the Wine Australia's funded *China Wine Barometer* provide detail on how imported and Chinese wines are perceived. According to Datamonitor International (2015), the four biggest Chinese players account for 60% of the volume of wine sold in China, with one company – Yantai Changyu – controlling nearly one quarter of the market. Discussions with wine distributors in China about the imported wine market lead to repeated comments about the size of the domestic market. It is often said that four out of five bottles of wine sold in China are from Chinese-grown grapes. Therefore, despite the increasingly deep understanding of the imported wine market in China by practitioners, those who know the market well are often incredulous at the lack of awareness of the power and market share of local producers. There is a tendency to focus on the tip of the iceberg. If so many are misinformed about this, what else is misaligned in our collective knowledge about retail in the China wine market?

Not unlike retail in the USA at the turn of the 20th century where consumers asked a salesperson at the counter for items, a lot of traditional retailing in China has typically been small businesses operating out of miniscule spaces, prohibiting the product displays that are common to Western shopping contexts. The influx of foreign hypermarket brands into China as well as the creation of national brands based on this format has changed the way the Chinese shop, at least in the major Tier 1 cities where all but a few of the biggest international wine brands are playing the brick-and-mortar game. Lannes et al. (2012) concluded through a vast exploration of shopper behaviour in China that supermarkets and hypermarkets are seeing rapid growth in Tier 1 cities and accounting for more than half of all fast moving consumer goods (FMCG) sales. Romaniuk and Sharp (2015) show evidence that repertoire buying exists in emerging markets including China, which makes them similar to more developed Western markets. The evolution of large format retailers in China is changing the route-to-market of goods and creating the shelf space for wine distributors to fill and for consumers to choose from. Lannes et al. (2012) also illustrates the growth of the e-channel in the Chinese wine market. However, this channel still accounts for a very small share of total product sales in China.

Datamonitor International (2015) suggest that approximately 45% of wine sales occur in either a hypermarket or supermarket. Cohen et al. (2014a,b) demonstrate that among regular drinkers of imported wine in China, penetration is 94% for hypermarkets, 90% for speciality wine retailers, and 85% for online wine retail. It should be noted that this research investigated 15 known channels in China and penetration was above 50% for 14 out of 15 channels. This suggests that consumers are using a broad repertoire of retail channels. However, other than large format retailers, like hypermarkets and online retail, which distribute nationally, all other channels are localized in specific regions.

Some store audits the authors of this paper conducted in 2013 in Shanghai, Guangzhou and Chengdu gave us some other useful insights about the way wine is retailed in China. At the time, the wine category typically occupied two retail aisles. This comprised an aisle of Chinese wines and an aisle of imported wines. These aisles were cluttered with promotional material hanging from the ceiling, pasted as large stickers on the aisle floor and overabundance of shelf-talkers, which typically boasted two-for-one deals rather than any substantive brand information. In addition to the printed collateral material, due to the low cost of labour in China there were one to two salespeople — almost always female — standing in the aisles to provide sales support. It was clear that the only manner in which recommendations could be made was pointing out the most expensive bottle in the classification the shopper was perusing. The Chinese wine aisles were almost always arranged by brand. The imported wines were typically ranged by country of origin and then, within that, usually a breakdown by style. Despite the ever-present sales force, very little effort was ever placed on maintaining the order of the ranging. The research reported below coincides with the store audits described here. It should be noted that the audits of hypermarkets were replicated in 2015 and the categories look markedly different. The salespeople are gone and the category has been reduced drastically in size. The wine category now typically occupies one aisle, which is roughly 67% represented by Chinese wines. The remaining 33% are imported wines. This is probably a direct reflection of sales performance in China, which resulted in category consolidation.

THE CONCEPTUALIZATION OF STORE IMAGE

The concept of SI has been extensively unravelled in the literature. Martineau (1958) defined the concept as the way customers see stores both functionally and psychologically. Kunkel and Berry (1968) expanded this definition, arguing that for customers to develop an image of the store they need to experience the store first and compare this experience with their expectations. The outcome of this comparison determines future visits and repurchase decisions. A radical turning point in the conceptualization of SI happened when Lindquist (1974) brought forward the idea that SI is a multidimensional concept, its components can be singularly measured, and their contribution to the overall SI vary both in relation to the stores observed and the people evaluating them. More specifically, Lindquist (1974) grouped several factors in nine main dimensions — merchandise, service, clientele, physical facilities, convenience, promotion, store atmosphere, institutional factors and posttransaction satisfaction. Since then, many other authors have tried to define the quantity and quality SI should comprise, with the quality and quantity of dimensions varying between authors. For example, Doyle and Fenwick (1974) included five dimensions — product, price, assortment, styling and location; Nevin and Houston (1980) only three dimensions — assortment, facilities, and market posture; while Ghosh (1990) went back to classification similar to Lindquist (1974), as he conceptualized SI into eight factors — location, merchandise, store atmosphere, customer service, price, advertising, personal selling and sales incentive programmes. This is similar to Burt and Carralero-Encinas (2000), who reviewed a variety of SI studies published between 1974 and 1996 to also come up with eight dimensions — physical characteristics, pricing policy, product range, customer service, character and store reputation. It is important to point out that Burt and Carralero-Encinas (2000) did not adopt a scale validation approach (Churchill, 1979) to generate the factors and the dimensions used in the research. Their choice seemed to be totally arbitrary, although based on a subjective evaluation of what was previously published in the literature. This approach seems to be analogous to that adopted by Thang and Tan (2003), for whom the selection of the factors and dimensions was still qualitative, but with evidence that the choice of factors and dimensions was based on theoretical conceptualization. This led the authors to define eight dimensions, similar to those proposed by Lindquist (1974), with the exception of the clientele dimension, which the authors decided to delete. Semeijn et al. (2004) proposed three main dimensions — merchandise, layout, service — while Chang and Tu (2005) used only four dimensions — facilities, store service, store activities and convenience.

All the above mentioned papers refer to the concept of SI in relation to traditional brick-and-mortar retailers. However, the growth of online sales for FMCG (Euromonitor International, 2014) would make the conceptualization and the results of these studies less relevant, as brick-and-mortar retailers have different characteristics from online retailers. The seminal paper in this regard was published by van der Heijden and Verhagen (2004), who explored the impact of the online component in a multichannel retailing strategy and website presentation on SI perceptions. Following Churchill's (1979) scale validation approach, the authors identified seven elements of online SI — usefulness, enjoyment, ease-of-use, style, familiarity, trust and settlement performance. Elliott and Speck (2005) conceptualized online SI in six factors — ease-of-use, product information, entertainment, trust, customer support and currency — but this time the dimensions have been generated based on a qualitative analysis of previous SI research. More recently, Aghekyan-Simonian et al. (2012) examined the impact of two major risk reducing factors for online apparel shopping — product image and SI — adopting a modified version of a SI scale proposed by Yun and Good (2007), which was, in turn, developed via qualitative review of traditional and online SI studies. Chang and Teng (2013) and Chen and Teng (2013) also adopted the SI scale from van der Heijden and Verhagen (2004) to measure the relationship between online SI and purchase intentions towards online travel agents, travel related products and IT products.

Despite the abundance of SI papers in the marketing field, we face a paucity of SI studies in the wine marketing literature. Lockshin and Kahrimanis (1998) represent the only research which specifically investigated consumers' evaluation of wine retailers. The authors included seven dimensions — price, wine range, staff qualities, wine tastings, presentation and store layout, overall image of the store and miscellaneous (including membership clubs, parking, opening hours and distance to home and work) — finding that staff, product range and prices were the most important elements for the evaluation of wine retailers. In a broader sense, in fact, the wine marketing literature tended to focus more on the elements driving the choice of wine in a retail store rather than on the actual elements of the store itself. One of the most cited papers in this regard is Goodman (2009), who investigated the factors driving the choice of wine in the retail sector in 12 countries. The results showed that previous trial and recommendation were highly important across most markets, with the exceptions in some markets of influencers such as 'brand' (China and Brazil), 'food matching' (France and Italy), 'origin' (France) and 'grape variety' (Austria). Quinton and Harridge-March (2008) observed the importance of trust between buying wine in store versus online, finding that it is important to have an online service mix that instils trust for the first-time online buyer. Orth and Bourrain (2005) looked at the influence of ambient scent on wine buying behaviour, and observed that more pleasant scents increased variety seeking and curiosity-motivated behaviour. This had effects on the importance of the standard elements consumers use in deciding which wine to buy, such as label colour, taste, and grape variety. Finally, Lockshin and Knott (2009) measured the effect of free wine tastings on sales before, during and after the tasting period. Free tasting improved sales on the day by over 400% compared to before and after the tasting.

To sum up, this literature review shows the importance of SI in the marketing literature, but a lack of SI studies in relation to online stores and wine retailers. Lannes et al. (2012) conducted a comprehensive analysis of the shopper behaviour of Chinese consumers in hypermarkets, however their analysis never included measurement of store perceptions nor did it specifically explore the category of wine. It is, therefore the intention of this research to fill this gap, by analyzing how consumers perceive the main brick-and-mortar and online wine retailers in China.

SAMPLE AND METHOD

The data were collected in October 2013 through an online survey, generating 1094 completed questionnaires. The sample was sociodemographically representative in terms of age, gender and income of the upper-middle class urban population aged 18−49 living in Beijing, Shanghai, Guangzhou, Chengdu, Shenyang and Wuhan, who drink imported wine at least twice a year. After removing incomplete surveys and those whose response patterns indicated they were not responding to the questions properly, the sample was reduced to 966 analyzable questionnaires. The majority of respondents were 30−39 years old (42%), male (67%), earning more than RMB 10,000 (AUD1500) per month (50%), living in Shanghai (43%), Guangzhou (19%) and Beijing (20%).

The questionnaire included questions relative to different aspects of attitudes and behaviour towards wine in general and specific items related to the retail sector, but for the purpose of this chapter, we will focus on the perception respondents have about different traditional and online retailers in relation to wine across different SI dimensions.

The list of traditional and online retailers included in this research came from the ranking of wine retailers consumers were most aware of in China (Wine Intelligence, 2013) in conjunction with a qualitative review of the most popular retailers undertaken by the authors during multiple visits to China in 2013. The hypermarkets included in the study are, in alphabetical order: Auchan, Carrefour, Liahua, Lotus, Metro, RT-Mart, Tesco and Walmart. In addition to these brands, it was decided to include another option in the form of "my local wine store". This option reflects the fact that the grocery retail structure is very fragmented, with the leading grocery retailer, China Resources, holding a value share of only 3% of the market by value in 2012 (Euromonitor International, 2013). Traditional retailing still plays a fundamental role in China especially in areas where modern retailers have not yet established a significant presence. The online wine retailers included in the study are: Juixian.com, Firstcellars.com, Pinwine.com, Tmall.com, Yesmywine. com and Winenice.com.

The list of items chosen to evaluate the perception towards brick-and-mortar retail stores was adapted from the items developed by Lockshin and Kahrimanis (1998) and Burt and Carralero-Encinas (2000) to measure retail SI. From there, the list of items relative to online retailers was created, making sure the items used for the online stores matched as closely as possible with those developed for the physical retailers. Two exceptions need mentioning. First, instead of items measuring the perception of staff in online stores, we included items on the overall perception of the website. Secondly, instead of retail location items, we included items on the security of financial transactions and delivery options, as suggested by Van der Heijden and Verhagen (2004). The full lists of items for the two retail typologies are included in the Appendix.

A *pick-any* approach (Driesener and Romaniuk, 2006) allowed us to collect information about the association of each SI item with each of the physical and online retailers. This methodology was first developed in the branding literature (Bogomolova and Romaniuk, 2010; Nenycz-Thiel and Romaniuk, 2009), but it has been applied to other research fields, such as tourism (Bowe et al., 2013), pricing (Sjostrom et al., 2013), sensory analysis (Jaeger et al., 2013) and wine (Corsi et al., 2011). The method consists of showing respondents a list of items for each of the dimensions researchers want to investigate. For each dimension respondents are asked to indicate which, if any, brand (in our case retailers) they would associate with each item. Respondents select as many items as they want and can link the same attribute to multiple retailers. Unlike other forced-choice methods, the *pick-any* approach allows obtaining similar information to other forced-choice approaches, but it is quicker to understand and complete (Bogomolova and Romaniuk, 2010).

Correspondence analysis (CA) was used to analyze the data. This multivariate statistical technique is conceptually similar to principal component analysis (PCA), but instead of using continuous variables, it is applicable to categorical data. As in PCA, the output of CA is a set of coordinates onto the *i* dimensions of a CA plot for each of the items included in the analysis (in our case wine retailers and descriptors). For ease of interpretation, the plot is often reduced to two dimensions. However, different to PCA, where each axis can be defined by the factor scores each original variable is loaded into, the axes in CA have no other meaning than a bidimensional representation of the associations between the items displayed in the plot (Beh, 2004; Greenacre, 2007).

RESULTS

The results for the brick-and-mortar retailers reveal two groups of retailers, plus 'my local wine store', which is positioned far from the retail chains and defined by different SI elements (Fig. 6.1). Walmart and Carrefour are clustered together and are mainly characterized by elements relative to the products carried. The two chains are perceived to carry a wide selection of wines (#1), including reliable private labels (#4). The wines are of good quality (#2), generally available in stock (#6), easy to find on shelf (#7) and can easily be returned (#5). Some characteristics also emerge in relation to pricing. Respondents perceive that the wines stocked by these two retailers are good-value-for-money (#12), perhaps due to the fact that discounts are available (#10), and that prices are easily visible on shelf (#9). Finally, these two retailers are considered to be totally reliable (#23), trustworthy (#24) and located in convenient locations (#25).

The second group of retailers comprise Auchan, Tesco, Lotus and RT-Mart. These players seem to be characterized by a more balanced mix of the four SI dimensions. In terms of products, these chains are perceived to carry fashionable wines (#3) and to be chosen for online purchases too (#8). The prices are considered low compared to similar retailers (#11),

Store Image perception map for brick-and-mortar wine retailers in China

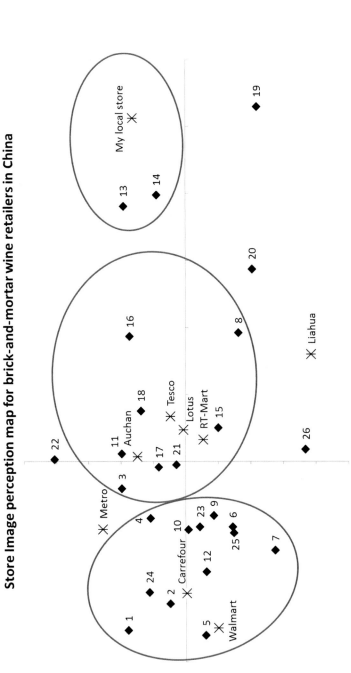

Figure 6.1 SI perception map for brick-and-mortar wine retailers in China.
Note: Brick-and-mortar wine retailers are represented by the asterisks, while SI factors by the diamonds.

and, in terms of overall SI, respondents feel that the stores are clean and tidy (#17), have an excellent atmosphere (#18), and are more suitable to serve the middle class (#21). Different from Walmart and Carrefour, these retailers are characterized by good perceptions of staff: friendly personnel (#16) who provide good customer service (#15).

'My local wine store' prevails over corporate retailers only in terms of personnel. When purchasing at a local store customers state they can rely on staff, with whom they can develop a good relationship (#14) and who are able to give recommendations about the wines (#13).

Interestingly, two retailers — Metro and Liahua — do not seem to be associated with any dimension in particular, though Metro is relatively close to Auchan. Similarly, other general SI dimensions such as being a world-class retailer (#22), having a Chinese appeal (#20), or projecting a conservative image (#19) do not belong to any retailer in particular. Finally, a previous purchase from a retailer (#26) is another characteristic not associated with any chain, as respondents are likely to have purchased from one or more of the retailers presented in this research.

The analysis of online wine retailers shows four groups of stores, two of which are characterized by a homogenous mix of the five SI dimensions, while the other two retailers emerge in relation to general SI aspects and security of transactions and delivery options (Fig. 6.2).

Yesmywine.com and Juixian.com are thought to carry a wide selection of wines (#1), which are also fashionable (#3). They offer price discounts (#8), they have an attractive website (#12), respondents frequently see advertising by these online retailers on the Internet (#22), and they have total trust in online transactions with these stores (#21).

Pinwine.com and Winenice.com are also appreciated for their products and value, which are perceived to be always in stock (#6), can be easily returned (#5), are of good-value-for-money #10), and offer a range of private labels consumers find to be reliable (#4). The website is fun (#11) and customers find the navigation a pleasurable experience (#15). In terms of security, the most important aspect associated with Pinwine.com and Winenice.com is that personal data are safely kept confidential (#24), thus contributing to an overall reliable image of these retailers #20).

Tmall.com, the largest of the operators considered in this study, is exclusively characterized by the security of transactions and delivery options. This online retailer offers safe (#25) and fast financial transactions (#26), has a number (#23) of safe (#28) and fast (#27) range delivery options.

Store Image perception map of online wine retailers in China

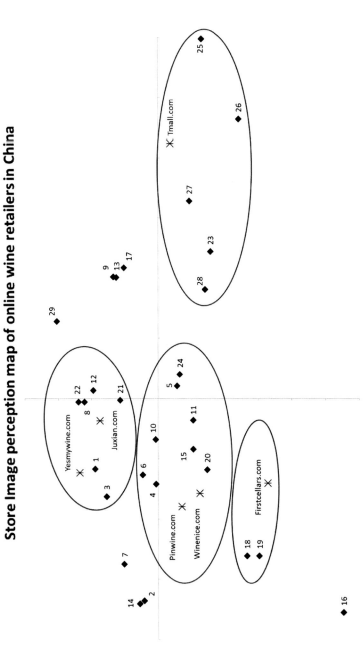

Figure 6.2 SI perception map for online wine retailers.
Note: Online wine retailers are represented by the asterisks, while SI factors by the diamonds.

Finally, Firstcellars.com is mostly associated with the ability to serve the middle class (#18) and is perceived to be a world-class retailer (#19).

As above, several SI dimensions do not seem to be connected with any specific online retailer. In terms of products, none of the retailers is thought to stock good quality wines (#2), nor do they seem to have a website providing good recommendations about the wines (#14). The prices offered by these retailers seem to be comparable, as no store is perceived to offer low prices compared to the others (#7). Also, prices seem to be hard to identify in any of the websites, as no store is perceived to make prices clearly visible (#9). This is reflected in the fact that none of retailers have an easy to navigate website (#13). Finally, no website in particular has a clear Chinese appeal (#17) or projects a conservative image (#16), and respondents do not seem to have shopped at any online retailer more than another (#29).

DISCUSSION AND CONCLUSIONS

This is the first study to consider the SI and attributes of major wine retailers in China. The brick-and-mortar retailers seem to fall into two groups plus the local wine store. Consumers see local shops as providing good customer service, while the Walmart—Carrefour grouping is not recognized for this. The third grouping is located between the other two. This means that wineries needing some personal selling would do better to look for distribution in stores in the groupings in the middle or right hand side of Fig. 6.1, while wineries with substantial advertising would likely do better in the group with Walmart or Carrefour. This is a surprising result. The image of stores in the middle cluster is better, but our evidence from another component of the survey is that consumers shop at a number of these major store brands. It is also interesting to note there seems to be no image differences between the international chains and the major Chinese one.

There are more differences among online retailers than major brick-and-mortar ones. This is mainly due to the different business models. Tmall.com is a general retailer across hundreds of product categories, whereas some of the online retailers are wine-specific and others are alcohol retailers with some wines. Yesmywine.com and Juxian.com are perceived to advertise more and have the perception of repeat purchase, which seem to go together. Pinwine.com and Winenice.com are known for private labels and for secure personal data, while Tmall.com has secure transactions and better delivery. None of these image attributes would seem of major importance to wine producers, but might be useful to the stores themselves for improving their position in the market. It also seems clear that there is potential to gain customers by developing an easy to navigate website, clearly marked prices, and wine recommendations. Some of the larger wineries or even wine regions might choose to ally with a particular retailer and help develop the recommendation part of the website.

Any wine brand and its associated distribution chain can benefit from understanding the landscape of retail offerings to wine consumers. There are many options for selling wine to retail consumers, but not all will suit each wine brand. All grocery chains and hypermarkets rely on individual brands building their awareness outside the retailer. Advertising, sales promotions and tastings are necessary to build consumer awareness before using one of these major retailers successfully. This is as true in China as it is in any wine market with large chain retailers. Most consumers shopping in these large stores are buying multiple items and do not shop there specifically for wine. They will likely buy wines they are aware of and have tasted previously as the authors found in other parts of the *China Wine Barometer*. So, wineries aiming to build a presence in China with a good marketing and promotion programme should definitely consider these major retail channels. Smaller wineries with small budgets will likely find it difficult to sell much wine through these retailers.

The largest hypermarkets, Carrefour and Walmart, do not seem to provide a good consumer experience, and thus, more brand building is necessary to succeed in these. The other large chains (Auchan, Tesco, Lotus, and RT-Mart) are very price oriented, so the ability to discount below the normal sales price is part of the success factors for selling there. These retailers have the image of being service oriented, so distributors with good in-house training programs may do well to target these retailers for brands with high awareness and good advertising.

It may be difficult to navigate the local convenience and independent wine store scene in China without a good local partner. However, this research shows that imported wine buyers find the local stores friendly and consumers can establish a relationship with them. This could be highly beneficial for some smaller brands wishing to penetrate specific localities in China.

Online retailing is structured differently to brick-and-mortar retailing. There are major players, like Tmall.com, with the platform selling anything one could think of. But there are also major national online alcohol and specialty wine retailers, which are not comparable to the grocery retailing space. Probably the most important difference among the online retailers is that Yesmywine.com and Juixian.com are thought to be both less expensive and to advertise a lot on the web. These outlets could be the first point of call for wine brands looking to reach a wide audience and having some promotional dollars to spend. Overall, online wine buyers view all the retailers' websites as difficult to use and hard to find the actual prices. This seems to be an opportunity for one or more of these companies to differentiate themselves by improving in these two areas.

One key fact learned about retailing in China from this research is that all of the major retailers, brick-and-mortar and online, are patronised by the majority of imported wine buyers. There is no one single retailer distinctively capturing the market and most are seen as fairly similar to each other. For wine brands exporting to China this reduces some of the difficulty in choosing exactly which outlets to focus on, as most of these heavy buyers visit most stores and websites.

Admittedly, this is a first research effort at understanding the wine retailing landscape in China. Further research can be used to clarify some of the issues found here. The research did not investigate the importance of the various SI attributes for consumers in choosing which store(s) to patronize. If convenience is the major factor, because most stores are seen as similar, then location becomes the most important factor in a wine retailer's success. If customer service is important for some groups of consumers, then certainly some retailers deliver better than others; but if customer service is not important, those retailers might be wasting funds building such attributes. The research also did not look at what consumers see as missing in the retail offer, except for the poor performance of online retailers in website navigation, pricing and wine recommendations. There must be some factors not investigated for brick-and-mortar retailers that provide a difference that drives patronage. If not, then location is the main driver of consumer preference. Another aspect the research did not take into account is retailing in smaller Chinese cities. It might be that the smaller cities are mirrors of the larger cities, but possibly slower to develop. If this is true, then we can predict the development of retailing in the smaller cities and perhaps as these retailers develop, they can take into account some of the issues raised in this research. The characteristics of the sample restrict the generalizability of our results across the

Chinese population. Future research should capture the perceptions of light and non-buyers to test for differences. In consideration of the state of the current knowledge base of the Chinese wine market, understanding our current customers is the first stage of this process. Finally, this research did not investigate the retailers themselves and look at their plans for evolving in the future. This type of research could be meshed with consumer perceptions and help deliver a better model for wine retailing in the future.

REFERENCES

Aghekyan-Simonian, M., Forsythe, S., Kwon, W.S., Chattaraman, V., 2012. The role of product brand image and online store image on perceived risks and online purchase intentions for apparel. J. Retailing Consum. Serv. 19 (3), 325−331.

Beh, E.J., 2004. Simple correspondence analysis: a bibliographic review. Int. Stat. Rev. 72 (2), 257−284.

Bogomolova, S., Romaniuk, J., 2010. Brand equity of defectors and never boughts in a business financial market. Ind. Mark. Manag. 39 (8), 1261−1268.

Bowe, J., Lockshin, L., Lee, R., Rungie, C., 2013. Old dogs, new tricks − rethinking country-image studies. J. Consum. Behav. 12 (6), 460−471.

Burt, S., Carralero-Encinas, J., 2000. The role of store image in retail internationalisation. Int. Mark. Rev. 17 (4/5), 433−453.

Chang, C., Tu, C., 2005. Exploring store image, customer satisfaction and customer loyalty relationship: evidence from Taiwanese hypermarket industry. J. Am. Acad. Bus. 7 (2), 197−202.

Chang, E., Teng, Y., 2013. Research note: e-store image, perceived value, and perceived risk. J. Bus. Res. 66 (7), 864−870.

Chen, M., Teng, C., 2013. A comprehensive model of the effects of online store image on purchase intention in an e-commerce environment. Electron. Commer. Res. 13 (1), 1−23.

Churchill Jr., G.A., 1979. A paradigm for developing better measures of marketing constructs. J. Mark. Res. 16 (1), 64−73.

Cohen, J., Corsi, A.M., Lockshin, L., 2014a. Are Australian wines well known in China? Wine Viticulture J 29 (1), 62−63.

Cohen, J., Corsi, A.M., Lockshin, L., 2014b. Forget special occasions, it is time to relax in China. Wine Viticulture J. 29 (4), 66−67.

Corsi, A.M., Cohen, J., Lockshin, L., 2015. What every wine brand needs to know about on-premise in China. Wine Viticulture J. 30 (1), 67−68.

Corsi, A.M., Mueller, S and Lockshin, L., 2011. Competition between and competition within: the strategic positioning of competing countries in key export markets. Paper presented at the 6th International Conference of the Academy of Wine Business Research, Bordeaux, France, 9th−11th June.

Datamonitor International, 2015. Wine in China. Available at: <http://www.datamonitor.com/store/Product/china_wine?productid=MLIP1635-0005>.

Doyle, P., Fenwick, I., 1974. Shopping habit in grocery chains. J. Retailing 50 (4), 39−52.

Driesener, C., Romaniuk, J., 2006. Comparing methods of brand image measurement. International Journal of Market Research 48 (6), 681−698.

Elliott, M.T., Speck, P.S., 2005. Factors that affect attitude toward a retail website. J. Mark. Theory Pract. 13 (1), 40−51.

Euromonitor International, 2013. Grocery retailers in China. Available at: <http://www.portal.euromonitor.com.ezlibproxy.unisa.edu.au/Portal/Pages/Search/SearchResultsList.aspx>.

Euromonitor International, 2014. Online grocery: strategies for growth. Available at <http://www.euromonitor.com/online-grocery-strategies-for-growth/report>.

Euromonitor International (2015). Wine in China. Available at: <http://www.euromonitor.com/wine-in-china/report>.

Ghosh, A., 1990. Retail Management, *2nd ed* The Dryden Press, Chicago, IL.

Goodman, S., 2009. An international comparison of retail consumer wine choice. International Journal of Wine Business Research 21 (1), 41−49.

Greenacre, M., 2007. Correspondence Analysis in Practice, *2nd ed* Chapman & Hall/CRC Interdisciplinary Statistics, Boca Raton, FL.

Jaeger, S.R., Chheang, S.L., Yin, J., Bava, C.M., Gimenez, A., Vidal, L., et al., 2013. Check-all-that-apply (CATA) responses elicited by consumers: within-assessor reproducibility and stability of sensory product characterisations. Food Qual. Preference 30 (1), 56−67.

Kunkel, J.H., Berry, L.L., 1968. A behavioural conception of retail image. J. Mark. 32 (4), 21−27.

Lannes, B., Chong, K., Han, W., Leung, P., Liu, F., Kou, M., et al., 2012. What Chinese shoppers really do buy will never tell you. Available at: <http://www.bain.com/publications/articles/what-chinese-shoppers-really-do-but-will-never-tell-you.aspx>.

Lindquist, J.D., 1974. Meaning of image − a survey of empirical and hypothetical evidence. J. Retail. 50 (4), 29−38.

Lockshin, L., 2014. China and wine: its impact on the global wine trade. Wine Econ. Policy 3 (1), 1−2.

Lockshin, L., Kahrimanis, P., 1998. Consumer evaluation of retail wine stores. J. Wine Res. 9 (3), 173−184.

Lockshin, L., Knott, D., 2009. Boozing or branding? Measuring the effects of free wine tastings at wine shops. Int. J. Wine Bus. Res. 21 (4), 312−324.

Martineau, P., 1958. The personality of the retail store. Harvard Bus. Rev. 36 (1), 47−55.

Nenycz-Thiel, M., Romaniuk, J., 2009. Perceptual categorization of private labels and national brands. J. Prod. Brand Manag. 18 (4), 251−261.

Nevin, J.R., Houston, M.J., 1980. Image as a component of attraction to intra-urban shopping area. J. Retailing 56 (1), 77−93.

Orth, U.R., Bourrain, A., 2005. Ambient scent and consumer exploratory behaviour: a causal analysis. J. Wine Res. 16 (2), 137−150.

Quinton, S., Harridge-March, S., 2008. Trust and online wine purchasing: insights into UK consumer behaviour. Int. J. Wine Bus. Res. 20 (1), 68−85.

Romaniuk, J., Sharp, B., 2015. How Brands Grow 2. Oxford University Press, Melbourne, Australia.

Semeijn, J., Van Riel, A.C.R., Ambrosini, A.B., 2004. Consumer evaluations of store brands: effects of store image and product attributes. J. Retailing Consum. Serv. 11 (4), 247−258.

Sjostrom, T., Corsi, A.M and Lockshin, L., 2013. Do consumers perceive luxury and premium attributes to belong exclusively to higher-price points? Paper presented at the Australian and New Zealand Marketing Academy Conference, Auckland, New Zealand, 2nd−4th December.

Thang, D.C.L., Tan, B.L.B., 2003. Linking consumer perception to preference of retail store: an empirical assessment of the multi-attribute store image. J. Retail. Consum. Serv. 10 (4), 193−200.

Van der Heijden, H., Verhagen, T., 2004. Online store image: conceptual foundations and empirical measurement. Inf. Manag. 41 (5), 609–617.

Wine Intelligence, 2013. China Wine Market Landscape Report - Wine Consumption Behaviour in China. Wine Intelligence, London, UK.

Yun, Z.S., Good, L.K., 2007. Developing customer loyalty from e-tail store image attributes. Manag. Serv. Qual. 17 (1), 4–22.

APPENDIX

Table 6.1 List of items for brick-and-mortar retailers SI

Dimension	#	Items
Product range	1	The retailer carries a wide selection of wines
	2	The wines stocked by the retailer are of good quality
	3	The wines sold by the retailer are fashionable
	4	The retailer's private label brands are reliable
	5	The retailer operates an easy return policy for wines
	6	The retailer always carries the wines that I want in stock
	7	The wines that I want are easy to find on shelf
	8	I buy on-line from this retailer
Price	9	The retailer makes the prices of the wines easily visible on the shelf
	10	Discounts are available from the retailer
	11	Prices for wines are low compared to similar retailers
	12	You get good value for money on the wines sold by the retailer
Staff	13	The staff is able to give recommendations about the wines
	14	The staff develop a good relationship with the customers in the store
	15	The retailer personnel are helpful
	16	The retailer personnel are friendly
General image and location	17	The retailer's stores are clean and tidy
	18	The retailer's stores atmosphere is excellent
	19	The retailer projects a conservative image
	20	The retailer has a clear Chinese appeal
	21	The retailer serves the middleclass
	22	The retailer is a world class wine retailer
	23	The retailer transmits a reliable image
	24	I find the retailer totally trustworthy
	25	The retailer's stores are located in convenient locations
	26	I have shopped at this retailer previously

Table 6.2 List of items for online retailers SI

Dimension	#	Items
Product range	1	The online retailer carries a wide selection of wines
	2	The wines sold by the online retailer are of good quality
	3	The wines sold by the online retailer are fashionable
	4	The online retailer's private label brands are reliable
	5	The online retailer operates an easy return policy for wines
	6	The online retailer always has the wines that I want in stock
Price	7	The online retailer makes the prices of the wines easily visible on the website
	8	Discounts are available from the online retailer
	9	Prices for wines are low compared to similar online retailers
	10	You get good value for money on the wines sold by the online retailer
Website image	11	The website is fun
	12	The website is attractive
	13	The website is easy to navigate
	14	The website provides good recommendations about the wine
	15	I have great pleasure browsing through the website
General image	16	The online retailer projects a conservative image
	17	The online retailer has a clear Chinese appeal
	18	The online retailer serves the middle class
	19	The online retailer is a world class wine retailer
	20	The online retailer transmits a reliable image
	21	I find the online retailer totally trustworthy
Financial transactions and delivery options	22	I frequently see advertisement about the online retailer on the internet
	23	The online retailer offers a wide range of delivery options
	24	The online retailer keeps my personal data confidential
	25	The online retailer has safe financial transactions
	26	The online retailer has fast financial transactions
	27	The online retailer delivers wine fast
	28	The online retailer delivers wine safely
	29	I have shopped at this retailer previously

CHAPTER 7

Wine Consumption in China: Regional Differences in Territorial Brand Perceptions

D. Menival[1] and H. Han[2]
[1]ESC Dijon/Burgundy School of Business, Dijon, France
[2]Neoma Business School, Reims, France

INTRODUCTION

The wine industry has become increasingly globalized over the last decade. This trend is quite long-standing (Anderson et al., 2003) but concerns now more than 40% of the world wine production in 2014, according to the International Organization for Wine and the Vine (OIV). Exports and imports mainly result from European and American producing countries. However the stronger development of imports is now outside Europe and concerns more and more new markets. Among them, China should become a major market in the next few years.

Given the growing importance of wine as a status symbol amongst younger, wealthier and more educated consumers in China (Balestrini and Gamble, 2006; Liu and Murphy, 2007; Camillo, 2012; Noppe, 2012), there is plenty of scope for further expansion in this market. While the range and availability of foreign wine in the Chinese market is growing, in general Chinese consumers' wine knowledge remains relatively limited (Jin, 2004; Hu et al., 2008). As with less knowledgeable drinkers in other markets, Chinese wine consumers generally use extrinsic cues, including country of origin (COO), in wine purchase decisions (Yu et al., 2009; Liu et al., 2014).

This insight leads us to focus on the Chinese perception of foreign wines through the notion of territorial brands. Brands are traditionally seen as belonging to an enterprise. Some, however, operate collectively, and in some cases this collective operation may relate to place (Skinner, 2008). Further, it can be suggested that there are two parts of the definition of a brand; the view of traditional marketing is that it gives value to

The Wine Value Chain in China.

its producer (Kotler et al., 1994). However, a more recent perspective adds that it is also a differentiated product which benefits consumers above its merely functional purpose (De Chernatony and MacDonald, 2003). Accepting these two elements of the definition of a brand, it has been argued that certain products that are environmentally rooted in a specific place, display specific attributes which are the direct result of that environment, and adopt the name of that place, operate as a brand, the territorial brand.

A territorial brand is a form of location-related brand, but specifically one where the product sold is inextricably linked to its origin because without the environmental factors provided by the origin, the product would be different (Charters et al., 2013, Charters and Spielmann, 2014). The territorial brand includes tourism and some food and drink products, as well as other goods such as Cuban cigars, Kashmir wool and Venetian glass. As will be shown, a territorial brand is linked to a regional brand, but is not identical. It may also be a destination brand (although that is not inevitable) and it can overlap with the COO cue.

Thus, a territorial brand is one which belongs to all the producers in a definable territory, and which necessarily exists because the product they make can only be created in that place and cannot be replicated anywhere else. The territorial brand consequently operates alongside and in cooperation with a number of individual proprietary brands of the same product (e.g., separate brands of Brie cheese in France), or subbrands producing an element of that product (farms producing milk or factories creating cheese). There may also be subterritorial brands; thus Brie de Melun operates as in this way in relation to the territorial Brie cheese brand.

A territorial brand is a complex structured entity, yet one which has very clear consumer recognition as a brand in its own right. Beyond a defined and commonly shared origin, three major aspects characterize a territorial brand.

1. There is a tendency to coopetition (Nalebuff and Brandenburger, 1997) which means the existence of both competition and cooperation of all actors of a specific sector. That leads them to share one vision and understand a common culture, history, story and mythology (Zineldin, 2004; Gnyawali and He, 2008). This is fundamental if individual demands and expectations are to be subsumed into the common territorial good.

2. There is territorial brand manager who can catalyze individual marketing and promotional activities to avoid strong damage to the

territorial brand (Charters et al., 2011). This brand manager may well have the power to regulate production in order to maintain a common level of quality. It provides a framework for reinforcing coopetition and it defends the position of all actors by the guarantee of one collective image.

3. As with any strong brand, there must be clear added value for both producers and consumers. Thus, for instance, purchasers of Brie cheese know that they are going to consume something that is produced to controlled standards, tends to come with a consistent style (which they may like) and is a recognized name and thus generally acceptable if given to guests.

With the existence of a territorial brand, individual brands can benefit from a shared common image and its resultant reputation and reinforce their own position with consumers, thus adding a premium to the price paid. However, is this reputation useful for opening up new markets? If not, what prevents it from happening? To answer this question we decided to focus on perceptions of champagne and bordeaux in China.

TERRITORIAL BRANDS IN WINE: CHAMPAGNE AND BORDEAUX

China is clearly becoming an important market for champagne and bordeaux, as for other wines. Foreign wines are becoming more and more a lifestyle fashion especially for the emerging middle and upper classes (Liu and Murphy, 2007) who can now find foreign wines such as champagne in their market thanks to more open policies since 2001 (Hu et al., 2008).

Whilst champagne brands and bordeaux estates are very strongly marketed by their individual owners, much more than most wines made in other European wine regions, we can easily find the characteristics of territorial brands in these wine industries.

First, the actors in champagne have purpose and a common story thanks to the development of local coopetition. This situation has origins which go back several centuries and which are based on the idea of the mutual reliance of growers (who provide the raw materials) and the houses (the merchants who market the high-volume brands); these two groups have a common heritage and vision of their wines as the international medium of celebration *par excellence*. This all contributes to maintain and reinforce the territorial brand.

Secondly, the CIVC (Comité Champagne) is the brand manager. It markets the product, carries out research and development into production, protects its intellectual property, mediates between the conflicting parts of the (regional) enterprise, and has responsibility for quality control. It is also used as a means of controlling the flow of wine onto the market in response to demand, in order to avoid surpluses.

The final evidence of the territorial brand in champagne comes from the use of the champagne name. It is often argued by producers that champagne is not a brand, rather it is an protected designation of origin (PDO). But if one considers how the name "champagne" gives value both to producers and consumers by identifying the product and underlining that it has added value (Aaker, 1991; Kotler et al., 2006), then it is a brand. Further, that name is used as a guarantee of quality by many consumers worldwide who cannot name a specific individual brand of wine.

Apparently, the coopetition is less strong for bordeaux. There are 60 PDOs that have a widely varying level of reputation, so that cooperation seems harder to achieve than in Champagne. However, there is a current collective communication suggesting that bordeaux is synonymous of one style of red wine (effectively ignoring the white wines made there) which brings several styles and sub-regions together.

As for champagne, there is a brand manager which develops, defends and reinforces this style and approach, the Comité des Vins de Bordeaux (CIVB). The CIVB represents the three traditional groups of actors in the bordeaux industry: growers, brokers and merchants. It manages the territorial brand of bordeaux in three ways: (1) communication about "bordeaux" to the world, (2) providing economic information about markets and production, and (3) developing production techniques which guarantee the same basic quality for all bordeaux wines. Thus "bordeaux" is also used as "brand", by the bordeaux actors as well as the consumers. Its position is less strong than for champagne but nevertheless exists for a large part of producers who can benefit from its high reputation (Gergaud and Livat, 2010).

METHOD

Our knowledge about the Chinese market is incomplete, as wine consumers are recent and in constant evolution. Therefore, we decided enhance our understanding of this development by using qualitative data collection processes, which are the best for exploratory projects

(Calder, 1977). Interviews were undertaken in Chinese and translated into English by a Chinese academic who was a member of the research team. During and following the data collection stage, the researchers met regularly to evaluate the process; data analysis was a regular and cross-comparative process (Janesick, 1994), although the two researchers took responsibility for various aspects of the project.

We used a purposive sampling method, advertising the survey on databases of alumni from educational institutions with which the researchers had affiliations, as well as through social media contacts with wine. In 2013, 40 interviews were arranged for this study over Beijing and Shanghai which are the two most important centres for the Chinese wine market (2012). Twenty people lived in Shanghai and 20 people in Beijing. Our sample was constituted by consumers who displayed similar characteristics to Chinese wine consumption patterns previously defined by Li et al. (2011) and Camillo (2012):

1. They belong to the middle and upper classes.
2. They consume a small quantity of wine per year.
3. They live in Beijing and Shanghai.

Information about the informants is contained in Table 7.1.

Table 7.1 Interviewee profiles

ID-Beijing	Gender	Age	Occupation	ID-Shanghai	Gender	Age	Occupation
B1	F	27	Project Executive	S1	F	40	Doctor
B2	M	32	IT support director	S2	F	32	Administration assistant
B3	M	31	Project Executive	S3	F	39	Marketing Manager
B4	M	29	Staff member	S4	F	36	CEO
B5	M	29	GD	S5	F	24	Staff member
B6	M	29	Sales Director	S6	F	26	Product Manager
B7	F	29	Quality Manager	S7	M	40	Marketing Manager
B8	M	45	Director of department	S8	M	26	Staff member
B9	F	45	Director of department	S9	F	30	Project Executive
B10	M	39	Marketing Manager	S10	M	35	Deputy chief editor

(*Continued*)

Table 7.1 (Continued)

ID-Beijing	Gender	Age	Occupation	ID-Shanghai	Gender	Age	Occupation
B11	F	28	Project Executive	S11	M	31	Owner of enterprise
B12	M	34	Owner of enterprise	S12	F	27	Marketing Manager
B13	F	30	Staff member	S13	M	36	GM
B14	M	39	GM	S14	M	37	Engineer
B15	M	44	Staff member	S15	M	33	Regional head (bank)
B16	M	35	GM	S16	F	23	Import Manager
B17	F	39	Owner of enterprise	S17	M	33	Staff member
B18	M	35	Staff member	S18	F	32	Staff member
B19	F	38	Accounting	S19	M	26	Staff member
B20	M	36	Doctor	S20	M	25	Staff member

GD, General Director; GM, General Manager

We concentrated on three main questions about (1) their perception of both foreign wine and (2) bordeaux and champagne. The third question was about the definition of a famous wine.

FINDINGS

We started our interviews with a general question about foreign wines. This showed the strength of bordeaux in the Chinese market conversely to champagne. Then, whilst Chinese consumers are considered by researchers to have poor general knowledge of wine, our results show that they have a clear understanding of what their wine preferences are and, interestingly enough, the differences are not homogenous between the two cities.

Foreign Wines are Better than Chinese Wines

The distinction between Chinese wines and foreign wines quickly appeared for interviewees. Whatever their location, they considered Chinese wines inferior to foreign wines.

First, the wine security seemed a major perception in both Shanghai and Beijing — 'our wines do not respect the rules and many of them are adulterated' and 'Chinese wineries use cheap, foreign, bulk wine to fill their bottles'. This was explained by the idea that Chinese wines have an industrial production process which pollutes them and the location of production:'some local wines have been made by industrial methods and lead to global pollution'.

In addition, our sample explained the consumption of local wines due to both their low price and easy to find — '[Chinese wines] are produced in huge volumes and have a huge network of retailers' — 'There are a different large set of categories which are easy to buy'. Conversely, foreign wines were perceived as healthier and with higher quality —'They have strict control over the process of fabrication and use less chemical material'. More generally, interviewees considered foreign wines to have a stronger culture, personality. and history.

Even though some interviewees cited other origins, they almost all put French wines on the top of their preferences. For 29 consumers (of a total of 40), French wines were the most famous foreign wines and had the best image of all red wines — as one said, 'French wines have a high distinction, high quality and huge set of choices'. Then the same sample explained that bordeaux is the prototype of French wines — 'The taste of bordeaux is very good. It represents the French red wines I prefer'. This relationship is reinforced by the incredible presence of bordeaux brands, with eight consumers citing only brands from the region to illustrate foreign brands. Therefore, for Chinese consumption, bordeaux are the French red wines.

This great success is mainly explained by the idea that everybody knew bordeaux and consequently has a high social image. Ten consumers seemed to appreciate this social position more than its taste — the Chinese know bordeaux and its chateaux. Therefore these wines are perfect for dinners between friends and/or for business.

However, this domination was nuanced by the occasional citation of other foreign wines. This appeared when consumers were more focused on taste than price. In this context, Australian wines were considered good for 5 consumers: 'Australian and New Zealand wines present good quality for lower prices than bordeaux'.

Champagne Remains Outside Chinese Culture

Conversely to bordeaux, champagne was never cited naturally by interviewees. Therefore we asked them to expand on their perception of champagne. Ten consumers explained that champagne is appropriate for celebration and events: 'champagne is for winners (like in Formula 1) and parties'. Some others added weddings and special occasions such as a new job or a new contract — 'When I was younger, friends from Hong Kong bought a bottle. I understood champagne was for celebrations, new contracts, birthday parties, exactly like in Hong Kong movies'. Champagne was never considered like still wine; it is mysterious and often unknown — 'champagne is for ceremonies but is still quite unknown in China where the local champagne [sparkling wines] is preferred'.

However, although this link was understood, champagne in such situations was not really seen to be adapted for Chinese consumers and stayed mainly allied to occidental values. Whilst these values were quite clear for consumers, they have not led to a change in consumption practices: 'Sometimes, we are invited to visit bars and we never drink champagne'. 'For almost all parties and professional dinners, champagne is absent.' Worst, nine defined champagne 'as sparkling white wine' and did not make any distinction from other sparkling wines. This amalgam led them to consider champagne as too expensive for 'just sparkling white wine.'

Some Regional Reasons to Explain the Perception of Foreign Wines

Whatever their geographic origin, interviewees developed similar reasons to prefer foreign wines. For 23 people from Beijing and Shanghai, foreign wines had the advantage of being from several origins and then proposed several attractive origins which make choices easier. 'In face of the numerous marques of foreign wines in the Chinese market, we should pay attention in their origins.' However, the proportion of answers led us to distinguish different trends between Beijing and Shanghai.

Firstly, it seems that, compared with the consumers in Beijing, the consumers in Shanghai are more interested by the wine's taste than anything else. Twelve people from Shanghai, versus six from Beijing explained their preference of foreign wines due to their taste: 'Most foreign wines are very pure and natural'. The Shanghainese were more concerned with the intrinsic quality: 'aftertaste', 'fine and smooth'. Three of them looked for a pure wine and did not like Western wine producers tailoring their product to Chinese palates.

Secondly, Shanghainese (nine participants) were more concerned with well promoted brands than Beijingers (two participants) to explain the attractiveness of foreign wines.

Thirdly, six Beijingers versus one Shanghainese appreciated the cultural aspect of foreign wines. For them, foreign wines have higher cultural identity: 'Foreign wines have their cultural existence'. Therefore, they preferred foreign rather than Chinese wines because the former were more steeped in culture than domestic wines.

Lastly, 12 Beijingers considered the social attributes of foreign wines as important as compared with three Shanghainese. These former used foreign wines as tool to improve their social image and to communicate their economic welfare to the community: 'in China, wine is used for the communication and it can strengthen friendship'. Moreover, the social attributes seemed negatively considered by two Shanghainese: 'Drinking wine can improve your identity at the social occasion, that's why in China, wine is accepted more by the fashionable society'.

How Region Explains the Differences Between Champagne and Bordeaux

Faced with the irrelevance of champagne in the life of Chinese consumers, we sought for reasons. Half the consumers explained that champagne was too expensive. They did not understand why it has higher price than other sparkling wines, especially with a taste too far removed from that sought by the Chinese. 'In China, the price is high and its taste stays acid. I do not like champagne.' The other half focused on a lack of collective promotion. They explained that champagne is unknown due to the lack of presence in the public media and remains too mysterious for consumers: 'With champagne, unlike bordeaux, it seems that there is no common organization. Promotion is too weak in media and magazines'. They thought champagne needs to promote its culture to explain why it is different from other sparkling wines, especially those which are produced in China under the same name.

But this lack of collective promotion did not have the same importance according to the location of consumers. Twelve Shanghainese firstly explained the taste of champagne does not fit Chinese taste in comparison with the bordeaux which are interesting tastes. 'Even though it's a very important French wine, I don't really know it. Its taste is good but too smooth, with no tannin. It's for Chinese girls and reserved for weddings, celebration.' Only two Shanghainese considered the importance of bordeaux according to its culture and six according to their famous brands.

The situation is different for the Beijingers. The international image of champagne is well known for the Beijingers but few of them spoke about its taste. Champagne stays out of their habits because it is unknown by a majority:

The champagne problem is lack of recognition with the consumers. There is only a small group which includes it and which accepts it. It is especially the

Chinese who have spent time abroad who know champagne well. For the moment, celebration, marriage and romantic moments are the images of the champagne. But, for the most part at banquets and an evening, champagne is almost absent. It is not very strong. Even if there is more and more champagne, I do not think that many Chinese distinguish champagne from other efferves-cent wines (the same shape, even labelling). Besides it is much expensive. To succeed, the French government has to make efforts to promote the culture of the champagne. For instance, in wedding ceremonies, we have glass tower of champagne but nobody knows that it is to be drunk, they think that it is just for the atmosphere.

Here we find the importance of the social attributes of what is foreign for the Beijingers and the importance of taste for the Shanghainese. Obviously this gap is not so simple and clear. Both locations included outliers not belonging to the mainstream. However, the trend was clear, especially when we asked them how to define famous wines.

Twenty-six Chinese consumers spoke about quality and taste before any other aspect of wine. 'The components to define a famous wine are the taste, the origin, the year and the ageing.' The 14 others spoke about the reputation before anything else. 'Being famous for a wine means that there are many consumers who know it. A famous product gives confidence about the quality.' For the first sub-group, only eight came from Beijing whilst they were 12 for the second one.

DISCUSSION AND CONCLUSION

Our findings highlight the success of foreign wines compared with Chinese wines. Whatever the city, Chinese consumers seem more confi-dent in the quality and origin of imported wines. This confirmed previ-ous studies which noticed that Chinese consumers use COO cues considerably during wine purchases (Balestrini and Gamble, 2006), giving a real advantage to the well-established regions of the world (Zhang et al., 2013). It also shows that domestic wines are still a victim of the series of crises of wine adulteration and their impact on the consumers (Zhang, 2005; Eves and Cheng, 2007; Bing et al., 2011).

However, this success does not benefit all foreign wines. Our findings show that, conversely to bordeaux, champagne has failed to succeed in the Chinese market. Some could say this market is new hence key cham-pagne actors need time to master it. However, this argument is weak when we see how bordeaux has succeeded in becoming 'The Best Red Wine'. Champagne is seen as too expensive compare to its perceived quality whilst some bordeaux brands reach incredible prices in the market. Another answer could be that the taste of bordeaux appeals to Chinese palates, whilst champagne is too acidic. However, past studies have noted that heavy, tannic red wines have been difficult for Chinese consumers to adapt to (often cutting it with lemonade). Nevertheless, they have become big fans of this style over the last decade.

One real reason for this gap between champagne and bordeaux come from regional differences. Chinese consumers of wine seem to be in the context of *indigenizing* as defined by Üstüner and Holt (2009). For these authors, the form of national identity construction does not play off the cultural dominance of the West and is much more about constructing status for the middle and upper classes of the new industrialized countries. Indeed, due to rapid economic growth, personal income has largely increased in China and a new group of wealthy known as the 'new rich' has emerged in society (Wu, 1997). With the rise of individual income, the Chinese middle and upper classes 'demand more convenience and quality' (Hingley et al., 2009, p. 46), show more interest in branding (Kim et al., 2009) and purchase more luxury products (Blackwell et al., 2001). These consumption patterns explain the flow of foreign products in China, wines among them (Hu et al., 2008). In this context, the new Chinese consumers perceived wine — especially foreign wine — as a status symbol to aide social standing (Yu et al., 2009).

Nevertheless, this position seems quite restrictive. Our findings show that the middle and upper classes in Shanghai do not have not the same reason to choose foreign wines as consumers in Beijing. Beijingers are more attracted by cultural factors and social effects whilst Shanghainese pay more attention to well promoted brands and to taste. Here we have a kind of regionalization of the cultural globalization in Chinese wine market. The indigenizing (Üstüner and Holt, 2009) of Western culture diffused by foreign wines is mainly confirmed in Beijing but less in Shanghai. Foreign wines are used by Beijingers to construct status for the middle and upper class whilst Shanghainese tend to consume foreign wines more for their intrinsic attributes.

These local differences are not specific to the wine market. As explained by Hegarty and O'Mahony (2001), food has more than utilitarian aspect and usually reflects the culture where ingredients are blended and cooked. For Cook and Crang (1996), wine is among the best example of combination between production and culture, being a food which can reflect the local culture of its region of origin. Moreover, for Hall et al. (1997), the elements of culture should not be ignored for the identification of wine selection. Therefore, due to the main origin of exported wines, Chinese consumers are confronted by Western culture.

China is made up of multiple heterogeneous regional markets (Ralston et al., 1996; Schmitt, 1997; Schmitt, 1999; Cui, 1999; Veeck et al., 2007) have revealed that these regional markets present different factors as history, location, economic development, education and technology. Therefore, regional variations cannot be disregarded as part of any attempt to explore Chinese markets and consumers (Siu and Ho, 2001). Cui and Liu (2000) noticed different degrees of recognition for the foreign brands for cities like Guangzhou, Shanghai and Beijing. Similarly, Wei and Pan (1999) showed that compared with Beijing, Shanghai consumers were more interested by fashion brands. Moreover Zhang et al. (2008) pointed out that consumers in Shanghai pay more attention to style, workmanship, colour and brand, whilst in Beijing the colour is less important. Whilst these studies are quite old, they highlight the persistence of gaps between Shanghainese and Beijingers. On the one hand, Beijing is the political power centre in the North and the people of Beijing see themselves as the political and cultural guardians of China (Schlevogt, 2001). In traditional Chinese culture, aspects such as the family orientation, the concept of the 'middle way', *guanxi*, harmony, face and collectivism influence the consumer's motivation and behaviour (Lu, 2002). This is confirmed in Beijing where imported products symbolize higher social status (Wang and Chen, 2004).

On the other hand, Shanghai is considered the dominant commercial centre. Traditional culture is less emphasized in the South and the Shanghainese are even accused by the northern Chinese of having destroyed traditional structures that were based on family ties (Schlevogt, 2001). In attracting the attention of foreign companies, Shanghai is also becoming the seed bed of a new middle-class society. Whilst being not the richest, this class is well educated and may be the most loyal consumers of foreign products (Safier, 2001).

Finally, whilst our results are limited by the qualitative nature of the investigation, we have to consider that selling wines in Beijing is not the same as selling them in Shanghai. This point is important both in terms of the final consumers and to the importers who need to develop their business. Transferring values through wine is one important step, but guaranteeing the integration of these values into consumption patterns is a greater challenge. That point emphasizes the cultural gap between the North and the South of China and how it has evolved.

REFERENCES

Aaker, D., 1991. Managing Brand Equity: Capitalizing on the Value of a Brand Name. Free Press, New York.

Anderson, K., Norman, D., Wittwer, G., 2003. Globalization of the world's wine markets. World Econ. 26 (5), 659−687.

Balestrini, P., Gamble, P., 2006. Country-of-origin effects on Chinese wine consumers. Br. Food J. 108 (5), 396−412.

Bing, Z., Sirion, C., Combs, H., 2011. Green product consumer buyer behaviour in China. Am. J. Bus. Res. 4 (1), 55−77.

Blackwell, R.D., Minard, P.W., Engel, J.F., 2001. Consumer behaviour, *9th ed.* South-Western/Thomson Learning, Mason, Ohio.

Calder, B.J., 1977. Focus groups and the nature of qualitative marketing research. J. Market. Res. 14 (August), 353−364.

Camillo, A.A., 2012. A strategic investigation of the determinants of wine consumption in China. Int. J. Wine Bus. Res. 24 (1), 68−92.

Charters, S., Spielmann, N., 2014. The characteristics of strong territorial brands: the case of champagne. J. Bus. Res. 67 (7), 1461−1467.

Charters, S., Mitchell, R and Menival, D., 2011. The territorial brand in wine, 6th AWBR International Conference, Bordeaux Management School, 9−10 June.

Charters, S., Menival, D., Senaux, B., Serdukov, S., 2013. Value in the territorial brand: the case of champagne. Br. Food J. 115 (10), 1505−1517.

Cook, I., Crang, P., 1996. The world on a plate. J. Mater. Culture 1 (2), 131−153.

Cui, C., 1999. Segmenting China's consumer market: a hybrid approach. J. Int. Consum. Market. 1 (1), 55−76.

Cui, G., Liu, Q., 2000. Regional market segments of China: opportunities and barriers in a big emerging market. J. Consum. Marketing 17 (1), 55−72.

De Chernatony, L., MacDonald, M., 2003. Creating Powerful Brands. Butterworth Heinemann, Oxford.

Eves, A., Cheng, L., 2007. Cross-cultural evaluation of factors driving intention to purchase new food products- Beijing, China and south-east England. Int. J. Consum. Stud. Vol. 31, 410−417.

Gergaud, O and Livat, F., 2010. Collective reputation effects: an empirical appraisal. American Association of Wine Economists, AAWE working paper No. 73.

Gnyawali, D.R., He, J., 2008. Impact of co-opetition on firm competitive behaviour: an empirical examination. J. Manag. 32 (4), 507−553.

Hall, J., Shaw, M., Doole, L., 1997. Cross-cultural analysis of wine consumption motivations. Int. J. Wine Market. 9, 83−92.

Hegarty, J.A., O'Mahony, G.B., 2001. Gastronomy: a phenomenon of cultural expressionism and an aesthetic for living. Int. J. Hospitality Manag. 20 (1), 3−13.

Hingley, M., Lindgreen, A., Chen, L., 2009. Development of the grocery retail market in China: a qualitative study on how foreign and domestic retailers seek to increase market share. Br. Food J. 111 (1), 44−55.

Hu, X., Li, L., Xie, C., Zhou, J., 2008. The effects of country-of-origin on Chinese consumers' wine purchasing behaviour. J. Technol. Manag. China 3 (3), 292−306.

Janesick, V.J., 1994. The dance of qualitative research design. In: Denzin, N.K., Lincoln, Y.S. (Eds.), Handbook of Qualitative Research. SAGE Publications, Thousand Oaks, pp. 209−219.

Jin, W., 2004. The forecast of wine market in China. SINO-Overseas Grapevine Wine 4, 69–74.

Kim, S., Song, Z., Byun, C., 2009. A study on factors affecting brand preference: focusing on the Chinese mobile phone consumer. Bus. Educ. (Korea Association of Business Education) 58, 63–84.

Kotler, P., et al., 1994. Marketing, *3rd ed*. Prentice Hall, Sydney.

Kotler, P., Adam, S., et al., 2006. Principles of Marketing. Pearson Prentice Hall, Sydney.

Li, J.G., Jia, J.R., Taylor, D., Bruwer, J., Li, E., 2011. The wine drinking behaviour of young adults: an exploratory study in China. Br. Food J. 113 (10), 1305–1317.

Liu, F., Murphy, J., 2007. A qualitative study of Chinese wine consumption and purchasing. Int. J. Wine Bus. Res. 19 (2), 98–113.

Liu, H.B., McCarthy, B., Chen, T., Guo, S., Song, X., 2014. The Chinese wine market: a market segmentation study. Asia Pac. J. Market. Logistics 26 (3), 450–471.

Lu, l., 2002. A preliminary study on the concept of health among the Chinese. Couns. Psychol. Q. 15 (2), 179–190.

Nalebuff, B.J., Brandenburger, A.M., 1997. Co-opetition: competitive and cooperative business strategies for the digital economy. Strategy Leadersh. 25 (Nov/Dec), 28–35.

Noppe, R.P., 2012. Rise of the Dragon: The Chinese Wine Market. Dissertation submitted to the Cape Wine Academy, Cape Town, South Africa.

Ralston, D.A., Yu, K.-C., Wang, X., Terpstra, R.H., Wei, H., 1996. The cosmopolitan Chinese manager: findings of a study of managerial values across the six regions of China. J. Int. Manag. 2 (2), 79–109.

Safier, M., 2001. Transforming Shanghai: landscapes of turbo dynamic development in China's 'world city'. City Vol. 5, 67–75.

Schlevogt, K.A., 2001. Institutional and organizational factors affecting effectiveness: Geoeconomic comparison between Shanghai and Beijing. Asia Pac. J. Manag. 18 (4), 519–551.

Schmitt, B., 1997. Who is the Chinese consumer? Eur. Manag. J. 15 (2), 1991–1994.

Schmitt, B., 1999. Consumer segmentation in China. In: Rajeev, B. (Ed.), Marketing Issues in Transitional Economies. Kluwer Academic Publishers, Boston, pp. 73–84.

Sin, L., Ho, S., 2001. An assessment of theoretical and methodological development in consumer research on greater China: 1979–1997. Asia Pac. J. Market. Logistics 3 (1), 3–42.

Skinner, H., 2008. The emergence and development of place marketing's confused identity. J. Market. Manag. 24 (9-10), 915–928.

Üstüner, T., Holt, D.B., 2009. Toward a theory of status consumption in less industrialized countries. J. Consum. Res. 39 (June), 37–56.

Veeck, G., Pannell, C., Smith, C., Huang, Y., 2007. China's Geography: Globalization and the Dynamics of Political, Economic and Social Change. Rowman & Littlefield Publishers, Lanham.

Wang, C.L., Chen, Z.X., 2004. Consumer ethnocentrism and attitudes towards domestic and foreign products. Eur. J. Market. 34 (9/10), 391–400.

Wei, R., Pan, Z., 1999. Mass media and consumerist values in the People's Republic of China. Int. J. Public Opin. Res. 11 (1), 75–96.

Wu, Y., 1997. Wealth and spending patterns in China. Int. J. Soc. Econ. 24 (7/8), 1007–1022.

Yu, Y., Sun, H., Goodman, S., Chen, S., Ma, H., 2009. Chinese choices: a survey of wine consumers in Beijing. Int. J. Wine Bus. Res. 21 (2), 127–138.

Zhang, X., 2005. Chinese consumers' concerns about food safety case of Tianjin. J. Int. Food Agribusiness Market. 17 (1), 57–69.

Zhang, X., Grigoriou, N., Li, L., 2008. The myth of China as a single market: the influence of personal values differences on buying decision. Int. J. Market Res. 50 (3), 377−402.

Zhang, H.Q., Yuan, J., Ye, B.H., Hung, K., 2013. Wine tourism phenomena in China: an emerging market. Int. J. Contemp. Hospitality Manag. 25 (7), 1115−1134.

Zineldin, M., 2004. Co-opetition: the organization of the future. Market. Intell. Plan. 22 (7), 780−789.

CHAPTER 8

Wine Purchasing Behaviour in China

H. Liu and B. McCarthy
James Cook University, Townsville, QLD, Australia

INTRODUCTION

With the rise of China's middle class, the country is undergoing a social transformation. One of the most striking changes is the rapid increase in wine consumption. In 2013, China (including Hong Kong) consumed 155 million nine-liter cases (equivalent to 1.87 billion bottles) of red wine and became the world's largest consumer of red wine (Vinexpo, 2014).

China's red wine consumption almost tripled between 2007 and 2013, although there was a 7.4% decline in 2013 in comparison to 2012, which was thought to be due to years of stock building and the government crackdown on luxury gift-giving and excessive spending in 2012 (The Wall Street Journal, 2014). China has attracted the attention of domestic Chinese and international wine marketers in response to its rapid rise in demand. Wine marketers from France, Australia, Italy and the USA are some of the international sellers seeking an opportunity to expand their market share in China (Morrison and Rabellotti, 2014).

In the long run, the fundamentals for Chinese wine consumption growth are expected to remain strong (Anderson and Wittwer, 2013). Firstly, China has a large local wine industry, attracting and dispensing capital across the world (Morrison and Rabellotti, 2014). Secondly, per capita wine consumption in China is still low, compared to those of other wine producing countries. For example, China's annual adult wine consumption per capita was 1.4 L in 2013, far less than 54 L for France and 48 L for Italy (Bouzdine-Chameeva et al., 2013). Thirdly, wine in China is regarded as a healthier drink than the traditional grain-based alcohol, namely Baijiu and Mijiu, and it offers the sophistication some Chinese consumers crave (Liu et al., 2014). Last but not least, there is a rapidly expanding middle class and these new consumers will spur growth. The wealthy middle class that has emerged in China has become more and more sophisticated and Westernized, and drinking wine has become one of their habits (Zhou et al., 2014). Therefore, it is expected that Chinese wine consumption will continue to increase.

The emerging wine consumers are found to be more sophisticated and educated than before and pay more attention to variety and also to some intangible features, such as history, authenticity and the intrinsic quality of wine (Morrison and Rabellotti, 2014). It is believed that young and wealthy Chinese consumers in urban areas belong to this group (Barton et al., 2013). However, little research has so far investigated this increasingly important cohort. This research aims to fill the gap by investigating this group of emerging wine consumers in China.

LITERATURE REVIEW

China has a more than 2000-year long history of producing and drinking grape wine (Winechina, 2005). In fact, grape wine is not a brand new drink to the Chinese, but was a scarce one for many years. However, constrained by soil and weather conditions, Chinese wine production has remained low until recent decades and its consumption has been far behind other alcoholic beverages, mainly Chinese liquors distilled from grains or rice. Due to scarcity, only royal families, senior officials, and very rich people had the privilege of drinking wine on important occasions. Even in the 1970s, Chinese wine production was about only 85 million liters per year and its per capita wine consumption was almost negligible (Bouzdine-Chameeva et al., 2013). However, the situation has changed dramatically since 1978 when China started its economic reform.

With the expansion of China's domestic wine production, drinking wine started as a fashion, and slowly gained popularity among Chinese consumers. At the same time, wine imports in China also became easier and have increased by over 26,000% during the period 2000−11 (Muhammad et al., 2014). In 2014, China imported 383 million liters of wine, of which one-third was from France (Administrative Office of China Food and Drinks Fair, 2015). Today, wine, including different varieties of imported wine, has become widely available in the market of urban China and foreign wine is no longer strange to many ordinary Chinese consumers.

As China has gone from obscurity to being an important participant in the global market of the wine trade within a relatively short period of time, there has been limited quantitative analysis. However, several studies have investigated various aspects of wine consumption behaviour. A review of the literature is of help to better understand the factors contributing to wine consumption in China.

Wine is regarded as a special and luxurious food item that is desirable to have because of its scarcity (Camillo, 2012). Based on this perception, drinking wine has evolved as a way of showing hospitality and aiding in social communications in China (Li et al., 2011). This is particularly true when the Chinese buy wine as a gift or for special occasions (Qing and Hu, 2015).

Although wine is regarded as a symbol of foreign lifestyle, most Chinese consumers are found to have little knowledge of wine (Hu et al., 2008; Liu and Murphy, 2007). It is found that many Chinese consumers evaluate wine quality from where the wine is produced and the impact of the country-of-origin (COO) on wine choice becomes even more significant if the wine is bought for business use (Balestrini and Gamble, 2006). As a result, COO of wines functions as a quality signal in China and red wine retailers often display the wine according to the country in which the wine was produced, making it easier for consumers to use COO as a choice criterion.

It is also noted that, although wine knowledge based on the exporting country is limited, French wine is believed to be associated with the highest quality by some Chinese consumers. As such, COO is seen as a symbol of face and social status (Charters, 2006; Somogyi et al., 2011). This helps to explain why Chinese demand has been high for luxury French iconic wines and Australian branded super premium wines. Although the limited sample size and geographical location in these studies make it difficult to generalize to all consumers, they do provide some evidence that the COO is important to wine sales in China.

Furthermore, the Chinese were also found to value branded wines and to relate branded wines to success, prosperity and enhanced social status. A consumer survey in Shanghai and Guangzhou, China's two wealthiest cities, shows that red wine lovers believe branded red wine represents the Western lifestyle, good social image, and elegant behaviour (Liu and Murphy, 2007). In addition, Wilson and Huang (2003) found that translating the name of a foreign wine into a Chinese name with a positive connotation is one of the most appealing approaches for foreign wines to attract Chinese consumers. The translation of Australia's Penfold into Chinese, *benfu* (literally, stride to being rich), is a great example (Zhou et al., 2014).

Moreover, rising incomes, competitive prices, education, moving away from high volume Chinese spirits, being seen as trendy, and the growing influence of foreign eating and drinking habits are regarded as key drivers for wine consumption growth in China (Camillo, 2012; Barton et al., 2013). In addition, most wine consumers live in urban China, rather than rural areas (Wang and McCluskey, 2010). There are three major reasons: first, urban residents are more likely to have higher disposable income to support the consumption of relatively expensive products, such as wine; second, urban areas are more influenced by Western lifestyle and wine drinking is one of them; third, the availability and accessibility of wine in urban China is much better than its rural counterpart (Liu et al., 2014).

Existing studies have also found that wine's health-related attributes can be a factor that affects consumer choices. For instance, Chinese consumers believe drinking red wine has health benefits, particularly in maintaining a healthy cardiovascular system. Less alcohol content in wine is also believed to be healthier, compared to traditional Chinese liquor, which contains higher alcohol levels (Liu and Murphy, 2007). Zhang et al. (2008) found that some women aged in their 50s or above believe drinking red wine is helpful to make them look younger.

Available literature is of great value in helping to understand that wine consumption behaviours in China are affected by income, price, COO, health concerns and other social factors. However, the weakness of existing studies is obvious as well. First, many studies have based their conclusions on a limited sample. For example, studies have focused only on well-developed cities in China such as Hong Kong, Shanghai, Beijing, Hangzhou and Guangzhou (Hu et al., 2008; Liu and Murphy, 2007; Wilson and Huang, 2003; Yu et al., 2009). Others have studied special consumer groups such as Chinese residents in Adelaide (Somogyi et al., 2011) and Chinese immigrants in the US (Guinand, 2005). Second, most of the studies have used descriptive statistics and analysis, for example Balestrini and Gamble (2006), Camillo (2012), Goodman et al. (2007), Li et al. (2011) and Wilson and Huang (2003). However, it is worth trying other methods or techniques to gain more insights into the market. Last, as the Chinese wine market is an emerging one, more research is called for to investigate its diversity and dynamics.

The chapter concentrates on factors affecting wine purchasing decisions in China with a special focus on young and wealthy people in urban China. Section 3 outlines research methods. Data information is given in

Section 4. Section 5 presents and discusses the results of data analysis and reports the research findings. Section 6 concludes with contributions and limitations of the study, along with suggestions for future research.

RESEARCH METHOD

A quantitative approach is adopted in this study. Discrete choice models, namely, a binary and an ordered probit model, are used to identify the factors affecting wine purchase behaviour.

In general, the behaviour of a large number of consumers is expressed in terms of aggregate quantities such as market demand for either a commodity or a service and this behaviour is a consequence of individual consumer decisions (Mansfield, 1996). In contrast to this, cross-sectional models based on survey data can be developed in a discrete choice framework. Given the dichotomous, ordered nature of survey data, discrete choice models can be used in modelling consumer decisions to estimate the likelihood of purchasing. A binary probit model is used to discuss the determinants of wine purchase decision and an ordered probit model is used to explain why consumers consume more wine.

The binary probit model is used for explaining a dichotomous dependent variable with the empirical specification formulated in terms of a latent-response variable. It has been widely used in diverse fields; originally in toxicology and now it has gained popularity in econometric analyses (Ben-Akiva and Lerman, 1985; Maddala, 1983). In this study, the dependent variable may take on only two values to indicate whether a consumer wants to buy wine or not. In the binary model, we assume that the decision of the household consumer to buy wine or not depends on an unobserved utility index that is determined by explanatory variables in such a way that the larger the value of the index, the greater the probability of the household buying wine.

An ordered probit model represents situations in which a discrete outcome represents a greater preference for, or propensity to buy a product. The assumptions of the ordered probit model include a list of explanatory variables that affect the dependent variable and are exogenous, i.e., uncorrelated with either the normally distributed latent disturbance or the prediction error from the model.

The dependent variable in an ordered probit model may give different degrees of willingness to buy products, in accordance with the variables developed from a survey. In the survey, consumers chose the answers on a

Table 8.1 Definitions of independent variables used in probit regression models

Independent variables	Description
Income	Monthly household income level (1−8)
Age	Age group (1−5)
Education	Highest education level attained (1−8)
Gender	Dummy variable, 1 stands for male
Marriage status	Dummy variable, 1 stands for married
Presence of kid(s)	Dummy variable, 1 stands for having kid(s)
City tiers	City tiers 1−3 (first tier cities include Beijing, Shanghai, Tianjin and Chongqing, second tier cities include capital cities at provincial level and special economic zone cities and the third tier cities include the rest of areas surveyed)
Purchasing wine for multiple purposes	Dummy variable, 1 stands for multiple purposes for purchase
Overseas experience	Dummy variable, 1 stands for having overseas experience
Brand	Importance 1−7
Price	Importance 1−7
Taste	Importance 1−7
Good for health	Importance 1−7

Likert scale basis to show how often the households buy wine, which indicates preference or propensity for wine.

The independent variables used in probit models are shown in Table 8.1.

DATA

The questionnaire was first developed in English and discussed with professionals in the field of consumer research and other related sectors. This was later translated into Chinese and pre-tested on randomly-chosen male and female consumers from different age and income categories in China. This random population commented on the content and design of the questionnaire, especially on the length and structure, thus leading to a shorter and more user-friendly version. As a result, 16 questions were included in the survey which were questions designed to elicit sociodemographic information, purchase outlets used, price paid per wine bottle, wine attributes sought, frequency of wine consumption, sources of information used, and so forth.

A wine consumption survey was conducted between January and June 2015, by means of a self-administered, online, highly structured questionnaire. The researcher's professional networks were initially used in order to overcome the low response rates associated with surveys in general, including mail surveys, email and online surveys. The researcher approached potential respondents in a face-to-face manner and invited them to participate in the study by visiting the survey's website. Participants in MBA courses held in various regions of China were initially targeted as they matched the profile of red wine consumers in China. In addition, the postgraduate student population has been targeted before in studies on wine drinking behaviour (Li et al., 2011; Yu et al., 2009).

The snowball sampling technique was then used as it helps reduce search costs and helps reveal hidden populations (Dragan and Isaie-Maniu, 2012). Snowballing, or targeting colleagues and friends of the researcher, as a stepping stone to finding other suitable respondents, is a common practice in Chinese studies (Liu and Murphy, 2007) and in qualitative studies in general (Frankel and Devers, 2000). In a high-context and collectivistic society like China, characterized by strong kinship ties and interdependence, networking is critical when doing business (Gong et al., 2004). No incentives were used to solicit participation due to budget constraints as well as the risk of introducing some form of bias into the results.

Given the rapid adoption of the internet, online surveys are becoming a viable method of data collection. Internet research is appealing because it is a cost- and time-efficient way of accessing a large number of participants (Sue and Ritter, 2007). Furthermore, China has the world's largest online population with 129 million residential broadband accounts in 2011 (McKinsey Global Institute, 2013). By administering the survey online and guaranteeing confidentiality, it counteracted potential obstacles relating to the collection of sensitive data in a culture characterized by high 'face' consciousness.

This survey covered Chinese consumers in urban China as indicated by the literature. A total of 538 valid samples were obtained.

Table 8.2 gives a demographic profile of respondents. Females are slightly overrepresented in the survey, with 50.56% of females in the sample compared to 49.44% males. The Chinese census data show more males (51.23%) than females (48.77%) in the general population (National Bureau of Statistics of China 2014). A gender bias may be due to the

Table 8.2 Basic statistics of survey samples

Gender	Male	49.44%
	Female	50.56%
Age	18−24	13.94%
	25−34	44.24%
	35−44	31.41%
	45−54	7.43%
	55 and above	2.97%
City Tier	1st	36.43%
	2nd	39.78%
	3rd	23.79%
Education	Primary	0.19%
	Middle school	0.19%
	Senior high school	2.23%
	Technical/vocational	0.56%
	Junior college	6.32%
	Undergraduate	42.75%
	Postgraduate	47.21%
	Other	0.56%
Household monthly income (renminbi)	3000 and below	2.23%
	3001−5000	11.15%
	5001−8000	22.12%
	8001−10,000	28.25%
	10,001−20,000	22.86%
	20,001−30,000	8.74%
	30,001−50,000	3.53%
	50,001 and above	1.12%
Overseas experience	Yes	30.29%
	No	69.71%

recruitment process or to females being more interested in the topic than men.

This sample consists mostly of young people, with 90% of respondents under 45 years old. In contrast to Chinese census data, which shows that around 70% of the population fall into the 15−59 age bracket, this is due to the fact that it is a wine consumption survey sample and not a general population sample. As drinking wine is regarded as a symbol of Western lifestyle (Curtis et al., 2007), younger people are more inclined to become a wine consumer than older people.

With regard to education, 47.21% of all respondents are educated up to postgraduate level and 42.75% are educated up to undergraduate level.

Analysis of statistical data show that 27% of the population of tertiary age were in tertiary education in 2011 (UNESCO, 2013) so this sample is more educated than the general population, which is in line with the literature claiming that Chinese wine consumers are found to be more educated (Morrison and Rabellotti, 2014).

Monthly household income was classified into eight categories and 73.23% of all respondents report their household income per month falls into the 5001−20,000 renminbi bracket. According to Chinese census data, the annual average per capita disposable income of urban households was 28,844 renminbi in 2014. This sample is skewed towards the higher income categories. It might be due to (1) the fact that more than 76% of respondents are from China's 1st and 2nd tier cities and the wealthy coastal cities; and (2) the sample is more educated than the general population, hence their income is higher.

In summary, the respondents in the survey are young, wealthy and well-educated consumers living in urban China. This is the cohort that is relatively unknown in the existing literature.

RESULT AND DISCUSSION

A binary probit model was used to analyze the determinants of wine purchase decisions. The dependent variable in this model is the binary variable: to purchase or not purchase wine. Independent variables are determined based on the existing literature and survey questions. As a result, income, gender, age, marriage status, presence of child(ren), city tiers (where the respondent lives), overseas experience and importance of brand, price, taste and health are included in the model. Education is not included due to its high relevance to income. All analyses were conducted using STATA. Table 8.3 presents details of parameter estimates.

The results show that the binary probit model performs well in explaining wine purchase decisions (Table 8.3). Pseudo R^2 of 0.54 indicates joint significance of all regressor coefficient estimates.

As expected, the coefficient of being a male is positive and highly significant, indicating that gender is an important factor that affects whether or not to purchase wine. The coefficient of income is positive and highly significant, indicating wine consumption is driven by income increase. Overseas experience is found to be a positive and highly significant factor affecting wine consumption in China. The brand of wine is found to be major consideration when making wine purchase decisions.

Table 8.3 Estimates of binary probit model

Variables	Coefficient.	Std. Err.	Z	p > z
Male[b]	3.2074	0.2379	13.48	0.000
Age[a]	− 0.1687	0.1057	− 1.60	0.101
Marriage[a]	− 0.3626	0.2072	− 1.75	0.080
Child	− 0.1823	0.2100	− 0.87	0.385
Income[b]	0.1159	0.0711	1.63	0.049
Overseas[b]	0.2570	0.1708	1.50	0.052
City	0.0699	0.1084	0.64	0.255
Brand[b]	0.2032	0.0645	3.15	0.002
Price[a]	0.3011	0.0689	0.45	0.062
Taste	0.0754	0.0819	0.92	0.357
Health	0.0644	0.0773	0.83	0.405

Note: [a]Indicates significance at 10% level. [b]indicates significance at 5% level.

The coefficient of age is negative and significant as expected, revealing that young people are more likely to purchase wine than the old. Older people are not likely to buy wine because of two reasons: (1) as wine is a Western food item to Chinese consumers, young people are more open to new food concepts and more willing to try something different than the old ones; and (2) older people are more likely to stick to the traditional alcoholic drinks (Pan et al., 2006), therefore, they do not like the taste of wine.

It is surprise to see that the price of wine does not play as statistically significant (at 5% level) a role as brand does in wine purchase decision. This is probably because the brand is regarded as a proxy for COO, that affects wine purchase decisions. Interestingly, marriage is found to have a negative and significant impact on wine purchase.

In summary, gender, income, overseas experience and brand of wine are found to be the main determinants of whether or not to purchase wine. In addition, age, marriage and price of wine also affect the purchasing decisions significantly.

An ordered probit model was used to explain the frequency of wine purchase. The dependent variable in this model is frequency of purchasing wine (1−6, from never to once a week). Independent variables include income, gender, age, marriage status, presence of child(ren), city tiers (where the respondent lives), overseas experience, purposes of wine purchase and importance of brand, price, taste and health. Table 8.4 presents the parameter estimates. Pseudo R^2 of 0.43 indicates joint significance of all regressor coefficient estimates.

Table 8.4 Estimates of ordered probit model

Variables	Coefficient.	Std. Err.	z	p > z
Male[b]	0.2956	0.1003	2.95	0.043
Age	0.0143	0.0691	0.21	0.386
Marriage	0.1644	0.1261	1.30	0.152
Child[b]	− 0.3838	0.1286	− 2.98	0.003
Income[a]	0.1925	0.0436	4.42	0.053
Overseas	0.1121	0.1039	1.08	0.181
City[a]	− 0.1157	0.0691	− 1.67	0.094
Multipurpose[b]	0.3831	0.1012	3.79	0.023
Brand[b]	0.1734	0.0386	4.49	0.019
Price[a]	0.1816	0.0412	4.41	0.084
Taste[b]	0.1402	0.0461	3.04	0.002
Health	0.0154	0.0438	0.35	0.267

Note: [a]Indicates significance at 10% level. [b]indicates significance at 5% level.

Similar to the binary probit model, the coefficient of being a male is positive and highly significant, indicating that gender plays an important role in affecting the frequency of wine purchase. As expected, the presence of child(ren) is found to be a negative and highly significant factor. It is reasonable that the parents do not want their child to perceive themselves as alcoholic addicts. In addition, purchasing wine for more than one purpose is found to contribute to more frequent wine purchasing behaviour significantly. Furthermore, brand and the taste of wine are important considerations when purchasing wine more often.

As expected, the coefficient of income is positive and significant, indicating wine is a normal good in China. Therefore, wine consumption will continue to rise as income increases. Not surprisingly, living in big (or capital) cities has a positive impact on frequency of purchasing wine. As explained in Table 8.1, city tiers are closely related to various level of economic development and also to exposure to foreign cultures. Municipalities, such as Beijing, Shanghai, Tianjin and Chongqing, have large populations, including foreign communities. Therefore, the city tier affects wine consumption and purchasing behaviour as expected. Moreover, price is found to be an important factor affecting the frequent wine buyers.

In summary, gender, presence of child(ren), purchasing wine for multiple purposes, brand and taste of wine are found to be the significant factors affecting frequency of wine purchase. In addition, income, city tiers (where the respondent lives), and price of wine are also found to be significant considerations when studying frequent wine purchasing behaviours.

CONCLUSIONS AND IMPLICATIONS

China is not commonly associated with wine, but it can now be described as nothing less than an important participant in global wine trade (Muhammad et al., 2014). The present study gives an insight into consumer demand for wine by investigating the wine attributes sought by Chinese consumers and their purchasing decisions.

Rising incomes and prices have generated the rapid increase in wine consumption, but they cannot fully explain the changes that have occurred (Muhammad et al., 2014). This study shows that gender, income, overseas experience and brand of wine also strongly influence wine purchasing decisions. A simple portrait of a wine buyer in China is a rich male with overseas experience, whose preference for wine is brand-driven. However, a frequent wine buyer is a male without child (ren), buying wine for various reasons, whose preference for wine is brand and taste-driven. The latter represents the profile of an important group of wine consumers in China.

As all the respondents are from urban areas, 90% of the sample is young and 85% fall in to the higher income bracket, this study is, in fact, an investigation on young and wealthy Chinese consumers in urban areas, who are believed to be the major source of the increased wine consumption in future (Barton et al., 2013).

Understanding the Chinese local wine markets and consumer preference for wine products is important for wine producers. The results provide meaningful and insightful marketing suggestions for the foreign and Chinese wine producers, such as the target market and pricing strategy. Such information provides a valuable basis for developing efficient marketing strategies and equipping the sellers with ideas for wine marketing, for which there is a potential high demand.

This study also challenges the stereotype of Chinese consumers as novice consumers who lack wine experience. It shows the dynamic nature of the Chinese wine market and the recent emergence of the knowledgeable wine consumer. It signals that Chinese consumers have started caring about the quality of wines and enjoying drinking quality wines. As such, wine price will not be the only influential factor affecting wine purchasing decision, but quality also matters. This has important implications for developing wine markets in China.

REFERENCES

Administrative Office of China Food and Drinks Fair, 2015. *China imported wine index and market report 2014—2015* (in Chinese). Administrative Office of China Food and Drinks Fair, Beijing.

Anderson, K., Wittwer, G., 2013. How large could Australia's wine exports to China be by 2018? Wine Viticulture J. 28 (6), 60—64.

Balestrini, P., Gamble, P., 2006. Country of-origin effects on Chinese wine consumers. Br. Food J. 108 (No. 5), 396—412.

Barton, D., Chen, Y., Jin, A., 2013. Mapping China's middle class. McKinsey Q. McKinsey.

Ben-Akiva, M., Lerman, S., 1985. Discrete Choice Analysis: Theory and Application to Travel Demand. The MIT Press, Cambridge, MA.

Bouzdine-Chameeva, T., Pesme J. and Zhang, W. (2013). Chinese wine industry: current and future market trends.AAWE Conference, Stellenbosch, South Africa. <http://www.wine-economics.org/aawe/wp.../07/Bouzdine_Pesme_Zhang.pdf> (accessed 15.07.2015).

Camillo, A., 2012. A strategic investigation of the determinants of wine consumption in China. Int. J. Wine Bus. Res. Vol. 24 (No. 1), 68—92.

Charters, S., 2006. Wine and Society: The Social and Cultural Context of a Drink. Elsevier Butterworth-Heinemann, Oxford.

Curtis, K., Mccluskey, J., Wahl, T., 2007. Consumer preferences for western-style convenience foods in China. China Econ. Rev. Vol. 18, 1—14.

Dragan, M., Isaie-Maniu, A., 2012. Snowball sampling developments used in marketing research. Int. J. Art Commer. Vol. 1 (No. 16), 214—223.

Frankel, R., Devers, K., 2000. Study design in qualitative research: developing questions and assessing resource needs. Educ. Health Change Learn. Pract. 13 (No. 2), 251—261.

Gong, W., Li, Z.G., Li, T., 2004. Marketing to Chinese youths: a cultural transformation perspective. Bus. Horiz. 47 (No. 6), 41—50.

Goodman, S., Lockshin, L., Cohen, E., 2007. Influencers of consumer choice — comparing international markets. Bus. Market. Export 22 (3), 87—91.

Guinand, L., 2005. The Chinese taste for wine. Wines Vines42—44.

Hu, X., Li, L., Xie, C., Zhiu, J., 2008. The effects of country-of-origin on Chinese consumers' wine purchasing behaviour. J. Technol. Manag. 3 (No. 2), 292—306.

Li, J., Jia, J., Taylor, D., Bruwer, J., Li, E., 2011. The wine drinking behavior of young adults: an exploratory study in China. Br. Food J. 113 (No. 10), 1305—1317.

Liu, F., Murphy, J., 2007. A qualitative study of Chinese wine consumption and purchasing: implications for Australian wines. Int. J. Wine Bus. Res. 19 (No. 2), 98—113.

Liu, H., McCarthy, B., Chen, T., Guo, S., Song, X., 2014. The Chinese wine market: a market segmentation study. Asia Pac. J. Market. Logistics 26 (3), 450—471.

Maddala, C., 1983. Limited-Dependent and Qualitative Variables in Econometrics. Cambridge University Press, Cambridge.

Mansfield, E., 1996. Microeconomics. W.W. Norton & Company, Inc, New York.

McKinsey Global Institute, 2013. China's E-tail revolution: online shopping as a catalyst for growth, McKinsey Global Institute, Seoul and San Francisco, CA. Available at: <http://www.mckinsey.com/insights/asia-pacific/china_e-tailing> (accessed 15.10.2013).

Morrison, A. and Rabellotti, R., 2014. Gradual catch up and enduring leadership in the global wine industry, AAWE Working Paper No. 148, 1−34. Available at: <http://econpapers.repec.org/paper/agsaawewp/164650.htm> (accessed 28.07.2015).

Muhammad, A., Leister, A., McPhail, L., Chen, W., 2014. The evolution of foreign wine demand in China. Aust. J. Agric. Resour. Econ. 58, 392−408.

National Bureau of Statistics of China, 2014, China Statistical Yearbook (in Chinese), National Bureau of Statistics of China, Beijing.

Pan, S., Fang, C., Malaga, J., 2006. Alcoholic beverage consumption in China: a censored demand system approach. Appl. Econ. Lett. 13 (No. 15), 975−979.

Qing, P., Hu, W., 2015. Self-consumption, gifting, and chinese wine consumers. 2015 Agricultural & Applied Economics Association and Western Agricultural Economics Association Annual Meeting, San Francisco, CA, July 26−28.

Somogyi, S., Li, E., Johnson, T., Bruwer, J., Bastian, S., 2011. The underlying motivations of Chinese wine consumer behaviour. Asia Pac. J. Market. Logistics 23 (No. 4), 473−485.

Sue, M., Ritter, A., 2007. Conducting Online Surveys. Sage Publications, Thousand Oaks, CA.

The Wall Street Journal, 2014. China is now world's biggest consumer of red wine. Available at: <http://blogs.wsj.com/scene/2014/01/29/china-is-now-worlds-biggest-consumer-of-red-wine/> (accessed 16.11.2014).

UNESCO, 2013. UIS Statistics in brief − education (all levels) profile − China. Available at: <http://stats.uis.unesco.org/unesco/TableViewer/document.aspx?ReportId¼121&IF_Language¼eng&BR_Country¼1560 > (accessed 17.05.2013).

Vinexpo, 2014. The wine and spirits market in China. Available at: <http://www.vinexpo.com/media/cms_page_media/437/IWSR%20-%20Chine%20-%20ANG.pdf> (accessed 16.05.2015).

Wang, H., McCluskey, J., 2010. Effects of information and country of origin on Chinese consumer preferences for wine: an experimental approach in the field., Agricultural and Applied Economics Association. Available at: <http://ageconsearch.umn.edu/handle/61330> (accessed 25.07.2014).

Wilson, I., Huang, Y., 2003. Wine brand naming in China. Int. J. Wine Market. 15 (3), 52−63.

Winechina, 2005. Wine history in China. Available at: <http://www.winechina.net/view_news.asp?news_id = 20> (accessed 16.05.2014).

Yu, Y., Sun, H., Goodman, S., Chen, S., Ma, H., 2009. Chinese choices: a survey of wine consumers in Beijing. Int. J. Wine Bus. Res. 21 (No. 2), 155−168.

Zhang, J., Casswell, S., Cai, H., 2008. Increased drinking in a metropolitan city in China: a study of alcohol consumption patterns and changes. Addiction 103 (3), 416−426.

Zhou, Z., Liu, H., Cao, L., 2014. Food Consumption in China: The Revolution Continues. Edward Elgar Publishing, Cheltenham, UK.

PART III

Markets and Distribution

CHAPTER 9

David versus Goliath: Market Entry Strategies of Small and Medium Sized Wine Estates

J.H. Hanf[1] and P. Winter[2]
[1]Geisenheim University, Geisenheim, Germany
[2]Georg Müller Stiftung, Eltville am Rhein, Germany

INTRODUCTION

Direct sales and sales via specialized wine retail stores have been the dominant sales channels used by small and medium sized wine estates. However, changing consumption habits and lifestyle trends create high competition within these typical distribution channels. Particularly in saturated markets (e.g., Germany) small and medium wine estates face strong competition from other domestic wine producers as well as imported wines. Thus, small and medium wine estates are increasingly considering other distribution channels or new markets.

The development of the Chinese wine market over the past 10 years indicates that it is one of the few wine markets where consumption has been growing steadily (Euromonitor, 2014a). Additionally, forecasts by Euromonitor (2014b) and other market research institutes indicate that Chinese wine consumption will continue to grow. Thus, this market is currently — and will be in the future — a very attractive export destination for many small and medium sized wine estates. However, despite its great potential, the Chinese market also has many obstacles which may lead to disappointing outcomes of export activities.

Creating and implementing a successful exporting strategy is a very demanding task for any producer. However, often small and medium sized wine estates are new to the export market; thus, they lack appropriate capabilities and knowledge. In comparison to large companies, these wine estates generally have fewer resources available for export activities. Overall, export is a huge challenge for them, demanding adjusted export strategies.

In this context, the aim of this chapter is to elaborate on export activities of small and medium sized wine estates, addressing the challenges and obstacles. Hence, we will conduct a literature review on market entry strategies and on challenges of internationalization. Afterwards we present a case study.

This case study is based on the small *Verband deutscher Prädikatsweingüter* (VDP)[1] wine estate Georg Müller Stiftung. After being the wine-growing estate of the village of Hattenheim (1913—72) and the City of Eltville (1972—2003), the wine estate Georg Müller Stiftung was purchased by Peter Winter in 2003. Peter Winter was the Chairman of the Executive Board of one of the ten largest wine companies worldwide[2] and with four decades of international experience[3] — particularly in Asia — he restructured the wine estate in such a way that export is key to success. Moreover, from the beginning China was considered as one of the main target markets. Today, roughly 10 years after the reorganization of the wine estate it can be considered as one of the German benchmarks[4] for exporting wine to China.

MARKET ENTRY STRATEGIES IN LIGHT OF INTERNATIONALIZATION OF ENTERPRISES

Internationalization of Enterprises

Internationalization can be classified according to the direction of the process as outward (export of products, foreign production, licensing and franchising) and inward internationalization (e.g., foreign sourcing,

[1] The VDP is an elite group of some 200 quality-oriented German vintners who are committed to terroir-driven viticulture at the highest level. It was founded in 1910 as Verband Deutscher Naturweinversteigerer e.V., Association of German Natural Wine Auctioneers. Today it consists of 13 regional associations, one for each region in the German wine classification system (VDP, 2015).

[2] With a turnover of €520 million in the year 2002, WIV Wein International *AG* (until 1986 known as Ferd. Pieroth GmbH) was the 7th largest wine company worldwide according to Rabobank survey in 2003. It has been and still is the worldwide largest direct selling company in the wine business.

[3] Peter Winter worked from 1964 until 2003 in various positions at WIV Wein International AG. From 1967 to 1975 he was Managing Director of Pieroth Ltd, Great Britain; from 1976 to 1986 Managing Director of foreign subsidiaries, and from 1986 to 2003 Chief Executive Officer of WIV. Additionally, Peter Winter has been the President of the German Wine Exporters Association for 16 years; he has been their Honorary President for one year.

[4] Whereas the average export price per liter for German wine was €4.49 in 2015, in the same year the average export price of Georg Müller Stiftung to China was €18.67 per liter.

import of management ideas) (Welch and Luostarinen, 1993). Scholars have asked how international companies can be successful in other countries. The market imperfection (Hymer, 1976), resource advantage (Hunt and Morgen, 1996; Hunt 2002) and eclectic (Dunning, 1980, 1981, 1988) theories argue that enterprises should possess internationally exploitable, firm-specific advantages to compete in foreign countries and compensate for the costs of these the new, international, conditions. These advantages, such as efficient management skills, explain the competitiveness of multinational firms in new markets. The firm-specific advantages are asset-specific (ownership of specific assets such as financial capital, specific brand name) and transaction-specific (the advantages as a result of multinationality, e.g., the ability of a multinational enterprise to decrease the transaction costs compared to their competitors and external markets) (Dunning, 1981, 1988, 1993; Johanson and Wiedersheim-Paul, 1975; Johanson and Vahlne, 1977). Particularly, market imperfections enable companies to exploit their firm-specific advantages (Hymer, 1976; Malhotra et al., 2003).

Developing a market entry strategy involves a thorough analysis of potential competitors and possible customers (Janssen, 2004). Some of the relevant factors that are important in deciding the viability of entry into a particular market include trade barriers, localized knowledge, price localization, competition and export subsidies (Pearce, 2006). Thus, a market entry strategy is the planned method of delivering goods to a new target market and distributing them (Janssen, 2004). Some of the most common market entry strategies include directly setting up an entity in the market, directly exporting products and indirectly exporting using a middleman or other distributors. Others include licensing, franchising, joint ventures and producing products in the target market (Johnson and Tellis, 2008). In the context of China, joint ventures have been particularly important to enter markets, especially during the beginning of Chinese economic reform in the 1980s. For example, 1980 Rémy Cointreau ventured into China to set up the first joint venture enterprise, Dynasty Wine Ltd. A further example is Changyu Pioneer Wine Company, which entered into cooperation with Castel Group in France to establish the first professional chateau in China. Additionally, Changyu Pioneer Wine Company has formed a joint venture with a Canadian company to build the world's largest ice wine production facility near Huanlong Lake in Liaoning province in 2006.

Foreign exchange risks are an important challenge in the context of market entry strategies (Homaifar, 2004). Currency crises of the 1990s and early 2000s, such as the Mexican peso crisis, Asian currency crisis, 1998 Russian financial crisis, and the Argentine peso crisis, led to substantial losses from foreign exchange and led firms to pay closer attention to their foreign exchange risk (Eun and Resnick, 2011). Foreign exchange risk is a financial risk that exists when a financial transaction is denominated in a currency other than that of the base currency of the company (Levi, 2005). Foreign exchange risk also exists when the foreign subsidiary of a company maintains financial statements in a currency other than the reporting currency of the consolidated entity (Pilbeam, 2006). The risk is that there may be an adverse movement in the exchange rate of the denomination currency in relation to the base currency before the date when the transaction is completed (Dunn and Mutti, 2004). Firms with exposure to foreign exchange risk may use a number of foreign exchange hedging strategies to reduce the exchange rate risk (Wang, 2005). Transaction exposure can be reduced either with the use of the money markets, foreign exchange derivatives such as forward contracts, futures contracts, options and swaps, or with operational techniques such as currency invoicing and leading and lagging of receipts and payments (Moffett et al., 2009).

However, the most challenging decision that a company might face in internationalization is the degree of standardization or adaptation in its operations (Vrontis, 2003). The question of standardization or adaptation affects all avenues of a business's operations, such as research and development, finance, production, organizational structure, procurement and the marketing mix (Vrontis and Thrassou, 2007). Whether a company chooses to standardize or adapt its operations depends on its attitudes toward different cultures (Vrontis, 2005). These attitudes are defined by three orientations toward foreign culture: ethnocentric[5], polycentric[6] and geocentric[7] (Vrontis and Thrassou, 2007).

[5] The concept of 'ethnocentrism' assumes that people born into a particular culture — who grow up absorbing the values and behaviours of the culture — will develop a worldview that considers their culture to be the norm (Omohundro, 2008). As a result, ethnocentrism urges the use of standardization (Douglas and Wind, 1987).

[6] 'Polycentrism' is the opposite of 'ethnocentrism', highlighting cultural differences. Therefore, it urges the use of adaptation in every market, and its marketing mix differs, depending on the culture in which it operates (Vrontis and Thrassou, 2007).

[7] The geocentric orientation is a fusion of ethnocentric and polycentric orientations; it is understood that there are similarities and differences in cultures worldwide. Thus, this is more of a balanced approach to take in marketing strategies, cohabitating adaptation and standardization (Vrontis, 2005).

Standardization assumes a union of cultures with similar environmental and customer demand around the globe. Further, trade barriers are getting lower and technological advances and firms are displaying a global orientation in their strategy (Jain, 1989). Thus, one strategy can be created for the global market and standardizing the marketing mix elements can achieve consistency with customers as well as lower costs (Nanda and Dickson, 2007). Levitt (1983) argues that companies that are managed well have moved away from customizing items to offering globally standardized products that are advanced, functional, reliable and low priced. According to him, companies can achieve long term success by concentrating on what everyone wants rather than worrying about the particulars of what everyone thinks they might like.

Adaptation emphasizes the importance of customization (Czinkota and Ronkainen, 1998). The fundamental basis of the adaptation school of thought is that when entering a foreign market, one must consider all environmental factors and constraints such as language, climate, race, occupations, education, taste, different laws, cultures and societies (Soufani et al., 2006). Global companies have to find out how they must adjust an entire marketing strategy, including how they sell and distribute their product, to fit new market demands (Czinkota and Ronkainen, 1998; Vrontis, 2003).

Internationalization and Culture-Specific Consumption Preferences

Consumer behaviour theory assumes that consumers usually do not focus on the product as a whole, but on a combination of different product characteristics or attributes, which can be either concrete or abstract. Concrete product attributes are defined as being measurable in physical units (e.g., colour), whereas abstract attributes are an aggregation of several concrete attributes. Because of the consumers' selective and subjective allocation of cognitive resources, abstract attributes are perceived differently by each consumer. Thus, the main element of abstract attributes is that they are subjective in nature, as with style or taste (Olson and Reynolds, 1983; Reynolds and Gutman, 1984).

Whether the consequences brought about by attributes are positive (benefits) or negative (risks) depends on the consumers' personal values, which are defined as enduring beliefs that specific modes of conduct or end-states of existence are personally or socially preferable to opposite modes of conduct or end-states of existence. The expectation of achieving a personal value through the usage of a certain product is the actual buying motive (Grunert, 1994; Reynolds and Gutman, 1979).

Therefore, the formation of several preferences for certain products depends on values which people acquire during the process of socialization. Through this process, which starts within the family and continues through school and then throughout life, people develop their values, motivations and habitual activities. Furthermore, humans learn through imitation and by observing the process of reward and punishment to discover which values and what kind of behaviour is approved by a society (Engel et al., 1995). This process of socialization usually takes place against the cultural background, so that socialization also is the process of absorbing a culture (Kroeber and Kluckhohn, 1952).

The cultural level includes all kinds of different manners people learn while being brought up in certain society (e.g. the language, the physical distance from other people we keep to feel comfortable, the kind of food people eat, the drinks that people pair with food, how the food is prepared and the way food is eaten at a particular time of the day) (Hofstede, 1984; Hofstede and Hofstede, 2005). Hence, consumers from varying cultural backgrounds perceive food differently (Osinga and Hofstede, 2004).

Even if, through the globalization of markets, migration and worldwide web usage, cultural differences seem to decrease, culture-specific consumption patterns still exist (Craig et al. 2005; Watson et al., 2002). One extreme example of culture-specific consumption patterns is that of ethnocentrism. This behaviour is often motivated by patriotism and apparently rational, economic reasons in that the purchase of domestic products stimulates the economy and creates jobs, whereas purchasing foreign made products is viewed as harmful to the local economy and causes domestic unemployment (Orth and Firbasová, 2003). The recent OIV data (2015) indicates that more Chinese wine is drunk, possibly replacing imports.

All in all, consumers' respective cultural backgrounds have some impact on market entry strategies as more or less all marketing instruments are affected by culture. For example, consumers' willingness to pay is especially affected by their cultural background (Rewerts and Hanf, 2009a). The willingness to pay represents the valuation of products. Because consumers learned during the process of socialization which products they should approve of and which they should not, the socialization and thus the transmission of culture influences the appreciation of certain products as well as the willingness to pay (Rewerts and Hanf, 2009b). Another example is that culture can have an effect on the choice of certain types of wines which are preferred due to (religious) beliefs. Therefore, culture-specific preparations of food and culture-specific usage situations generally have to be considered in product development (Rewerts and Hanf, 2009a).

CASE STUDY: GEORG MÜLLER STIFTUNG SUCCESS IN CHINA

The wine-growing estate Georg Müller was established by Georg Müller, the co-owner of the famous Eltville sparkling wine cellar Matheus Müller, in 1882. The estate was a founding member of the Association of German Predicate Wine Estates (VDP) in 1910. With a document signed on December 6, 1913, Georg Müller donated the wine estate — which by then had an excellent reputation and was well known far beyond the borders of the Rheingau — to his home community of Hattenheim and the wine estate became the Georg Müller Stiftung. The purpose of the donation was to use the profits to help the poor in the community and support charitable causes (Georg Müller Stiftung, 2015). Since 2003 it has belonged to Peter Winter, who was the chairman of the executive board of the largest wine direct sales company in the world until April 2003. Together with his team and his family, Peter Winter has made it his goal to set the highest standards of quality in terms of growing and caring for the vines and producing the wine (Georg Müller Stiftung, 2015).

Beginning in 2003, Peter Winter made an assessment of sales strategies. The German domestic market in 2003 was already saturated and very competitive, so he decided that exports should be one of the major sales channels in the future. Classical export markets of German wine in the neighbouring countries were chosen but because he already had four decades of international experience — particularly in Asia — he restructured the wine estate so that this region was to be the focus of the new export strategy. From the beginning, China was considered as one of the main target markets because Peter Winter had some unique, intangible resources.

As the Managing Director of foreign subsidiaries of WIV he was responsible for establishing a subsidiary in Hong Kong selling wine directly to end consumers in 1975. Subsidiaries in most of the 'Asian Tiger Countries' followed soon after. His first journey to mainland China was in 1979 and his first attempts to export wine to mainland China started in 1981. In 1984 he was responsible for a joint venture producing wine in China, and in 1992 a representative office was opened in Peking, exporting the sales concept of 'direct sales' to China. Thus, by 2003 he had been working with Chinese wine consumers for more than 20 years. He had a very good knowledge of their eating and drinking habits as well as their socialization regarding alcohol consumption. Thus, from the beginning his Pinot Noir had been used as 'door opener' to the Chinese market. Accompanying the Pinot Noir were white wines that go particularly well with the Chinese cuisine. Still today red wines and expensive white dessert wines are very important for the sales portfolio. Knowing China from direct sales, Peter Winter deliberately decided that his small wine estate would not use a broad market entry approach but would use a niche market approach addressing selected importers engaged in Horeca and selling to rich private clients.

Peter Winter's knowledge of the Chinese drinking culture combined with his business experience in China and his knowledge of Chinese business etiquette opened him the doors to his business partners, too. Thus, Georg Müller Stiftung had no trouble finding import agents so they could export directly. His knowledge of trustworthy importers particularly helped the Georg Müller Stiftung to overcome risks and disadvantages which are often attached to exports. Knowing his importers for many years, Peter Winter also knows many of their customers which are hotels, restaurants, wine retail stores and the abovementioned private clients. Thus, he knew from the beginning that the wine supply had to be flexible and adjusted to the needs of each commercial customer. He dealt with this issue in such a way that the wine sold under the umbrella brand Georg Müller Stiftung has the same design and marketing philosophy globally, and only limited adjustments regarding the sugar content and therefore taste are made. However, in order to adapt to local needs Peter Winter introduced subbrands as well as wine sold under the labels of his commercial customers. The more the subbrands are adapted, the more the wine inside the bottles is adapted as well. Moreover, Peter Winter has also founded a small winery so that he is able to sell wines that are sold under the label "Peter Winter Wines" to Chinese importers. This strategic action allows Georg Müller Stiftung to increase its supply flexibility and supply credibility. Thus, Georg Müller Stiftung combines aspects of standardization and adaptation at the same time (i.e., its marketing approach is geocentric in nature).

Further, Peter Winter knows the importance of visiting his customers personally and still flies to China three or four times a year. Because travel costs have decreased over time he states that today the business trips to

China are not much costlier than those to other destinations. During his regular visits he always organizes or participates in events such as food pairing seminars with his importers or together with their commercial and private customers. In this context, Peter Winter stresses the importance of both consumption preferences and culture-specific social graces and socio-cultural hierarchies. In addition to his polycentric behaviour, seniority[8] also helps him to establish, maintain and foster business relations. The combination of visits to fairs, (end) customer presentations and business meetings is essential to his effectiveness. Despite his experience in China, Peter Winter is accompanied by a native Chinese speaker regardless of whether he is attending a fair or a customer event. Particularly today, as he changes his business focus from first tier cities to second and third tier cities, Peter Winter believes the support of native Chinese speakers is very important. In these cities lessons learned ten years ago are still of high value today.

Because of his experience working with a variety of secure foreign exchange risks while working in the large international company, Peter Winter was often able to turn those risks into 'foreign exchange gains.' Those experiences still benefit him today. For instance, when Georg Müller Stiftung is invoicing in Renminbi, a foreign exchange risk markup is added.

Ultimately, Peter Winter has successfully restructured the Georg Müller Stiftung, which is growing in acreage and sales. Today the Georg Müller Stiftung sells around 15,000 L for around €280,000 to China. These 15,000 L amount to only 0.5% market share of the total volume of German wine exported to China. However, they account for 2% market share of the total value of German wine exported to China. The average price per 750 mL bottle of Georg Müller Stiftung wine is €14, and is more than 400% higher than the average of all German wine exported to China (€3.37 per bottle). Exports to China represent today 20% of the total volume produced by Georg Müller Stiftung and 30% of the annual turnover. Peter Winter's unique market knowledge combined with a unique network of trustworthy people who deliver location-specific and firm-related benefits such as transaction-specific advantages are the main reasons for this success.

---

[8] The 50th anniversary of Peter Winter significantly devoting all his passion and efforts to wine industry was in 2014 (Georg Müller Stiftung, 2015).

SUMMARY AND 'LESSONS LEARNED'

Despite the fact that literature concentrates mainly on large scale producers, our case study shows that small and medium sized wine estates are able to successfully establish themselves in the market. To a certain extent, winning the battle against the large corporations is just like David versus Goliath.

The quintessence of the case study of Georg Müller Stiftung is that regardless of the size of the company (large scale or small scale), long term vision and a sound business strategy must be used to succeed in the Chinese market. Furthermore, the vision and strategy need to be formulated with a deep understanding of the Chinese people and market. Particularly for small scale producers, this means abandoning a producer orientation and adopting a customer-orientation.

This implies that the owner and/or the managers must regularly visit China; in the beginning at least two to three times per year, later that can perhaps be scaled back. Wine representatives must regularly attend fairs such as Vinexpo Asia in Hong Kong, Hong Kong International Wine & Spirits Fair, or ProWein in Shanghai. In this context, the EU and the German government — as well as the German Wine Institute (DWI) — often offer attractive support.

Once the first contact is made, the choice of a good importer is crucial. A small estate must have some reliable personal contacts (as in the case of Peter Winter) or support organizations (e.g., DWI) to help match estates with importers. However, just finding an importer is not enough. Instead, an attractive incentive system for the importer(s) has to be worked out and to be set up.

It is not enough to travel just once to China hoping to make a good deal. Instead a successful business requires a long term strategy, capital, time, courage and even more far-sightedness. Last but not least, the glue that holds all of these success components together is *Guanxi*. Hence, the most important investment is in the establishment of reliable, trustworthy and strong personal relations with Chinese key customers such as importers.

REFERENCES

Craig, C.S., Greene, W.H., Douglas, S.P., 2005. Culture matters: consumer acceptance of U.S. firms in foreign markets. J. Int. Market. 13 (4), 80–103.
Czinkota, M.R., Ronkainen, I.A., 1998. International Marketing, 5th ed. The Dryden Press, London.
Douglas, S.P., Wind, Y., 1987. The myth of globalization. Columbia J. World Bus. 22, 19–29.

Dunn Jr., R.M., Mutti, J.H., 2004. International Economics, *6th ed.* Routledge, New York, NY.

Dunning, J.H., 1980. Toward an eclectic theory of international production: some empirical tests. J. Int. Bus. Stud. 11, 9−30.

Dunning, J.H., 1981. The Eclectic Theory of the MNC. Allen & Unwin, London.

Dunning, J.H., 1988. The eclectic paradigm of international production: a restatement and some possible extensions. J. Int. Bus. Stud. 19, 1−31.

Dunning, J.H., 1993. Multinational Enterprises and the Global Economy. Addison Wesley, Wokingham.

Engel, J.F., Blackwell, R.D., Miniard, P.W., 1995. Consumer Behaviour, *8th ed.* The Dryden Press.

Eun, C.S., Resnick, B.G., 2011. International Financial Management, *6th ed.* McGraw-Hill/Irwin, New York, NY.

Euromonitor, 2014a. Passport: Alcoholic Drinks in China. Euromonitor International, Market Research Report, London, United Kingdom.

Euromonitor, 2014b. Passport: Wines in China. Euromonitor International, Market Research Report, London, United Kingdom.

Georg Müller Stiftung, 2015. Homepage. <http://georg-mueller-stiftung.de/?page_id = 75&lang = en>.

Grunert, K.G., 1994. Subjektive Produktbedeutungen: Auf dem Wege zu einem integrativen Ansatz in der Konsumentenforschung. In: Konsumentenforschung (Ed.), Forschungsgruppe Konsum und Verhalten. Verlag Vahlen, München.

Hofstede, G., 1984. Culture's Consequences: International Differences in Work-Related Values, Abridged Edition Sage Publications.

Hofstede, G., Hofstede, G.J., 2005. Cultures and Organizations: Software of the Mind. McGraw-Hill, New York.

Homaifar, G.A., 2004. Managing Global Financial and Foreign Exchange Risk. John Wiley & Sons, Hoboken, NJ.

Hunt, S.D., 2002. Foundations of Marketing Theory. M.E. Sharpe, Armonk, NY.

Hunt, S.D., Morgan, R.M., 1996. The resource-advantage theory of competition: dynamics, path dependencies, and evolutionary dimensions. J. Market. 60 (4), 107−114.

Hymer, S.H., 1976. The International Operations of National Firms: A Study of Direct Foreign Investment. Massachusetts Institute of Technology Press, Cambridge.

Jain, S.C., 1989. Standardisation of international marketing strategy: some research hypotheses. J. Market. 53, 70−79.

Janssen, M.R., 2004. On durable goods markets with entry and adverse selection. Can. J. Economics 37 (3), 552−589.

Johanson, J., Vahlne, J.E., 1977. The internationalisation process of the firm: a model of knowledge development on increasing foreign commitments. J. Int. Bus. Stud.23−32.

Johanson, J., Wiedersheim-Paul, F., 1975. The internationalisation of the firm: four Swedish case studies. J. Manag. Stud.305−322.

Johnson, J., Tellis, G.J., 2008. Drivers of success for market entry into China and India. J. Market. 72 (May), 1−13.

Kroeber, A.L., Kluckhohn, C., 1952. Culture: a critical review of concepts and definitions. Papers of the Peabody Museum of American Archeology and Ethnology, 47(1). Harvard University, Cambridge (MA).

Levi, M.D., 2005. International Finance, 4th ed. Routledge, New York, NY.

Levitt, T., 1983. The globalization of markets. Harvard Bus. Rev. 61, 92−102.

Malhotra, N.K., Agarwal, J., Ulgado, F.M., 2003. Internationalization and entry modes: a multi-theoretical framework and research propositions. J. Int. Market. 11 (4), 1−31.

Moffett, M.H., Stonehill, A.I., Eiteman, D.K., 2009. Fundamentals of Multinational Finance, *3rd ed.* Addison-Wesley, Boston, MA.

Nanda, K.V., Dickson, P.R., 2007. The fundamentals of standardizing global marketing strategy. Int. Market. Rev. 24 (1), 46—63.

OIV, 2015. World Viticulture Situation. Presentation at the OIV World Congress, Mainz, Germany.

Olson, J.C., Reynolds, T.J., 1983. Understanding Consumers' Cognitive Structures: Implications for Advertising Strategy. In: Percy, T.J., Woodside, A.G. (Eds.), Advertising and Consumer Psychology. Lexington Books, Lexington, Mass.

Omohundro, J.T., 2008. Thinking Like an Anthropologist: A Practical Introduction to Cultural Anthropology. McGraw Hill, New York.

Orth, U.R., Firbasová, Z., 2003. The role of consumer ethnocentrism in food product evaluation. Agribusiness 19 (2), 137—153.

Osinga, S.A., Hofstede, G.J., 2004. What we want to know about our food: consumer values across countries. In: Bremmers, H.J., Omta, S.W.F., Trienekens, J.H., Wubben, E.F.M. (eds.): Dynamics in Chains and Networks, Proceedings of the 6th International Conference on Chain and Network Management in Agribusiness and the Food Industry, Ede, 27—28 May 2004, pp. 301—309.

Pearce, R., 2006. Globalization and development: an international business strategy approach. Trans. Corp. 15 (1), 39—74.

Pilbeam, K., 2006. International Finance, 3rd ed. Palgrave Macmillan, New York, NY.

Rewerts, A and Hanf, JH., 2009a. Values as driving forces of culture-specific consumption patterns — an empirical investigation of wine consumers. XXVII Conference of the International Association of Agricultural Economists, Beijing, China.

Rewerts, A., Hanf, J.H., 2009b. Warum kaufen wir? Werte als Ausloser von Konsumentscheidungen bei Lebensmittel. Berichte über Landwirtschaft 87 (3), 519—533.

Reynolds, T.J., Gutman, J., 1979. An Investigation of the Levels of Cognitive Abstraction Utilized by Consumers in Product Differentiation. Attitude Research Under the Sun. American Marketing Association, Chicago.

Reynolds, T.J., Gutman, J., 1984. Advertising is image management. J. Advert. Res. Vol. 24 (1), 27—36.

Soufani, K., Vrontis, D., Poutziouris, P., 2006. Private equity for small firms: a conceptual model of adaptation versus standardization strategy. Int. J. Entrep. Small Bus. 3, 498—515.

VDP. 2015, VDP. Die Prädikatsweingüter. <http://www.vdp.de/en/the-vdp/>.

Vrontis, D., 2003. Integrating adaptation and standardisation in international marketing, the Adapt Stand modelling process. J. Market. Manag. 19, 283—305.

Vrontis, D., 2005. The creation of the Adapt Stand process in international marketing. J. Innov. Market. 1 (2), 7—21.

Vrontis, D., Thrassou, A., 2007. Adaptation vs. standardisation in international marketing — the country-of-origin effect. J. Innov. Market. 3 (4), 7—21.

Wang, P., 2005. The Economics of Foreign Exchange and Global Finance. Springer, Berlin, Germany.

Watson, J., Lysonski, S., Gillan, T., Raymore, L., 2002. Cultural values and important possessions: a cross-cultural analysis. J. Bus. Res. 55, 923—931.

Welch, L.S., Luostarinen, R., 1993. Inward-outward connections in internationalization. J. Int. Market. 1 (1), 44—56.

CHAPTER 10

The Chinese Wine Market — An Analysis of Wine Distribution Channels in a Highly Competitive Market

T. Bouzdine-Chameeva[1], J.H. Hanf[2] and W. Zhang[1]
[1]KEDGE Business School, Bordeaux, France
[2]Geisenheim University, Geisenheim, Germany

INTRODUCTION

One of the critical success factors for any wine producer is the development of effective partnership relationships with its distributors (Thach and Olsen, 2006). The shortage of studies on the distribution channels in the wine sector has been identified by many authors (Beaujanot et al., 2004; Orth et al., 2007; Thach and Olsen, 2006). The need to determine the features of wine distribution channels in different countries is especially urgent, particularly when considering the rapidly growing Asian wine markets (Beverland, 2009; Bouzdine-Chameeva and Ninomiya, 2011; Bouzdine-Chameeva et al., 2014; Muhammad et al., 2014). Most existing studies focus either on Chinese consumers (Xu and Zeng, 2014) or on pure market characteristics from the econometric point of view (Capitello et al., 2015). The aim of our study is to examine the different aspects of the distribution channels for imported wine in China and discuss the possible future evolution of these channels. French wines serve as a yardstick because they occupy the leading export position in the Chinese market.

The research question posed in this chapter is related to the transfer of certain lessons from the mature wine market in Germany to the emerging Chinese wine market. Do the first signs of the changes in China's wine distribution system confirm the evolution and maturation of the Chinese wine market?

We first analyze the recent developments of China's wine market and then we compare this emerging but highly competitive market with the typical mature and highly competitive German market. The results of the analyses of the interviews performed in the three countries are presented in the last part of this chapter. We attempt to assess the distribution channels' functioning in both countries, and to understand the attitudes of wine players — importers and distributors in both markets as well as French wine producers and wine merchants — toward wines and the wine trade in general.

SETTING THE STAGE

According to the recent International Organization of Vine and Wine (OIV) data (Aurand, 2015) about 40% of world wine production is consumed outside European countries, compared to 31% in 2000. The wine markets have become more international: In 2000, 27% of consumed wines crossed one border; in 2014 this proportion increased to 43%. The world wine production consumption difference is positive, revealing a surplus of more than 33 million hectolitres (Mhl) wine supply which has remained stable for several years. As a result, the European Union has reduced its wine production; however at the same time new players (e.g., New World but also China) are increasing in production volume. Nevertheless, EU wine producers — particularly France, Italy and Spain — must export. Because Asian countries such as China, Japan and Taiwan have increased their wine consumption in recent years, they now represent export markets of high potential (Lee, 2009; Bouzdine-Chameeva and Ninomiya 2011). Hence, it becomes crucial to understand the foreign wine distribution systems of these markets and try to foresee their evolution — particularly as the Chinese wine distribution system has emerged and undergone fundamental changes during the last decade.

In this context, OIV data (OIV, 2012, 2013) shows that the Chinese wine market is one of the most dynamic and steadily growing markets of the world.[1] Hence, one could assume that the Chinese market has little competition. However, this simplified picture is only partly true. On the

---

[1] In 15 years, from 2000 to 2014, the wine production experienced growth of more than 10%, from 10.5 Mhl to 11.6 Mhl. Wine consumption follows a similar positive trend, increasing from 10.7 Mhl to 14.55 Mhl. Wine imports (including bottled wine, bulk wine, and sparkling wine) increased sharply from 0.125 Mhl to 3.8 Mhl (OIV, 2015). However, OIV (2015) states that both consumption as well as production decreased in 2013 as well as in 2014.

one hand, domestic wine production is increasing in China, but on the other hand, wine imports from around the world are also increasingly pouring into China. Whereas in tier two and tier three cities more and more wine is consumed, the growth is more moderate in tier one cities such as Shanghai, Beijing or Guangzhou. In these cities wine consumption is far above Chinese average consumption. As a result the competition within these cities is high, which reveals the first signs of wine market maturity. Additionally, recent OIV publications indicate that in the past few years wine consumption in China decreased, leading to an increase in market competition. Furthermore, due to policy shifts in the recent past, luxury wines are facing pressure. More moderately priced wines are in demand. In this particular segment the competitors from other southern European countries (e.g., Spain, Italy) as well as from the New World enhance competition.

Nevertheless, a priori the distribution channel systems in an emerging wine market like China and a typical mature wine market such as Germany should be completely different. The abovementioned changes indicate that a comparison might reveal valuable insights. Thus, the observations of the developments from the German market might provide insights on the future development of the Chinese market. Lessons could be learned regarding the mass distribution channels, the usage of generic selling offers, and the resulting price competition.

THE CHINESE WINE DISTRIBUTION SYSTEM DEVELOPMENT

China's long wine history tracks back almost 5000 years; however, the new chapter only began about three decades ago. Dynasty Wine Ltd., the first joint venture of Rémy Martin set up in the 1980s, witnessed the beginning of the radical Chinese economic changes. It can be seen as a turning point in the era of the development of the wine sector in China. Today, China has 799,000 ha under vine, which is the world's second largest growing area. Of those hectares, around 120,000 ha are being used for "wine" grapes, producing around 11 Mio hl (OIV, 2015) from more than a 1000 wineries (Fig. 10.1). Nevertheless, the Chinese wine market remains strongly concentrated. The sale volume of ChangYu, Cofco and Dynasty wines makes up about 40% of the Chinese wine market. These companies have well-developed national sales networks covering both off-trade and on-trade channels. However, the local brands are facing challenges from foreign wine brands in terms of price/quality ratio.

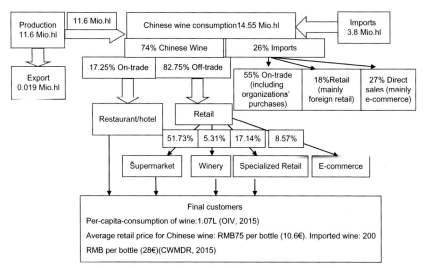

Figure 10.1 The distribution system of the Chinese wine market. *Adapted and updated from Bouzdine-Chameeva, T., Ninomiya, M., 2011. Bordeaux natural wines on the Japanese market: Analysis of supply chain system indolence. Supply Chain Forum Int. J. 12(2), 56–67. (Note: Mio.hl = million hectolitre)*

According to the companies' interim reports, Changyu's revenue declined in the first half of 2014 for the first time in five years, falling 2.51% year-on-year to 3.01 billion renminbi (US$470 million). Cofco's sales declined 2.1% year-on-year and the Sino-French joint venture Dynasty saw a 10.5% year-on-year slump in its income in 2013. The quality of Chinese wine has improved greatly in recent years, partly because of advice from French oenologists (Bouzdine-Chameeva et al., 2014).

At the same time, the evolution of the Chinese wine sector is heavily influenced by China's institutions and policies (Bouzdine-Chameeva et al., 2014). The volume gain of 583 million litres of wine consumption in the Chinese market from 1999 to 2004 was the result of government policies encouraging consumers to switch from drinking Baijiu to grape wine to preserve national stocks of rice for food.[2] This consumption policy resulted in growth of grape wine sales, while the anticorruption policy measures introduced by the government in 2013 have driven a decline of the top-end French wine sales. Thus, today's market for the medium range wines expands

---

[2] In the last decade the per capita consumption of wine in China had a strongly increasing tendency, though it still remains low (1.07 L in 2014) (OIV, 2015).

even more, which can be seen as a positive sign of the trend towards market maturity and global wine market evolution in China.

According to Tang (2006), more than 40% of Chinese wine consumption is due to organizations purchasing wines for business and relationship-building reasons. This channel of wine distribution is specific to the market in China. Companies and organizations serve wine to key stakeholders, important customers and government officials. French wines are bought in large quantities for cocktail parties or formal banquets for these dignitaries. The anticorruption drive has slowed the sales to organizations; therefore the orders for collective purchasing by companies and organizations have decreased since 2013.

The second major consumption category, accounting for nearly 22% of total wine consumption, is entertainment: an individual purchases wine for parties with friends or family celebrations (Bouzdine-Chameeva et al., 2014). Only 13% is for private consumption at home. There is an overwhelming preference for red (accounting for 85% of the whole consumption) in China. Customer preferences are also driven heavily by advertising, with top producers running extensive mass-marketing campaigns to build brand awareness. The brand-driven environment, with a lack of emphasis on taste preferences, has also affected the market for foreign wine. Regardless of brand or vintage, bordeaux and burgundy wines maintain strong reputations in the Chinese market. Developing a truly localized strategy for both packaging and marketing in response to specific consumer preferences is necessary in China today.

Foreign winemakers began making inroads into China once the import tariffs were dropped. Since China entered the World Trade Organization (TWO) in January 2005, the import duty on bottled wine has been reduced from 43% to 14% and on bulk wine from 43% to 20%. However, when the general total tax for bottled wine is calculated, it is still 48%. Facing some overproduction due to decreasing domestic consumption, some European producers hoped that increases in sales in China could more than offset losses at home. At the same time, the upwardly mobile Chinese population, eager to display their wealth and sophistication, has developed a taste for imported wine along with other foreign luxuries. Many small importers turned to the wine business after seeing the high increase of Chinese wine imports. Without a clear strategy and knowledge of the distribution channels, these small importers could easily quit the industry.

Currently, imported grape wine accounts for only 26% of volume sales in China (CWMDR, 2015), with domestic wine dominating. In 2014, France retained its grip on importers in China, representing nearly 34% by volume and 44% by value, followed by Chile, Spain, Australia and Italy (CIVB, 2015). Those countries — the Big Six — continue to account for more than 90% of bottled imports. The price of wines varies sharply; domestic wines are sold primarily at the lower end of the pricing spectrum, whereas imported wines are sold at the mid- to higher end. The average retail price at the lower end is RMB 20–30 (€2.50–€3.75) per bottle. Mid-range wines sell for RMB 30–80 (€3.75–€10) per bottle and are aimed at consumers with higher incomes and who are more exposed to wine. Premium wines sell for RMB 80 (€10) and upwards per bottle. Imported wines typically range from RMB 80–400 (€10–€50) per bottle and are in direct competition with high-end domestic wines. Numerous factors drive growth in imported wines: interest in Western culture, products and lifestyles; increasing incomes; the healthy image of wine compared to other alcoholic beverages in China; and the high quality perception of imported wines.

THE GERMAN MARKET

While many European wine markets are experiencing severe reductions in per capita wine consumption, the German wine market has had a stable consumption per capita of about 20 L still wine plus 4 L of sparkling wine for the past two decades. Since 2000, French imports to Germany have reduced by 6%; French wines lost their position to Spanish and Italian wines, which are more competitive in price.

Due to the population of Germany, the total wine market consisted of roughly 34 Mhl (including stocks) in 2014. About 30% of this amount is produced in Germany and about 70% is imported. The vast majority of imports is bulk wine. Compared to the market data revealed in Fig. 10.2, it is obvious that imports are gaining in market importance. As Fig. 10.2 reveals, in 2010 the three main distribution channels were discount retail chains (40% market share), supermarkets and direct-sales from the producers (Hanf et al., 2012). This situation has remained unchanged for the last five years.

However, market data from 2014 shows that discount chains have increased their market share to 49%, whereas supermarkets have lost market share, ending up with 26%. Direct-sales have also lost market share, at

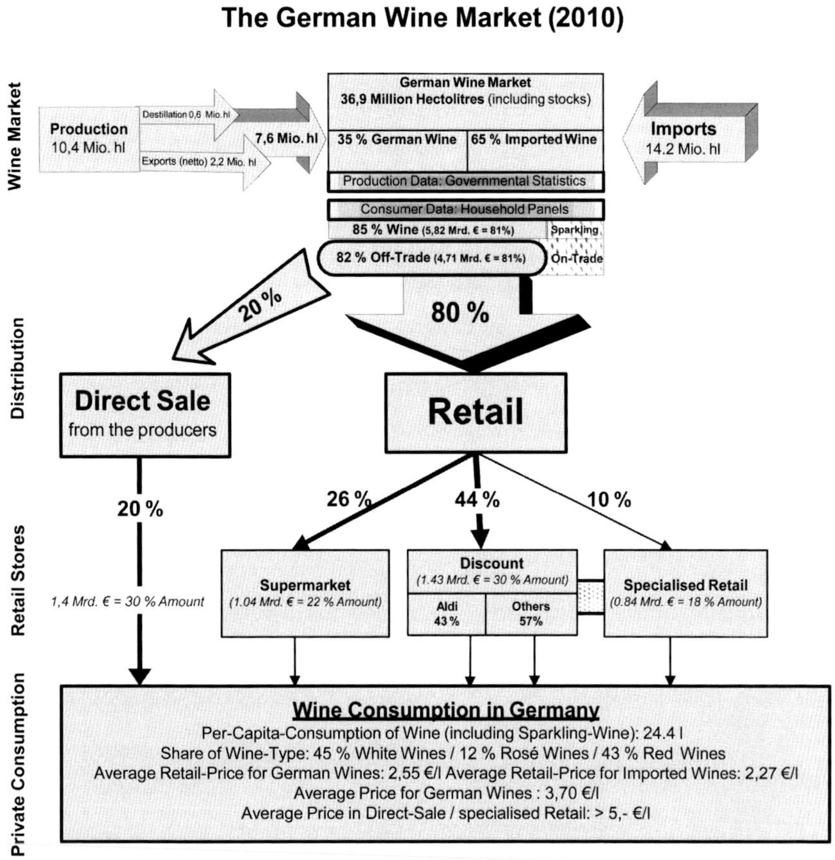

The German Wine Market (2010)

Figure 10.2 The German wine market. *Hanf, J.H., Belaya, V., Schweickert, E., 2012. Power play in the German wine business: are German wine co-operatives able to use their power to manage their business relationships? J. Econ. Behav. Stud. 4(4), 227–238*

about 13% today. Controversially, discount chains not only increased market share in terms of volume but also in value — the opposite of supermarkets. Again, the same picture can be revealed for direct-sales as they have lost both in value and volume. The main competitors for direct-sales are not the discount chains but specialized retailers, which have won market share both in value and volume terms (DWI, 2015).

The German wine market exemplifies developments in very competitive environments. Consumers are used to buying wine at food retailers, and they demand good, drinkable wine with a very good price quality relation (Hanf and Schweickert, 2007). As low-involved consumers, they search for easily accessible quality/differential indicators (Schweickert, 2007). Because taste and aroma are sealed in the bottle, they look for varieties or country-of-origin as fast indicators. Producers make wines with similar taste without off-flavours to satisfy their customers. Only recently has branding become more sophisticated in the German still wine market – quite the opposite of the sparkling wine market. A couple of years ago, Rotkäppchen, Germany's largest sparkling wine producer, entered the still wine market. Today it is Germany's largest branded wine producer. Current wine sales comprise about 50% red wine, roughly 38% white wine, and 12% rosé. More white wine is produced than red in Germany, indicating that more red wine is imported (DWI, 2015).

Without clear differentiation, consumers see wine as a homogeneous product. As a result, prices are comparatively low. For instance, the average price in German retailers has been around €2.50 per litre (Hanf et al., 2012). The increase of market share (volume and value) of discount chains indicates that German consumers are very satisfied with the clear structure but small assortment they offer. The increase of market share of specialized retailers, mainly on the costs of direct-sales, mirrors the growing reluctance of consumers to buy larger quantities directly and storing them at home. Thus, the ubiquity of supply is becoming increasingly important.

THE VIEWS OF GERMAN AND CHINESE WINE PLAYERS ON WINE DISTRIBUTION CHANNELS

To capture the differences in the attitudes about imported French wines in China and Germany, we conducted an extensive study in the three countries concerned. Semistructured interviews were conducted by one of the authors with different wine actors and specialists in France, China and Germany in 2013 and 2014 (see Table 10.1 for information on the

Table 10.1 The design of the 49 interviews

	France	China	Germany
Producers	10	4	2
Wine merchants/exporters	3	0	0
Importers/distributors	0	24	5
Wine brokers	2	0	0
Total	15	28	7

Figure 10.3 The cloud of the top concepts used by French, German and Chinese wine actors.

composition of the interviewers' set). The focus of the interviews was the use and performance of wine distribution channels in the three countries.

Each of the 49 interviews lasted an average of 70 minutes. The transcripts of these interviews, more than 1000 pages, contained 220,740 words. This exhaustive text corpus permitted us to perform contextual and content analysis using the qualitative data analysis software Alceste[3].

The cloud of the top 200 words used by all the participants is presented in Fig. 10.3. The two most cited words are 'wine' and 'wines'. The different use of these words illustrates the existence of the two obviously distinct ways to refer to wine. If the word 'wine' is used to designate a product with unique characteristics, the term 'wines' is used as a generic term of a trade product, putting more weight on economic aspects emphasized by the interviewed wine players who preferred this term to the term 'wine'. This is the case of Chinese wine actors. A more frequent use of the words 'market', 'channel', 'customers', 'price' and 'sell' by Chinese participants also suggests that they focus much more on commercial and trade features of the market rather than speaking of

---

[3] http://www.image-zafar.com/english/index_alceste.htm.

'wine' as a craft-made, specific product. Conversely, the German and French participants prefer the term 'wine' to 'wines'.

In all of the interviews, French producers and exporters bring up the word 'China' and refer to it more often than 'German market'. The concept of 'wine' for them is associated more recurrently with the words 'Chinese' and 'Chateau' and only afterward do economic topics such as 'market', 'business' or 'product' emerge.

In most of the interviews the Chinese importers placed more importance on the economic and commercial terms such as 'sell', 'customers', 'RMB' and 'price' rather than on the specificities of 'wine' itself (such as taste, vintage, brand, region, etc.). Meanwhile, German participants more frequently discuss 'wine', focusing more on its specific characteristics and referring to wine more as a unique product. This difference is clearly observed in Fig. 10.4.

Almost all of those interviewed in China emphasized the important role of organizational purchases in China. According to our interview

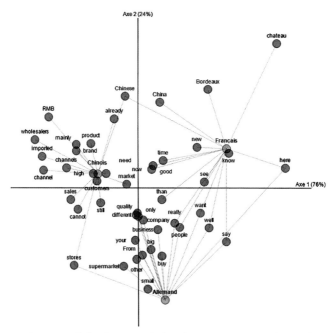

Figure 10.4 The use of the key words by the interviewees of the three different wine markets.
(Note that for each country on this graph the words are displayed via the meaning of Chi^2 at the 5% threshold).

data (Zhang, 2016), 70–80% of total sales of imported wines are through specific channels such as governmental organizations and corporations. This direct distribution channel of organization purchases remains uniquely and strongly specific to the Chinese system.

To deepen our analysis we introduced six major marketing categories (product, customers, price, channel, quality and brand) to analyze how these areas are represented in the German and Chinese interviews. In Table 10.2 we describe the words of each category used by wine specialists of the different countries.

When we cluster the words from the 'marketing' point of view, the factor which influences that channel choice is 'customers', followed by the concept of 'product'. The German respondents then referred more to the concepts 'price' and 'product', whereas the Chinese participants more frequently used the concepts 'customers', 'channels' and 'brands' (Table 10.3).

We implemented the Alceste method to perform a descending hierarchical classification proceeding by successive iterations from a factor analysis multiple correspondence. The data table included the column lemmas and/or text concepts described by the lines of the table. The first iteration led to a partition according to the first factorial. The iterations continued by partition of the class are more effective, as they exceeded a percentage of the total population that was set as the stop criterion (40% in this case). The results of this analysis are presented in Fig. 10.5 and confirm the differences among the six marketing categories.

To get a better understanding of the wine distribution channel practices and preferences, we created six categories: off-trade, direct trade and wholesalers and on-trade, government and e-commerce. The obtained results showed that the most discussed channel in both Germany and China is the 'off-trade' channel, followed by 'direct-sales'. In contrast, the e-commerce channel is addressed much less frequently (Fig. 10.6), which might be explained partly by the absence of the famous wine players using this channel among our interviewees.

The German participants evoked more 'on-trade', 'direct-sales' and 'e-commerce'. The Chinese wine players more frequently discussed the issues related to 'government', 'off-trade' and 'wholesaler'.

Government influence is a special issue for the Chinese market, particularly in reference to the anticorruption policies introduced in 2013. As we mentioned earlier, these policies have had a drastic impact on high-end wine consumption, especially for grand cru French wines.

Table 10.2 The contents of each of the six marketing categories per country

Countries	PRODUCT Germany, France	CUSTOMERS China	PRICE France, Germany	CHANNEL China	QUALITY French	BRAND China
R.:Key words	Product	Customer	Price	Channel	Quality	Brand
	Only	Buy	Sell	Channels	Good	Market
	From	Need	Rmb	Supermarket	High	Only
	Like	Chinese	High	Sales	Imported	Chinese
	One	People	Euros	Different	Local	Big
	About	Know	Same	Line	Still	Other
	Different	China	Bottle	Other	Really	Want
	Some	Who	What	Wholesalers	Bordeaux	Many
	Other	New	Germany	Stores	What	Stores
	Your	Company	Just	These	Time	Bordeaux
	New	Drink	Little	Restaurants	Say	Company
	Line	End		Large		Choose
	Same	Choose		Mainly		Another
	Small	Taste		Important		
	See	Business		Most		

(Each concept is presented by country; the words over-represented within the meaning of Chi^2 a: the 5% threshold)

Table 10.3 Marketing concept by country

	Germany (%)	China (%)
Product	41.0	26.3
Customers	23.9	36.6
Price	30.0	26.6
Channel	15.4	34.8
Quality	13.1	12.9
Brand	8.7	18.9
Total	100.0	100.0

(Note that $p = 0.00$; khi = 236.49; ddl = 10(TS). The relation is very significant.)

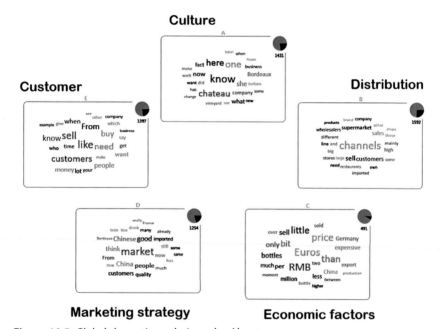

Figure 10.5 Global thematic analysis under Alceste.

According to the French wine and spirits export body (FEVS), total French wine exports to China in 2014 dropped by 3.3% in volume, which is equivalent to 1.7 billion bottles, while value exports sank by 1.7% versus 2013, to €7.44 billion.

Nevertheless, China has risen to the fifth biggest export destination for French wine and spirits, though the purchasing propensity — situated earlier in the high-end range — suddenly melted away in the first six months of 2014, falling by 9% in volume and by nearly a third in value.

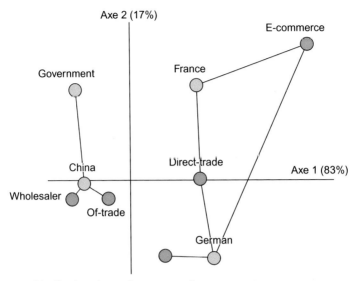

Figure 10.6 Distribution channel representation per country.
(Note: for each country distribution channels are over-represented within the meaning of Chi^2 at the 5% threshold.)

Anticorruption and frugality drives in China were the main causes. Despite the decline, France is still leading the pack for wine sales in China. It remains ahead of Chile, Spain and Australia, maintaining the same proportion of sales as last year (36% by volume), although the total volume of wine imported into China dropped for the first time in 2014. French wine exports to China, excluding Hong Kong, fell by 7% to 423 million euros, and shipments crept up by 0.1% in volume to 154 million bottles (CWMDR, 2015).

All of these fluctuations influence the interactions within the whole distribution system, and the importance of certain channels, on-trade channels in particular, might endure serious changes.

CONCLUSIONS: LESSONS LEARNED

First, there is not one Chinese wine market. Whereas more and more wine is consumed in tier two and tier three cities, in tier one cities (such as Shanghai, Beijing and Guangzhou) growth is more moderate, even stagnating. As a result competition within these cities is very high. Furthermore, due to policy shifts in the recent past, luxury wines are facing some pressure. Hence, more moderately priced wines might be in demand. The governmental procurement system shows certain signs of collapse because there is a decrease in sales volume while new sales channels (often online shops) are increasing in volume.

The average frequent wine consumer is getting younger and becoming more educated about wine, and therefore demanding a better quality/price relation. Furthermore, the traditionally more educated consumers have a growing affinity for French wines and are seeking the best value at lower price points. In this particular price segment the competition is growing and the desire for wines from southern European countries (e.g., Spain, Italy) as well as from the New World (e.g., Chile) is enhanced. They are the same competitors for French wine on the German market as well. Therefore, the comparison between these two markets becomes quite interesting because it provides noteworthy parallels and give insights for the future development of the Chinese market.

Our findings show a marked difference between the channel choices for the German and Chinese wine markets. Mature markets have focused primarily on off-trade channels (e.g., Bouzdine-Chameeva et al., 2014), whereas emerging, developing markets are more likely to choose on-trade channels (such as restaurants, hotels, etc.). It is only with the process of consumer education that the off-trade channels will begin to prevail. However, it also becomes clear that the evolution of channels in emerging markets generates certain bottlenecks. Autoregulation promotes transparency within the industry, and therefore the development of other channels comes into view, in particular those off-trade channels which are favoured in mature markets.

In the past two decades, the German wine market has witnessed high competition that has driven prices down and increased the quality of basic wines. As a result of the price competition, today's profits are rather low, and brand building appears to be an alternative for attracting consumers. Thus, the German market exhibits quite interesting lessons for the Chinese market regarding mass distribution channels, the use of various selling offers, price competition and the quest for eliminating poor quality wines. This might be good news for Chinese wine consumers because they can expect rather good quality for moderate prices.

The attitudes towards wine as a product are also different in China and Germany. Chinese wine actors began with a general attitude of 'wines' as a modern luxury product to sell, a trade product without any particular interest in its specificity. This attitude combined with governmental policies and changing laws and regulations explains the fluctuations of the wine market during the last three years. Nevertheless, the market continues to expand as the Chinese have gained experience with wine. Only a few years ago, they were either looking for big French châteaux to show off their status, or seeking basic functional benefits in domestic wines. Foreign trips, along with technology development and social media channels, have helped Chinese consumers become more proficient in their wine purchases.

French producers selling their wine in China today have to ask themselves whether providing France (or a French wine growing region) and good quality as key arguments for selling their wine will suffice in future. As the German market shows, brand building might be a way to avoid price competition to some degree. The education of Chinese consumers is underway, and the quest for high quality, the reference to wine as a unique product revealed at the mature German market, shows the possible trends of the evolution of the wine market in China.

REFERENCES

Aurand, J.M., 2015. The major challenges of the vitivinicultural sector: role and strategy of the OIV. Review at Clave Congress. Available at: http://www.clavecongres.com/.

Beaujanot, A., Lockshin, L., Quester, P., 2004. Distributors' business characteristics, buyer/seller relationship and market orientation: an empirical study of the Australian wine export industry. J. Market. Channels 12 (1), 79–97.

Beverland, M., 2009. Boundary conditions to business relationships in China: the case of selling wine in China. J. Bus. Ind. Market 24 (1), 27–34.

Bouzdine-Chameeva, T., Ninomiya, M., 2011. Bordeaux natural wines on the Japanese market: Analysis of supply chain system indolence. Supply Chain Forum Int. J. 12 (2), 56–67.

Bouzdine-Chameeva, T., Zhang, W., Pesme, J.-O., 2014. The evolution of wine emerging markets: the case of China. Asian J. Manag. Res. 4 (6), 277–292.

Capitello, R., Agnoli, L., Begalli, D., 2015. Chinese import demand for wine: evidence from econometric estimations. J. Wine Res. 26 (2), 115–135.

CIVB, 2015. Service Economie et Etudes Marche des Vin, Chine mdv.

CWMDR, 2015. Chinese Wine Market Development Report, pp. 78–81.

DWI, 2015. Deutscher Wein – Statistik 2015/2016. Deutsches Weininstitut GmbH, Mainz, Germany EU – 28 Wine annual report and statistics (2014). Available at: <http://gain.fas.usda.gov/Recent%20GAIN%20Publications/Wine%20Annual_Rome_EU-28_2-26-2014.pdf>.

Hanf, J.H., Schweickert, E., 2007. How to deal with member heterogeneity – management implications. Int. J. Cooper. Manag. 3, 40–48.

Hanf, J.H., Belaya, V., Schweickert, E., 2012. Power play in the German wine business: are German wine co-operatives able to use their power to manage their business relationships?. J. Econ. Behav. Stud. 4 (4), 227–238.

Lee, K., 2009. Is a glass of merlot the symbol of globalization? An examination of the impacts of globalization on wine consumption of Asia. Int. J. Wine Bus. Res. 23 (3), 258–266.

Muhammad, A., Leister, A.M., McPhail, L., Chen, W., 2014. The evolution of foreign wine demand in China. Aust. J. Agric. Resour. Econ. 58 (3), 392−408.

OIV, 2012. World Viticulture Situation. Presentation at the OIV World Congress, Izmir, Turkey.

OIV, 2013. World Viticulture Situation. Presentation at the OIV World Congress, Bucharest, Romania.

OIV, 2015. World Viticulture Situation. Presentation at the OIV World Congress, Mainz, Germany.

Orth, U., Lockshin, L., D'Hauteville, F., 2007. The global wine business as a research field. Int. J. Wine Bus. Res. 19 (1), 5−13.

Schweickert, E., 2007. Unternehmensstrategien in der Weinwirtschaft im Rahmen der EU-Weinmarktordnungspolitik. Dissertation, DLG-Verlag, Frankfurt, Germany.

Tang W.L., 2006. Make sure you understand consumer. J. of Chinese Famous Brands. March, 37−44.

Thach, E., Olsen, J., 2006. Building strategic partnerships in wine marketing: implications for wine distribution. J. Food Prod. Market. 12 (3), 71−86.

Xu, P., Zeng, Y.C., 2014. Factors that affect willingness to pay for red wines in China. J. Int. Consum. Market. 26 (5), 426−439.

Zhang W., 2016. Wine distribution channels evolution: the analysis and modeling of new developing wine market compared to mature wine market (from China to Germany). PhD thesis KEDGE Business School, France (under submission).

CHAPTER 11

Relationship Quality Between Portuguese Wine Producers and Chinese Distributors Insight and Recommendations

S.M.C. Loureiro[1] and N. Cunha[2]

[1]Instituto Universitário de Lisboa (ISCTE-IUL), Business Research Unit (BRU/UNIDE) and SOCIUS, Lisbon, Portugal
[2]University of Aveiro, Aveiro, Portugal

INTRODUCTION

The wine industry started in Europe, which transacted one of the world's oldest commodities. In the past 20 years, the European wine market has been confronted with major changes at economic and regulatory levels. The emergence of new producing countries has significantly increased the amount of competition, reinforcing the global dimension of the wine market (Cafaggi and Lamiceli, 2011).

In Portugal, several brands from regions such as Douro, Vinho Verde or Alentejo are internationally known. At the top of the list is Port wine from the Douro valley. The Douro valley was the first officially demarcated wine appellation in the world (in the 18th Century) created under the leadership of the Marquis of Pombal (Loureiro and Kaufmann, 2012) to assure the authenticity of its wines. Although many port-style wines are made around the world (Australia, South Africa and United States), the strict usage of the terms "Port" or "Porto" is reserved only for the wines produced in Portugal.

With regards to the Chinese wine market, this represents a relatively small market to Portuguese producers but with a huge potential, whose operation does not yet match the standards of a mature market, nor is it informed about prices, varieties and qualities. Yet, producers from around the world try to sell their products in this country which increases the popularity of wine (Agency for Investment and Foreign Trade of Portugal [AICEP], 2011).

The import of wine represents a significant market quota, yet the majority of the consumption is of local wine. Although China is one of the youngest wine producers, it is already in the 10 top producing countries (International Organisation of Vine and Wine [OIV], 2015).

Thus, Portuguese producers are confronted with three kinds of problems: First, the aggressive competition with local producers and with other exporting countries with a strong reputation. Second, how to define the best approach to start and develop a solid exchange relationship with a partner that is physically distant and that shares different cultural references. Third, which kind of behaviour is recommended to ensure the sustainability of this relationship?

The wine sector has unique characteristics regarding cultural issues which will be developed further in this chapter. Communicating a wine brand is an exercise that requires more than a perfect control of the visible aspects of the product or service operations. Other aspects should not be disregarded, such as: the location where the grapes were produced; the expertise of winemakers and their methods; the history of the company owner and the culture of the brand. In a market with thousands of brands, this requires the wine producer to be truly passionate about the sector, but at the same time, this will help to develop a perfect relationship with the main players of the distribution channel.

In the wine sector, the distributor is an important player who greatly influences the retailing of bottled wine to the consumer. Moreover, producers and distributors may work together by focusing on their customers and improving the relationship they have with them (Crosby et al., 1990).

OBJECTIVES

A proactive effort to achieve a strong business-to-business relationship is essential in order to develop loyalty and competitiveness (Athanasopoulou, 2009; Bobot, 2011; Crosby et al., 1990). Loyalty itself is an important relationship concept, as long as it is analysed as a long-term, committed and affect-laden partnership (Fournier, 1998). But what differentiates a single transaction from a relationship exchange is time; that is, a business relationship happens when there are repeated exchanges among all known participants committed to developing interactions according to their context (Fournier, 1998). The willingness and the ability to create effective long-term relationships with positive outcomes for both partners may be regarded as relationship quality (RQ) (e.g., Athanasopoulou, 2009; Bobot, 2011; Fournier, 1998).

A relationship implies interdependence and exchange between the partners. The partners' actions have an active influence on the creation and maintenance of dynamic and dyadic relationship (Bobot, 2011; Crosby et al., 1990; Dwyer et al., 1987; Fournier, 1998).

The quality of the relationship also demands the partners' ability to manage conflict situations (Bobot, 2011). However, what are the core constructs of RQ that can positively or negatively differentiate the business-to-business (producers and distributors) relationship? How does the country of origin of the wine producer influence the RQ with a Chinese distributor? What is the Portuguese producer's perspective in relation to the Chinese market and how do they deal with Chinese distributors?

Consequently, this study aims to: (1) present the core constructs of RQ that may differentiate positively or negatively the business-to-business relationships; (2) give an overview of major wine producing countries (old world and new world) from the perspective of the Chinese market; (3) highlight the characteristics of the Chinese wine market as an opportunity for Portuguese wine producers; and (4) to give insight and recommendations to develop a sustainable exchange relationship with a Chinese distributor.

BACKGROUND LITERATURE ON RELATIONSHIP QUALITY

A systematic literature review is employed to identify the core constructs of RQ that had been studied and analysed in past research. We used the Web of Knowledge database to search for articles from peer reviewed journals published between 1967 and 2014 (most journals do not have article accessed from online platforms before 1967) in top international journals of several fields, which are included in the "UQ Business School Adjusted ERA Rankings List" and incorporated in the Journal Quality List (Harzing, 2013). The range of initial filters employed[1] is followed by title reading, abstract reading and finally full paper reading. When we narrowed the focus of the study to the wine sector, we did not find relevant studies (meaning publishing in top journals) pertaining to this dyadic relationship.

When analyzing these set of articles, it is possible to consider two clearly distinct stages in the period under analysis (see Table 11.1).

---

[1] The collected articles were subjected to a careful selection using filter parameters such as: Source type – article; Language – English; Research Area – Business economics; Operations research management science; Social sciences and other topics; Psychology; Communication; International relations; Sociology.

Table 11.1 RQ articles published by year

Journal	Total	%	1984	1987	1990	1995	1996	1997	1998	1999	2000	2001	2003	2004	2005	2006	2007	2008	2009	2010	2011	2012	2013	2014
Industrial Marketing Management	12	14.29						1			1		1			2		1		2	2	1	1	
Journal of Business Research	10	11.90								1					1		2		1	2		2	1	
Journal of Business & Industrial Marketing	9	10.71			2													1	1	1	1		2	1
European Journal of Marketing	8	9.52														1	1		2	2		1	1	
Journal of Marketing	7	8.33	1				1				1	1		1		1		1						
Total quality Management & Business Excellence	6	7.14															2	1				2	1	
Journal of Marketing Research	4	4.76		1		1												1	1					
Journal of Business-to-Business Marketing	4	4.76													1	1						1		1
International Business Review	3	3.57																			1		2	
Subtotal	63	74.98	1	1	2	1	1	1		1	2	1	1	1	2	5	5	5	5	7	4	7	8	2
Other Journals	21	25.02						1	3	1	1				3			2	1	3	4	1	1	
Total	84	100	1	1	2	1	1	2	3	2	3	1	1	1	5	5	5	7	6	10	8	8	9	2

Source: authors' elaboration based on their systematic literature review.

Overall, and despite the initial interest in the 1990s [published in journals such as the *Journal of Marketing Research* (1987/1995), *Journal of Marketing* (1984/1990), *Journal of Business Research* (1996/1999) or *Industrial Marketing Management* (1997)], only from 2005 onwards did the number of articles published on the topic significantly increase. In fact, the study of the RQ in the relationship between producer and distributor has had a greater development since 2007, having 60% of the total references. Despite the decrease in the number of articles in 2014, if we take into account the general trend of research on RQ, then we can foresee that in the near future we will continue to witness a growth trend of research on this topic.

Overall, we highlight three constructs as the most frequently employed and analyzed by researchers into a producer−distributor channel context: trust, commitment and satisfaction. Trust occurs when both parties have expectations and mutual confidence in order to develop exchanges (e.g., Bobot, 2011; Crosby et al., 1990; Dwyer et al., 1987). Commitment is established when mutual motivation and efforts exist, therefore ensuring and maintaining an ongoing relationship, which is defined as very important for all parties (Bobot, 2011). Satisfaction is related to a positive affective evaluation, which results from the overall appraisal of the meaning and development of the relationship with other partners (Anderson and Narus, 1984; Crosby et al., 1990; Dwyer et al., 1987).

In second position, but still frequently analyzed by researchers, we may point out three other constructs: cooperation, communication and conflict. Cooperation happens when the behaviour of the partners is centered on searching together for solutions that satisfy the concerns and goals of both, which characterizes a win−win relationship with mutual transactional benefits (e.g., Anderson and Narus, 1990; Bobot, 2011; Claro and Claro, 2010; Lacoste, 2012). Communication refers to information that circulates between the partners in a downstream or upstream direction. In the first case, the information is related to consumers' demands, because is important for the producer to satisfy the current and future expectations of the customer (Claro and Claro, 2010; Fournier and Mick, 1999). A continuous communication between both parties helps prevent, support and solve problems and align the perceptions and expectations of both of them (Fyneset al., 2004). Conflict means the style of behaviour developed by the partners when a situation occurs making it more difficult to achieve their individual interests or the solution to their concerns (Anderson and Narus, 1984; Bobot, 2011).

METHODOLOGY

We collected data from both secondary and primary sources. The secondary sources are based on data taken from official statistical reports of the OIV, the Portuguese Institute of Vine and Wine (Institute of Vine and Wine, 2011), ViniPortugal (an interprofessional association of the Portuguese wine industry and the entity that manages the brand "Wines of Portugal"), and the Agency for Investment and Foreign Trade of Portugal (AICEP), which deals with the internationalization of Portuguese wine, as well as the wine partnership between Portugal and China.

The primary sources are the interviews, which were conducted with wine producers to obtain the main factors that may positively or negatively differentiate the RQ with Chinese distributors. The interviews began by explaining the purpose of the research and requesting that the interview be recorded, followed by the intended questions, according to Gubrium and Holstein (2001) and McCracken (1988). The average time for each interview was 50 minutes.

In order to carry out the first approach to the potential participants, we visited the main national wine fair, which ensured the presence of the major Portuguese wine producers. We went on to explain the main intention of the research and scheduled the interview with representatives of the major corporate brand producers, which characterizes the majority of the Portuguese producers and wine regions (31% Douro; 14% Alentejo, Dão, Bairrada and Vinho Verde; 14% other regions).

Thus, the sample is composed of 10 representatives of those major corporate wine brands, who deal with Chinese market (see Table 11.2). Their profiles are characterized by someone qualified to represent the company, who has a direct exchange relationship with a Chinese wine partner. As a result, our sample includes professionals having vast experience in the wine sector (30% had 5−9 years; 50% had 10−15 years; 20% had more than 15 years), that participate in the business with Chinese partners. 60% are Exporter Managers; 20% Marketing Managers; and 20% are Company CEOs. We also contacted the President of ViniPortugal, who has vast knowledge of the Chinese wine market.

The data analysis followed McCracken's process (McCracken, 1988), which moves from an analysis of the particular utterances as individual units up through higher and higher levels of generality. WEBQDA software (University of Aveiro and Esfera Crítica, 2015) allowed the selection

Table 11.2 Sample profile

Respondent	Position	Wine sector experience (years)	Wine region of the Producers
1	Export Manager	11	Douro
2	Export Manager	8	Douro/Dão/Bairrada/ Estremadura Vinho Verde/ Alentejo
3	Export Manager	7	Douro/Dão/Bairrada/ Alentejo/Vinho Verde
4	Export Manager/ Area Manager	10	Alenetejo/Douro/Tejo/ Beiras/Vinho Verde
5	Export Manager/ Area Manager	14	Douro/alentejo/Dão/ Bairrada/Vinho Verde Pennisula de Setubal/Beiras
6	Export Manager/ Area Manager	5	Douro
7	Marketing Manager	12	Douro
8	Marketing Manager	12	Douro
9	Company CEO	18	Bairrada/Dão
10	Company CEO	22	Douro

Source: authors' elaboration.

of the coding procedure and modification of the coding schemes as the analysis progressed and new factors or facets were uncovered.

RESULTS

The Chinese Wine Market and Consumption

In this subsection, we identify and present opportunities to be explored and barriers to be avoided by the Portuguese wine producers in the Chinese market. We also point out the main components of the marketing mix, as well as cultural issues.

The Chinese Market as an Opportunity for Portuguese Producers

A study carried out by the British Consultancy Wine Intelligence featured the Chinese market as a huge market at an early stage of development (Cardoso, 2012). Wine producers are faced with a good opportunity to export to this country, due to the size of the Chinese market, the rapid dynamic of its economy and the potential for the per capita growth in the consumption of wine (Santos, 2014). In 2012 the per capita consumption of wine in China was 0.69 litres, while in other main importing countries this amount is much higher, for example in the UK, it was 19.9 litres, and in the United States it was 9.2 litres. In the same period in Portugal, the consumption of wine per capita was 42.5 litres (Falcão, 2014).

On the other hand, China is already a highly competitive market, and so only Portuguese companies with consistent export experience and having the resources to make long-term investments will succeed (Agency for Investment and Foreign Trade of Portugal [AICEP], 2012). To successfully establish a business with China it is essential that Portuguese producers focus on building trust (ViniPortugal, 2015).

The Chinese Consumer Behaviour

The President of ViniPortugal reported, '*The behaviour of the Chinese market has shown itself to be somewhat unpredictable, maybe because there is in fact no wine culture, only a taste for "what is fashionable" and especially for French brands.*' (Monteiro, 2015, personal communication). He goes on to say that it is difficult to determine in which moments wine is consumed, '*it is a common question: "where are the wine consumers?"*'. He considers that the *ganbai* or *ganbei* is a simple act of drinking without taking into consideration tasting and savouring the aromas, the flavors and the harmonization (Monteiro, 2015, personal communication).

The best-known grape varieties such as Cabernet Sauvignon (for red) or Chardonnay (for white) have attracted more attention, although customers do not properly differentiate the flavors. The reason for this preference lies in the styles of bottle and other marketing communication activities, because the Chinese tend to perceive red wine as a healthy beverage and basically consume it outside the home (restaurants, bars, hotels, etc.) (AICEP, 2012). The consumer type is mostly young urban males (Institute of Vine and Wine, 2011).

Red wine is also associated with the core symbolic aspect of Chinese culture; success, fortune and luck. This product is much appreciated at weddings because it is seen as something that brings happiness and romance. White wine often has negative connotations for most of the population (white can symbolize sadness or even grief). But the main problem lies in the white wine called "Baijiu", which creates confusion with the very strong rice brandy, unpleasant to much of the population.

In terms of packaging and labels, it is relevant that the most auspicious colours are red and gold. The numbers are also very important, since the Chinese give gifts in even numbers and never in odd numbers because it represents bad luck. So, they usually buy two bottles at a time in a very appealing package (AICEP, 2012; Institute of Vine and Wine, 2011).

In China, wine is a means of showing respect towards the business partner. It is also associated with the image of the perfect lives of wealthy families. On TV, if the hero wants to seduce the heroine, the scene is often a restaurant where he has a glass of red wine waiting. That's why wine is associated with elegance, fashion, romance and passion (Institute of Vine and Wine, 2011).

The Chinese New Year is a very important season for the Chinese population and they really enjoy drinking and offering wine on this occasion. There is a strong tradition of exchanging gifts (equivalent to Christmas) where the wine offered is a sign of sophistication (and packaging matters). Imported wine has a huge social importance and status in these social occasions (Institute of Vine and Wine, 2011).

A Wine Product for the Chinese Market

The Chinese wine market is growing, mainly because of the producers adapting their product portfolios to the market changes in a context of an economic downturn and when there is an antiextravagance campaign. More mid-end products have been promoted and achieved good results in part due to a significant decline in premium wine. On the other hand, some companies have chosen to broaden their product line into more segments, including wedding and healthcare products, in order to catch the attention of the consumers (Euromonitor, 2015).

Globally, with regards to the bottled wine market, the Chinese prefer red wine due to its colour. Red is a welcome colour among the Chinese. White wine sales are around 20% and its core group of customers are expatriates. Rosé wine presents marginal sales, around 5% of the total. Other types of wine, such as sparkling, have reduced sales because knowledge among the Chinese population is limited, which translates into low consumption. The expatriated population maintains a certain consumption, but the enormous competition and meagre sales show the current consumption shortage in these short and medium term markets. Some Portuguese producers and distributors incorporate these products in small quantities in their portfolio in order to expand it and develop the market

(Institute of Vine and Wine, 2011). Thus, red wines not only dominate the market, but are also growing more significantly (Institute of Vine and Wine, 2011). The British Consultancy Wine Intelligence estimates that, in the near future, consumer trends in China will be leaning towards white or sweeter red wines (Cardoso, 2012).

Wine Prices in the China Market

The British Consultancy Wine Intelligence estimates that one-fifth of consumers account for 40% of sales. However, these consumers are only concerned about buying expensive wines for business and gifts, not for personal consumption. People buying wine to drink for pleasure account for half of total consumption, but only 30% of sales (Cardoso, 2012).

Chinese consumers tend to buy expensive bottles of wine with the purpose of drinking them during special occasions and not on a daily basis. Even so, Chinese consumers are changing and are starting to look for less expensive wines, as mentioned by the President of ViniPortugal (Santos, 2014).

Distribution Channel

Bottled wine is mainly sold in the east of China, where we may find more dynamic cities with higher wages and higher growth, and where we can find the home of more expatriates with a greater acceptance and knowledge of imported products. The south, with Guangzhou and Shenzhen at the top, is the second center of consumption (AICEP, 2012).

Usually in China, neither hotels and restaurants, nor retailers' channels negotiate directly with the producer. So, the first step for the Portuguese producers to consider when entering the Chinese market is to find a distributor for the hotels and restaurants and then for the supermarkets and specialty stores.

However, we can find only a few prestigious distributors and so they are being excessively contacted by wineries interested in the Chinese market, which means that their bargaining power is considerable. Furthermore, strategies have been clearly defined. They know quite well which wines are absent from their market, with regards to country of origin, type and price range (AICEP, 2012).

Currently, some Portuguese producers are opening representative offices in China, including creating distribution companies of wines from Portugal. Others prefer to do this with a local partner, i.e. Chinese distributing companies (AICEP, 2012; Cardoso, 2012).

Communication Strategy

Portuguese producers, who want to work in the Chinese market, should be well prepared with regards to the market, have a good communication strategy and the intention of building and maintaining a long-term relationship. The main factor to be preselected by Chinese distributors is international communication, in other words, being mentioned in prestigious international wine publications. A continued good score from Robert Parker is especially valued in China (AICEP, 2012).

The Chinese consumer has great difficulty in reading and verbalizing the brand names, due to linguistic difficulties with Western names. For them, the brands are mainly countries of origin, their cost and, to a lesser extent, some more well-known regions or grape varieties. These aspects are critical to any country and so Portuguese producers should use colour and iconic images of the country of origin of the wines (Institute of Vine and Wine, 2011).

Portuguese producers should participate in major events such as Vinexpo Asia-Pacific and China Wine & Spirits Awards, where Portuguese wines have been widely awarded, winning a significant number of medals (AICEP, 2012). To maximize results, Portuguese wine should also be present at the Hong Kong Wine & Spirits Fair, where many Portuguese producers make contact with potential Chinese buyers (AICEP, 2012; ViniPortugal, 2015).

Under the umbrella "Wines of Portugal", ViniPortugal has organized promotional campaigns in the major Chinese cities such as Beijing, Shanghai, Guangzhou, Qingdao and Dalian Xian. These campaigns are devoted to wine events designated as City and Grand Tastings.

The City Tastings include wine harmonization lunches with local cuisine and are presented by a well-known Chinese personality, like Jennifer Chen. These City Tastings are carried out in order to increase awareness of opinion leaders to Portuguese wines (AICEP, 2012). The Grand Tastings are annual events, which aim to increase awareness of the wines of Portugal and to promote the business potential for Portuguese economic agents, in particular producers (AICEP, 2012). With regards to local support, ViniPortugal has collaborated with a Chinese association of importers, the China Association for Importers & Exporters of Wine & Spirits, as well as with the Portuguese Embassy (Caeiro, 2015).

Seminars and training sessions can be considered as additional complementary events. They are attended by winemakers or other distinguished experts (ViniPortugal, 2015). For example, several workshops are being organized to increase the awareness of students, sommeliers, wine lovers and the final consumers of Portuguese wines. These events are organized in partnership with the Asia Wine Service & Education Centre (ViniPortugal, 2015).

In sum, ViniPortugal uses below-the-line strategies, with specialized events in the wine sector. These events and activities are organized with major industry professionals, opinion leaders, journalists and wine critics. Another good example is the publication of the *Portugal Wine Guide* in the Mandarin language (Cardoso, 2012).

Country of Origin Wine Image in China

Chinese consumers tend to prefer wines of their own country, but among the imported, French wine is their first choice, followed closely by Australian wine (OIV, 2015; ViniPortugal and Institute of Vine and Wine, 2014). French dominance is due to the production size, the organization of the market and the trinomial Luxury-Wine-France (the Chinese associate French wine with luxury), which transmits elegance and sophistication (Institute of Vine and Wine, 2011; ViniPortugal and Institute of Vine and Wine, 2014). France is the only country with a market share above 40%, representing three times more than Australia, the second major supplier and it is also the only country with region reputation and widespread acceptance of small producers. Wines from Australia, as well as Chile, are clearly geared towards the Chinese market. These two producing countries focus on very few brands and are consistent in terms of marketing. The United States, Italy and Spain also have good quotas. Another one that is worthy of note is Germany, with a very clear strategic choice in this market, has proven that even white wines can succeed.

Portugal is positioned as the 14th largest supplier of wine in China, and Portuguese wines have the 11th place in the price ranking (Table 11.3). This performance is well-known by the President of ViniPortugal. Portugal as a brand is not yet widely known in China and only football players have been recognized abroad (e.g., Figo and Cristiano Ronaldo). This lack of knowledge mainly relates to the profile of the proposal from Portugal Wines, thus creating incompatibilities between what they are looking for and what we have to offer. Jorge Monteiro explains that Portugal's offer — "A world of difference" — is based on the fact that wines can be of the

Table 11.3 Value and average price of major Chinese wine suppliers (China, Hong Kong and Macau)

Country supplier	Value				Average price		
	2014 (€)	Variation last year (%)	Variation last 5 years (%)	Share (%)	2014 (€)	Variation last year (%)	Variation last 5 years (%)
France	853,996,165	6	160	41	5.88	11	0
Australia	270,953,168	15	163	13	5.50	14	143
United Kingdom	164,064,622	0	50	8	98.52	−16	12
Chile	140,985,369	3	181	7	1.48	−6	57
USA	112,087,664	−16	92	5	4.70	−22	31
Italy	104,028,371	3	270	5	3.69	−3	17
China	100,144,127	307	6921	5	23.63	93	342
Spain	94,042,867	2	496	5	1.78	−10	14
Germany	36,946,133	16	176	2	6.46	8	12
Singapore	32,580,785	2	189	2	27.55	−22	100
New Zealand	27,157,200	8	172	1	8.58	8	48
Switzerland	25,516,759	−20	156	1	275.71	−2	123
South Africa	21,111,112	−6	194	1	2.75	−9	95
Portugal	18,521,928	14	148	1	2.99	7	15

Note: Value in Euros and price in Euros per litre.
Source: ViniPortugal (2015).

same quality as competitor countries, but have different profiles because they are produced with native varieties. Nevertheless, he goes on to refer to the fact that that the Chinese consumer will look for cheap wines, according to the Chinese Import Association (CAWS) (Monteiro, 2015, personal communication).

Organizational Culture in the Chinese Market

The organization culture in China is an important issue in any Portugal—China exchanges. According to Hofstede's (2001) cultural dimensions, Chinese society is a very pragmatic culture, and so Chinese people have an ability to easily adapt traditions to changed conditions, a strong propensity to save and invest, and perseverance in achieving results (long-term orientation). They accept inequalities among people, that is, the subordinate—superior relationship tends to be polarized and individuals are influenced by formal authority and sanctions, and are in general optimistic about people's capacity for leadership and initiative (power distance).

People act in the interests of the group and not necessarily of themselves ('we' and not 'I'). In-group considerations affect hiring and promotions with closer in-groups (such as family) receiving preferential treatment. Relationships with colleagues are cooperative for in-groups, but they are cold or even hostile towards out-groups. Personal business relationships prevail over task and company. The need to ensure success can be exemplified by the fact that many Chinese people will sacrifice family and leisure for work.

The Chinese are comfortable with ambiguous meanings because the Chinese language is full of ambiguities and can be difficult for Western people to follow. The Chinese do not put much emphasis on leisure time and control the gratification of their desires. Their actions tend to be restrained by social norms and they feel that indulging themselves is somewhat wrong (Hofstede, 2015).

Relationship Quality in the Wine Sector

The content analysis of the interviews with Portuguese wine producers allowed us to highlight four major RQ factors that should be developed in order to create and maintain a favourable relationship with distributors: (1) trust; (2) interdependence; (3) cooperation; and (4) long-term relationship. Table 11.4 shows several statements mentioning these factors.

1. *Trust* is a core factor in relationships with distributors. Trust represents a positive exchange relationship, alignment, and transparency.

    For the Portuguese producers interviewed it is fundamental to understand that, when creating an exchange relationship with Chinese distributors, they must bear in mind the way in which mutual trust is promoted by both. The producers mention that this factor needs time to grow and requires transparency in all exchange actions. Chinese partners tend to give special attention to personal and professional behaviour.

2. *Interdependence* is a second core factor, signifying the actions between producers and distributors and the dynamic of inter-influence with the purpose of reducing uncertainty. It is a relationship that ensures efficient coordination by both parties, as a whole.

    Portuguese producers should be aware that in order to ensure an efficient exchange relationship it is required that the parties work closely, as in a partnership, in which they promote a continuous sharing of information. This operational action is the basis for the Chinese distributor to act as an arm's-length operator and an extension of the Portuguese producer.

3. *Cooperation* occurs when the behaviour of the producers and the distributors is focused on finding solutions that are beneficial for both.

    It is difficult for Portuguese producers to have total knowledge of all the variables of the Chinese market. For them, it is crucial to listen and work with the Chinese partner as a team, in the development of solutions that will help the brand to be more competitive in this market. Personal involvement in this work is valued by the Chinese distributor.

4. *Long-term relationship* refers to an effective partnership that lasts. It is the perception of stability of the relationship, ensuring the sustainability of the partnership in the future.

To ensure the continuity of the exchange relationship, the Portuguese producers who were interviewed recommended that there be a long-term vision with regards to the behaviour with Chinese distributors. It is important that this personal behaviour be consistent with professional conduct in the business. Moreover, the producer's senior management staff must be available to attend social events, such as lunches or social drinking with the distributor's interlocutor.

Table 11.4 Constructs given by those interviewed

Construct	Respondent	Representative evidence from interviews
Trust	2	The positive exchange relationship created is very important.
	3	There are many moments in which we will have to be in line with each other.
	5	It is necessary to develop trust, mutual respect and an understanding that the Chinese market takes time to advance and develop, and therefore a long-term vision is needed.
	8	The relationship with distributors is established on the basis of trust; trust and assurance complete transparency.
	10	Complete openness and transparency.
Interdependence	1	This has to be a partnership.
	4	It's about being interconnected.
	5	The distributor will work the market as an extension of the producer.
	7	Talking is the first thing that someone should do.
	10	A relationship that requires daily contact, close daily contacts. It is a relationship based on an exchange of shared information.
Cooperation	3	We review and make common decisions
	5	To perceive the point of view of the distributor and try to find a solution to the problems that arise.
	7	It is essential that the business relationship be supported by a personal relationship. This is particularly true when the goal is to grow together, and not merely that of making a sale. A solid personal relationship, I would even go as far as to say one of friendship, solidifies business ties and so the Chinese customer becomes not only customer but a trading partner as well, the obvious and ultimate goal in a business relationship.
	8	We work a lot as a team, in other words, we practice decision making as a group.
	10	It's truly a partnership. It is working together.

(*Continued*)

Table 11.4 (Continued)

Construct	Respondent	Representative evidence from interviews
Long-term relationship	1	Building a sustainable relationship; a good relationship.
	5	It is having a good relationship and a continuous connection among the team (producer and distributor).
	6	Accumulating a business relationship with a private one (the Chinese do not distinguish one from the other, as they consider them to be interconnected).
	7	Visiting the customer, sharing a local meal with him, going out for a local drink together with him and his friends, etc., are all very specific and fundamental ways of developing the business relationship, sometimes more important than actually doing business.
	8	We have some sustainability values and in the long term we intend to build value for the company and for the distributor.

Source: Authors' elaboration.

Factors Influencing the Relationship with China

Producers allude to three main inhibitors or difficulties in the relationship with Chinese distributors, which are: (1) physical distance between Portugal and China, (2) knowledge about Portugal and its grapes and (3) communication and culture. Table 11.5 shows several statements expressing these concerns.

1. Physical distance between Portugal and China

   The physical distance creates difficulties in establishing and maintaining the relationship, particularly because the Chinese usually feel the need for several meetings (being physically present) before deciding on a deal. The Chinese also prefer that another partner, someone they know very well, give them a previous referral about those who they are going to negotiate with.

   So, first the producer must do their homework, by studying their potential partner in the Chinese market. A wrong choice could represent relevant money and time losses. Then, it is imperative that the Chinese distributor believes in the producer's capability, quality and honesty.

Table 11.5 Inhibitors given by those interviewed

Inhibitors	Respondent	Representative evidence from interviews
Physical distance between Portugal and China	1	Have the right partner.
	2	The agent/importer is very relevant and should be well positioned.
	3	Reverse visit, greatly cements commercial and personal relationships. Reassures the importer about the origin of products, it is formative and helps to develop good personal relationships, which is as important as delivering and receiving on time.
	4	A commitment to building an ongoing relationship of trust.
	5	If possible, plan visits to Portugal, owners, board members and top managers.
	7	Continued support and commitment to a close relationship.
	8	It is common to find Chinese business man who largely exaggerate their capabilities in order to achieve advantages in the prices of products. The trading companies often do not give out email addresses without evidence of existence facilities or personnel and sellers.
Knowledge about Portugal and wine grapes	1	Lack of knowledge of Portugal.
	3	Lack of knowledge of wine in general, and variety of Portuguese wine grapes.
	4	Do not allocate a budget to promote the wine during the New Year's celebrations or Fall Festival.
	10	Generalized lack of knowledge with regards to the wine product (from vitis vinifera) and its consumption.
Communication and culture	1	Difficulties in communication.
	2	Difficulties in negotiating.
	4	Unable to adapt products (image and taste) to the Chinese market (the Chinese have a very different taste/flavor/experience from that of Europe).
	5	Nothing is more inconvenient for a business relationship than to make the Chinese businessman "lose face" in relation to their local customers.

(Continued)

Table 11.5 (Continued)

Inhibitors	Respondent	Representative evidence from interviews
	9	Usually this leads to a total rupture of the relationship. Patience and resilience is key is Asian markets, especially in China.
	10	The Chinese people's distinctiveness regarding the complex process or route taken to attain a true and stable business relationship which works on a regular basis.

Source: Authors' elaboration.

To achieve this level of credibility, those interviewed recommend that the producer have the financial capability of promoting a visit of the Chinese distributor to Portugal to get to know the company, the family and the rest of the country and especially the main wine regions.

2. Knowledge of Portugal and its unique grape varieties

Although ViniPortugal and the Portuguese government have been making an effort to promote Portugal in China, wine producers consider that Chinese distributors still do not have any knowledge of Portuguese wine and grapes and demand more actions.

In comparison with France and Italy, the producers recognized that Portugal is an unknown wine country. They do not recognize the heritage of Portuguese wines and this creates difficulties in starting or upgrading the value of a relationship.

Furthermore, the interviewers stress that the wine producers should be prepared to allocate a promotional budget, giving more attention to the Chinese celebration seasons, when wine consumption is high.

3. Communication and culture

Language is a difficult issue, but more than this aspect we may consider the difficulty in understanding the Chinese culture, which reduces the possibilities of negotiation and establishing long-term relationships.

Portuguese producers mention that it is crucial to be aware of the relevant characteristics of Chinese culture. This factor could improve the product quality, taste and image expected by the consumers. On the other hand, it avoids making serious mistakes in the process of creating and developing the relationship. In this vein, to reach a solid business relationship with a Chinese distributor, it is necessary to know how to manage it with patience and resilience.

CONCLUSION

Key Summary

Portugal is an old and relatively small wine producer, but the wine has been regarded all over the world as being top quality, original and unique, having won several awards. Overall, Portugal and China have a long-term trade relationship (more than 500 years), however, only for the last 10 years has the Portuguese wine industry started to go further in promoting their wine in China, using below-the-line strategies, mainly through public relations with the help of ViniPortugal and the Ministry of Foreign Affairs. Examples of this are: wine tastings and annual wine events in the major Chinese cities, which include harmonization lunches of wines with local cuisine that are presented by a celebrated figure in China; seminars or training, attended by winemakers or other renowned experts; participation in major events such as Vinexpo Asia-Pacific, China Wine & Spirits Awards and Hong Kong Wine & Spirits Fair; collaboration with the China Association for Importers & Exporters and Asian Wine Service & Education Centre; and the publication of the Portugal Wine Guide in the mandarin language (AICEP, 2012; Cardoso, 2012; ViniPortugal, 2015).

The first step when going to China is finding an importer or a local distributor. This is a hard task because there is merely one small group of prestigious distributors. On the other hand, wine consumption in China has been growing, due to the increase of the middle class. For Chinese consumers, red wine is regarded as a healthy drink, connected to romance, success and luck and so they tend to prefer to drink red wine. From abroad, they want prestigious wine brands associated with good taste and pleasure.

Wine producers highlight four core factors of RQ between producers and distributors: trust, interdependence, cooperation and long-term relationship. Trust has been widely considered and analysed in literature (e.g., Bobot, 2011; Crosby et al., 1990; Dwyer et al., 1987). In the wine sector, achieving mutual confidence is crucial in developing trade. This is particularly true in the case of the Chinese market due to their cultural origin. The Chinese do not negotiate or maintain a relationship with those who they do not trust.

When establishing relationships with the Chinese, producers should be prepared to attend several less formal meetings. Because face-to-face meetings are considered more appropriate than virtual ones, producers (their representatives) should be resilient and count on frequent travel. In this vein, interdependence and cooperation emerge if producers from European countries are able to operate with 'we' instead of 'I'. A dynamic relationship between the producer's group and the distributor's reduces uncertainty (Bobot, 2011; Crosby et al., 1990; Dwyer et al., 1987; Fournier, 1998) and contributes to long-term relationships.

A long-term relationship is viewed in literature as important, but not a core factor of RQ which gains importance in the context of wine and particularly the Chinese market. As Hofstede (2001, 2015) mentions, Chinese people are oriented to making adaptations and persevere in order to achieve results and when they trust the other partner they maintain the relationship.

The inhibitors and difficulties of introducing and sustaining the wines in China mentioned by wine producers reflect that the efforts to promote and transmit the characteristics of Portuguese wine and grapes are not adequate. Even so, wine producers need to acquire more knowledge about the Chinese market and culture, as well as learn how to negotiate and be persevering and patient.

Managerial and Social Implications

The Chinese market is large but not easy to deal with. Based on the current study, it is possible to make several recommendations to Portuguese wine producers, which may be extended to other European wine producers.

First, before establishing contact, it is important to understand the Chinese culture and have a reliable linguist who works with the producer. The linguist should be updated beforehand by the wine producer about the context at hand, so that they may carry out a more appropriate translation.

Second, wine producers should distinguish between importers and distributors. Most of the time in China, they will deal with importers who resell the product in more or less opaque circuits. The Chinese entrepreneurs are extremely reluctant to reveal details of the deal, because in their mind, from the moment they purchase the products, they become the masters of the products' destiny. The circuit of the product can be extremely complex and even follow informal rules.

Third, wine producers should have knowledge about the distributors, understand the type of market portfolio they have, and decide who could be the best for that particular wine product and brand.

Fourth, producers should be prepared to travel to China and establish direct contact, and have several meetings before closing a deal. Even when the deal is apparently closed, it is important to realize that a signed contract only means the beginning of a business, not its conclusion. It is crucial to maintain contact with the distributor, to develop a long-term relationship.

Fifth, the Chinese give major importance to personal reputation and hierarchy. Therefore, when meeting someone for the first time, a business card should be given in English and Chinese and it is important to include academic and professional titles. Never call someone by their first name until they ask that you do so (position is very important). The Chinese like to work with people they know. Thus, producers should find an individual or an organization that can introduce them formally to the producer's representative. To formalize the deal, they insist that a senior representative of the company be present.

Sixth, during the meetings, be prepared for sentences like 'we will see', or 'let us think about it', which in Chinese society means 'no'. Avoid asking pointed questions (the Chinese live easily with ambiguities). Losing one's temper, confronting someone, putting someone on the spot, arrogant behaviour or failing to show proper respect can cause a loss of face ("Mianzi"). This is fatal in negotiations. Chinese teams need to have time during meetings to consult each other.

Seventh, patience and resilience are key characteristics. Do not expect decisions to be made at meetings. At some of the meetings, business is sometimes not even referred to. Meetings are merely a means of exchanging information, of creating true relationships. Expect frequent rescheduling of meetings. So, appointments should be set up a few weeks in advance and confirmed 1−2 days before the scheduled meeting.

Eighth, always remember that in the Chinese context, great importance is given to interpersonal relationships. Knowing how to respond positively to invitations for lunch or dinner and exchanging gifts are important moments needed to demonstrate esteem for the business partner and to promote their confidence.

Ninth, colour code, shape and packaging all have different interpretations in China. The producer's team should study and understand all of those meanings beforehand.

Tenth, the country of origin image is very important for the Chinese. Therefore, cooperatives, producer associations and the Portuguese Government should jointly develop a plan to promote Portugal in China. Although some effort has been made, producers should go further in coordinating the visibility of wine products and associating them to an icon that can symbolize Portugal.

ACKNOWLEDGMENTS

The authors want to express their appreciation for the contribution made by official entities, as is the case of: AICEP; IVV (Portuguese Institute of Vine and Wine); and ViniPortugal.

Similarly, the authors acknowledge the participation in the qualitative study by certain wine producers and exporters, notably: Bacalhôa Vinhos de Portugal; Dão Sul: Sociedade Vitivinícola, S.A.; J. Portugal Ramos Vinhos S.A.; Manuel dos Santos Campolargo, Herdeiros; Quinta do Quetzal; Quinta dos Avidagos; Quinta Nova de Nossa Sr^a. do Carmo S.A.; Symington Family Estates; Sogevinus Fine Wines; Sogrape Vinhos, S.A.

REFERENCES

Agency for Investment and Foreign Trade of Portugal [AICEP], 2011. China — Dossier de Vinhos. (pdf) Lisboa: AICEP. Available at: <http://www.ccilc.pt/sites/default/files/docs/dossier_de_vinhos_aicep.pdf> (accessed 17.09.2015).

Agency for Investment and Foreign Trade of Portugal [AICEP], 2012. China Acolhe Vinhos Portugueses. (online) Available at: <http://www.portugalglobal.pt/pt/portugalnewsarquivo2012/edicaoaicepportugalglobal/paginas/chinaacolhevinhosportugueses.aspx> (accessed 17.09.2015).

Anderson, J.C., Narus, J.A., 1984. A model of the distributor's perspective of manufacturer working relationships. J. Market. 48 (Fall), 62–74.

Anderson, J.C., Narus, J.A., 1990. A model of distributor firm and manufacturer firm working partnerships. J. Market. 54 (January), 42–58.

Athanasopoulou, P., 2009. Relationship quality: a critical literature review and research agenda. Eur. J. Market. 43 (5/6), 583–610.

Bobot, L., 2011. Functional and dysfunctional conflicts in retailer–supplier relationships. Int. J. Retail Distrib. Manag. 39 (1), 25–50.

Caeiro, A., 2015. Portugal já é o quinto fornecedor europeu de vinhos importados pela China. Lusa, (online) 11 April. Available at: <http://www.sapo.pt/noticias/portugal-ja-e-o-quinto-fornecedor-europeu-de-_552920a55be7b9130a305cb5> (accessed 17.09.2015).

Cafaggi, F., Lamiceli, P., 2011. Inter-firm networks in the European Wine Industry. Am. Assoc. Wine Econ. Available at: <http://cadmus.eui.eu/handle/1814/15654>.

Cardoso, M., 2012. Vendas de vinho para a China cresce 62% - Duplicar vendas, é meta para 2014. Expresso, Caderno Econ. 15 (December), 20–21.

Claro, D.P., Claro, P.B.O., 2010. Collaborative buyer–supplier relationships and down-stream information in marketing channels. Ind. Market. Manag. 39 (2), 221–228.

Crosby, L.A., Evans, K.R., Cowles, D., 1990. Relationship quality in services selling: an interpersonal influence perspective. J. Market. 54 (July), 68–81.

Dwyer, F.R., Schurr, P.H., Oh, S., 1987. Developing buyer–seller relationships. J. Market. 51 (April), 11–27.

Euromonitor, 2015. Country Report - Wine in China, June-2015. (online) Available at: <http://www.euromonitor.com/wine-in-china/report> (accessed 17.09.2015).

Falcão, A., 2014. Portugal e o mundo: os números do vinho e da vinha. Revista de Vinhos,4 (online) 26 June. Available at: <http://www.revistadevinhos.pt/artigos/show.aspx?

seccao=reportagens&artigo=15459&title=portugal-e-o-mundo-os-numeros-do-vinho-e-da-vinha&idioma=pt> (accessed 17.09.2015).

Fournier, S., 1998. Consumers and their brands: developing relationship theory in consumer research. J. Consum. Res. 24 (4), 343–353.

Fournier, S., Mick, D.G., 1999. Rediscovering satisfaction. J. Market. 63 (October), 5–23.

Fynes, B., De Búrca, S., Marshall, D., 2004. Environmental uncertainty, supply chain relationship quality and performance. J. Purchas. Supply Manag. 10 (4-5), 179–190.

Gubrium, J.F., Holstein, J.A., 2001. From the individual interview to the interview society. In: Gubrium, J.F., Holstein, J.A. (Eds.), The SAGE Handbook of Interview Research: The Complexity of the Craft, 2nd ed SAGE Publications, pp. 3–32.

Harzing, 2013. Journal quality list. Available at: <http://www.harzing.com> (accessed 14.11.2013).

Hofstede, G., 2001. Culture's Consequences: Comparing Values, Behaviors, Institutions, and Organizations across Nations, 2nd ed Sage Publications, Thousand Oaks, CA.

Hofstede, G., 2015. The Hofstede Centre. Available at: <http://geert-hofstede.com/countries.html> (accessed 10.08.2015).

Institute of Vine and Wine, 2011. O mercado Internacional do Vinho. Lisbon: IVV. Available at: <http://www.ivv.min-agricultura.pt/np4/371> (accessed 17.09.2015).

International Organisation of Vine and Wine, 2015. World vitivinicultural situation. Mainz. OIV Available at: <http://www.oiv.int/oiv/info/en-Bilan_OIV_ Mainz_2015> (accessed 15.09.2015).

Lacoste, S., 2012. Vertical coopetition: the key account perspective. Ind. Market. Manag. 41 (4), 649–658.

Loureiro, S.M.C., Kaufmann, H.R., 2012. Explaining love of wine brands. J. Promot. Manag 18 (3), 329–343.

McCracken, G., 1988. The Long Interview. Sage, Newbury Park, CA.

Santos, M.M., 2014. Vinhos lusos ganham terreno no gigante asiático. Revista Invest, (online) 28 Ju/n. Available at: <http://www.revistainvest.pt/pt/Vinhos-lusos-ganham-terreno-no-gigante-asiatico/A588> (accessed 14.09.2015).

University of Aveiro and Esfera Crítica, 2015. webQDA (computer program). Available at: <https://www.webqda.com/?lang> (accessed 10.09.2015).

ViniPortugal and Institute of Vine and Wine, 2014. China, Hong Kong, Macau – Evolução da posição competitiva dos vinhos portuguesas de 2008 a 2013. Lisbon. ViniPortugal. Available at <http://www.viniportugal.pt/docs/default-source/estudos-de-mercado/china-hong-kong-e-macau---estudo-de-mercado-2008-2013.pdf?sfvrsn=4> (accessed 15.03.2015).

ViniPortugal, 2015. Management Report of the Exercise 2014. Lisbon. ViniPortugal. Available at: <http://www.viniportugal.pt/docs/default-source/relat%C3%B3rios-e-contas/relat%C3%B3rio-de-gest%C3%A3o-2014.pdf?sfvrsn=4> (accessed 17.09.2015).

CHAPTER 12

Rough Seas Ahead: Quality Concerns for China-bound Wine Shipments

T. Atkin[1] and S. Cholette[2]

[1]Sonoma State University, Rohnert Park, United States
[2]San Francisco State University, San Francisco, United States

INTRODUCTION

In order to motivate the discussion on the importance of protecting wine, some background is provided, starting with relevant information concerning the markets and logistics infrastructure in both mainland China and Hong Kong. The severity and frequency of quality problems that arise from temperature fluctuations as wine moves through the supply chain to reach overseas markets such as China is presented. Total quality management (TQM) concepts are summarized, with a more detailed look at the metrics and certification programme defined by the Hong Kong Quality Assurance Agency.

The Chinese Wine Market and Infrastructure Challenges

Wine markets worldwide are becoming more international due to a reduction in both tariffs and non-tariff barriers to wine marketing. China is no exception to this trend, with entry into the World Trade Organization (WTO) leading to decreased import duties on wine. China's imports of bottled wine have risen dramatically from 221,000 cases in 2000 to nearly 29.6 million cases in 2012 (Insel, 2014). China is the fifth largest wine importing country by revenue (OIV, 2013). Bouzdine-Chameeva et al. (2014) report that imports comprise 25% of the bottled wine sales in China, and import sales are growing at four times the rate of domestically produced wines. As discussed in other chapters in more detail, wine consumption outpaces production in China (OIV, 2013), and Chinese consumers often prefer imports due to perceived quality and food safety concerns (Bouzdine-Chameeva et al., 2014).

Many wine producing countries are represented in this market: the top six countries that comprise the majority of the market share are, in decreasing order by revenue: France, Australia, Chile, Spain, Italy and the US (OIV, 2014). Wang (2014) reports that the top three sales channels are on premise (51%), supermarkets (28%) and specialty wine retailers (21%). Only the latter represents a reliable channel for foreign wines, and this channel is serviced by specialized wine importing and distribution agents such as Montrose, which operates in both mainland China (Shanghai) and Hong Kong (Rozelle et al., 2005).

China is experiencing insatiable demand for modernized transportation and logistics services. Less than 20% of China's warehouses are categorized as modern, as they are lacking automation and up to date technology. For example, trucks are often loaded and unloaded by hand due to the lack of raised loading bays and conveyor systems (Supply Chain 24/7 staff, 2014). The lack of modernization can lead to more cargo damage and higher inventory costs, especially in older facilities (Moradian, 2004). Chinese consumers' growing appetite for wine and other formerly-out-of-reach comestibles, such as meat, is stressing the capacity of the country's cold chain logistics. Goedde et al. (2015) report China's cold supply chain infrastructure would need to grow at a rate of 20% annually for the next 5 to 10 years to reach the level found in more developed nations. To cope with the surge in demand for modern warehousing, China may need to invest up to $2.5 trillion over the next 15 years (Supply Chain 24/7 staff, 2014).

The Hong Kong Wine Gateway

When studying the Chinese wine market, one must also specifically consider Hong Kong. Import duties on wine were abolished by the Hong Kong government in 2008 in order to promote local wine industry development (Chen, 2011). Further blessed with a prime geographic location, a highly developed logistical infrastructure, and clear legal and financial systems, Hong Kong has blossomed into the preeminent regional centre for the warehousing, trade, and auction of wines. Riding upon the strong growth of the Asian wine markets, Hong Kong has become the world's largest wine auction centre, handling over US$104 million in sales in 2014 (USDA, 2014). As the Hong Kong Government has signed an agreement with the General Administration of Customs to facilitate exports of wines to mainland China, Hong Kong has become a major point of entry for mainland China's growing wine market. Insel (2014) reports that 40% of imports that reach Hong Kong are ultimately destined for mainland Chinese customers. Although various agencies report Hong Kong figures as separate from those for Mainland China, these markets are clearly intertwined, and their interdependence can lead to confusion over some statistics. For example, while the OIV (2014) indicates US wines rank sixth in China, the USDA (2014) reports the US is the fourth largest wine exporter into Hong Kong.

Hong Kong and its vibrant auction market must be considered not only because it serves as an entry point for Chinese consumers, but also because of the associated operations that provide the requisite support for the sale of luxury wines. Hong Kong has become a nexus for academic researchers and practitioners alike in efforts to monitor and stabilize environmental conditions that could impact wine quality, such as Chen (2011)'s study on certifying wine storage. In addition, Lam et al. (2013) experimented with monitoring a variety of environmental conditions at a Hong Kong distributor using radio frequency identification (RFID) technology and proposed a storage and retrieval programme to best stabilize wines. In particular, the standards defined by the Hong Kong Quality Assurance Agency will be discussed later in the chapter.

The Wine Supply Chain

Wine is the most valuable and complex product in the food and beverage sector (Butzke et al., 2012). Yet the scarcity of intensive studies on how wine is distributed has been widely noted by many researchers (Beaujenot et al., 2004; Orth et al., 2007; Bouzdine-Chameeva and Zhang, 2013).

The wine industry has a complex, multistep distribution network with many players, and no single player takes responsibility for the entire process (Vogt and Jeannel, 2011). Consider a typical journey of a Northern Californian wine to Shanghai, China as follows. International shipment of wine is typically coordinated by freight forwarders, who arrange for a container to be delivered to the winery or an independently owned warehouse, where it will be loaded with pallets by warehouse personnel. The container is then sent by either truck or rail to the port of origin, Oakland, where it undergoes a relatively short waiting period before being loaded onto the carrier's vessel. After a multiweek voyage across the Pacific, the container is unloaded and waits at the destination port, where customs and other paperwork is handled by the freight forwarder and may add delay. An importing agent such as Montrose sends a truck to receive the container and unload it at its warehouse (Rozelle et al., 2005).

Winemakers go to great lengths to grow grapes and control wine production in order to generate the highest degree of quality. Yet once the wine is bottled, this level of attention declines even though a multitude of opportunities for deterioration arise as wine works its way through the supply chain. Wine producers typically have very little downstream visibility and generally have even less control (Chandes and Estampe, 2003), especially if they are small producers. However, proper handling of wine needs to be assured at all points along the supply chain: from producers to carriers, distribution warehouses, and retailers. The authors detail the consequences of improper handling and discuss performance metrics, focusing on a particular set defined specifically for safeguarding wine.

Temperature Quality Issues in the Wine Supply Chain

Butzke (2010) asserts the most common degradation of a wine's quality and value is the improper storage conditions that occur during the journey to the consumer that lead to elevated temperatures and/or temperature fluctuations. If the wine is to be stored and transported over a period of several weeks or months, the temperature should ideally stay between 10−16°C (50−60°F). This range needs to be maintained by every single link in the supply chain, and the chain breaks if even one link fails to maintain the required conditions.

Temperatures above 16°C (60°F) may change a wine's maturation process, affect varietal character, and shorten life expectancy. Temperatures over 30°C (86°F) for more than 18 hours can permanently degrade wine (Jackson, 2008). Rapid temperature changes generate fluctuations in wine volume, exerting pressure on the cork seal, which may ultimately rupture and allow oxygen into the bottle, thus ruining the wine (Jackson, 2008). However, in most cases, temperature-related damage may be difficult to detect because there may be no outward indication until the customer drinks the wine. President of eProvenance.com, Eric Vogt, estimates that about 2% of the wines shipped from Europe to the US are overheated long enough to suffer damage. MacCawley (2014) summarizes thousands of temperature monitoring data points that have been collected on ocean voyages, finding temperature variations are highly dependent on route and time of year, but that temperatures range between 10−45°C.

The damaging effects that extreme temperatures and excessive temperature fluctuations have on wine quality has been documented and decried by many. Robert Parker (2008) estimates that between 10% and 25% of the wines sold in American markets have been damaged because of exposure to extreme heat. A recent multiyear study found that that 9.6% of California wines shipped internationally were at risk of damage (eProvenance, 2010). Another analysis of 285 shipments from France to various Asian destinations (Canterbury, 2013) found that over 13% had noticeable damage.

Applying Total Quality Management to Wine Distribution

Performance measurement is one of the pillars of TQM initiatives. TQM represents an integrated business strategy intended to develop an awareness of quality in all organizational processes (Swink et al., 2014). These types of TQM efforts require appropriate performance measurement in order to make decisions based on data and enable continuous improvement. Programs such as the International Organization for Standardization (ISO) have created a family of standards to ensure that a firm's operating processes are well documented, consistently executed, monitored, and ultimately improved upon. Key performance indicators are critical to operations management across a variety of industry sectors (Gunasekaran et al., 2004).

Given the aforementioned problems associated with temperature fluctuations and extremes, it should not be surprising that many industry professionals are concerned about how wines are transported and stored (Atkin and Gurney, 2013). Although the wine industry as a whole has been slower than other sectors in implementing state of the art logistical practices (Cholette, 2009), some wine producers are starting to pay attention to performance measures that concern the storage and transportation of the wine. Constellation Brands Vice President of Logistics, Rick Anderson, reports that Turner Road Vintners Winery has achieved both ISO 9001 and ISO 9000 certification.

A more specific programme targeted at food production is ISO 22000:2005, which integrates the principles of hazard analysis and critical control point (HACCP) into its system (Aggelogiannopoulos et al., 2007). Aggelogiannopoulos et al. (2007) document the implementation at a Greek winery with an annual production of approximately 600,000 bottles and calculate the cost; consulting, registration and audit fees, training and improvements tallied over 30,000 Euros. These costs are not inclusive of hiring of a quality manager or continuing with ongoing reviews. Not surprisingly, many smaller producers are not able to afford the costs of formal, comprehensive certification, so only a few wineries have had their operations certified (Marshall et al., 2010).

Wine Storage Management Certification

While the industry as a whole has neither defined nor embraced a unified standard that caters to the particular needs of the wine industry, the most complete set of industry relevant key performance indicators has been created by the Hong Kong Quality Assurance Agency (HKQAA). Established by the Hong Kong Government in 1989 as a nonprofit distributing organization, the HKQAA created the Wine Storage Management Systems (WSMS) certification, which defines standards for warehouses, retailers, carriers, and freight forwarders (HKQAA, 2013). The intention was to enhance the confidence of consumers and wine collectors, in turn generating more business for Hong Kong companies and safeguarding the value of the wines traded in Hong Kong's markets.

Appropriate levels for temperature, humidity, and vibration are addressed, as shown in Table 12.1. Furthermore, these metrics distinguish

Table 12.1 Key performance indicators for the wine storage management system

	Fine wine	Commercial wine
Minimum storage temperature	11 °C	—
Maximum storage temperature	17 °C	22°C
Maximum daily fluctuation range	3 °C	5°C
Maximum annual fluctuation range	5 °C	10°C
Humidity as a running average	55−80%	>50%
Storage areas shall be isolated from external lights	Yes	Yes
Low UV lights (i.e. LED lights) shall be used to replace regular fluorescent lights	Yes	No
Storage areas shall not subject to continuous vibrations	Yes	Yes
Suspension systems underneath cellar floorings shall be installed if continuous vibrations occur	Yes	Yes
Regular maintenance shall be carried out on all requirements (refrigerators, humidifiers, etc.)	Yes	Yes
Calibration of conditional controllers and sensors shall be carried out	Once per year	Once per 3 years
Accuracy of temperature sensors	± 0.5°C	± 1°C
Accuracy of humidity sensors	± 5%	± 5%
Insurance coverage shall satisfy with contractual agreements with clients	Yes	Yes

Source: HKQAA, 2013. Wine storage management systems certification scheme handbook, Available at <http://www.hkqaa.org/en_certservice.php?catid = 9 > (accessed 1.06.2015).

between fine wines and commercial wines. The former are not only more expensive but typically involve extensive aging, thus meriting stricter quality controls (Chen, 2011). Other aspects that are monitored and assessed include processes such as equipment maintenance, security, inventory management, hygiene, and insurance.

The management systems of candidate companies are assessed by auditors, in a process similar to ISO 9000 programs. The first phase includes a documentation review and preliminary assessment of the Wine Storage Management Plan. In addition, temperature and humidity sensors are installed to gather information. During the second phase, collected data is analyzed to provide the basis for suggested improvements or maintenance of systems. Companies that meet the standards are then listed on the HKQAA website and may display certification badges for all schemes that they have qualified for, as seen in Fig. 12.1.

Wine Storage

Wine Transportation

Figure 12.1 HKQAA Certifications displayed by a wine importer. *This data has been modified for anonymity.*

RESEARCH METHODOLOGY AND FINDINGS

The current research was motivated by the aforementioned quality concerns and was conducted in two stages: (1) a set of interviews, that was later followed by (2) a survey. The methods for both are briefly described, and greater emphasis given to the exploratory results.

Interview Methodology

In the preliminary phase of the research, the authors met with industry professionals in a series of semistructured interviews. Rather than assume prior knowledge, the researchers desired to start with a blank slate. Hence interviews did not conform to specific questions, but were based around the following preselected research themes: Quality degradation during transport and storage, systems to protect wine quality, and standards (key performance indicators), with time allowed for free-form discussion.

Quality can be a sensitive topic, requiring a level of trust to be established between interviewer and interviewee. Such preexisting rapport and the length of the meeting limited the size of the potential pool of interviewees. The authors honed a short list of approximately 30 contacts possessed between the authors with the goal of soliciting input from actors across several stages of the wine supply chain involved in exporting to China. Twelve of these contacts were either willing or able to meet with the interviewers. Interviewees were allowed to make comments anonymously, but it was otherwise understood that unless anonymity was specifically requested, comments would be public, as would the names and firms. The majority of interviewees were willing to go on record on all but a few issues.

Lessons from the Interviews

Interviewees held positions at various points in the wine supply chain: winery owners/managers, freight forwarders, equipment suppliers, and warehouse managers. Members of the Hong Kong Quality Assurance Agency were also interviewed. As these interviews were conducted in person, most of the interviewees were based in California, although a few also worked elsewhere across the globe, most notably in Hong Kong. The small number of interviewees and their relative lack of diversity preclude generalizing these findings to all firms working within the wine supply chain. However, some common themes became apparent after these discussions and are grouped as follows.

Lack of Standardization Leads to Heterogeneous Responses

It quickly became evident that winery operators often do not know where to turn to assess and find ways to improve their logistics performance. In fact the underlying research was inspired by a consulting project with an unnamed high-end Napa Valley winery. Their warehouse had plenty of space and competent personnel, and the top level management had substantial experience in the wine industry. However, they wondered what they could do to further improve and in asking this question they found that there was no definitive resource available to assess the adequacy of their current practices or guide them to do better with respect to such issues as shipping procedures, floor plan, storage racking, and library storage.

Other winery professionals have been able to partner with suppliers and create their own best practices. Rick Anderson, Vice President of Logistics for Constellation Brands, has partnered with ProtekCargo to perfect a process for guarding wines from extreme heat or cold during cross country rail journeys that may last up to one week. Of course, smaller wineries often lack the scale or initial budget to attract potential partners.

Multiple Options Exist for Protection

Ideally, wines should be stored in refrigerated warehouses and shipped in refrigerated trucks and refrigerated containers with temperatures periodically recorded (Butzke, 2010). However, the expense can be prohibitive for many shippers, often three times the cost of a regular dry container (MacCawley, 2014), and refrigerated containers are not always available when they would be needed. The freight forwarders and suppliers interviewed provided some alternative suggestions when refrigeration is not possible or is too costly.

JIB International, a logistics provider in the Central Valley of California, recommended wrapping each pallet in an insulating blanket to protect the wine from extreme temperatures and perhaps more importantly, temperature variations. As the container is typically delivered to the port one day ahead of vessel loading, the best case scenario is for the wine to remain refrigerated while waiting to be loaded. They noted that this service can be provided by the Port of Oakland, but that it is rarely utilized due to expense.

Bob Brun of Embassy Wine Distributors recommends that shippers include instructions that the container be stored below the water line to keep it cool, removing the need for refrigeration. Positioning pallets away from container walls, ensured through use of inflatable air bladders, provides effective insulation. In fact, Vice President at ProtekCargo Justin Garcia points out that passive measures such as insulated wraps and proper spacing have one particular advantage over more active measures such as refrigeration: there is little chance of equipment failure, such as a power failure.

Lastly, several interviewees suggested additional measures that can be taken to monitor and protect the wine, including utilizing the following pieces of equipment:

- The COX Temperature Recorder is a battery powered instrument that tracks temperature over time, recording the data.
- J. F. Hillebrand's Vinliner Pallet Cover is a protective fabric with a foil layer that protects cargo from thermal shocks, odours, and humidity.
- ProtekCargo's SureTemp Container Liners are fitted to standard dry ocean shipping containers and protect against thermal shocks, container rain/sweat, and IR currents. Conductive heat transfer is reduced by up to 85% through positioning pallets with a 5 cm gap from the side walls.

Temperature Monitoring and Protection Yields Tangible Benefits

Discussions with interviewees showed that protection from even subtle or short-term changes in humidity or temperature can increase a wine's valuation. For example, the previously mentioned high-end winery that had lacked direction, looked to the HKQAA standards for inspiration. The criteria provided guidance and an objective set of key performance indicators upon which to base decisions. Several improvements were immediately identified and have been implemented.

The Sonoma Wine Company, a contract bottler, owns the first facility in Napa Valley to obtain ISO 22000 Certification. General Manager Mark Castaldi, attests that although the process took over a year and a half, it led to improvements in quality and consistency. He indicated that the certification has generated additional business opportunities, drawing overseas customers to use their facility to bottle imported bulk wines.

In both personal communication and a publicly available white paper (ProtekCargo, 2014), Vice President of Logistics Rick Anderson credits pallet placement techniques and thermal blankets with reducing damage to wines during shipment. He estimates Constellation has saved hundreds of thousands of dollars through preventing damages to inventory and the associated write-offs. On the receiving side, Christian Pillsbury, Associate Global Merchandise Manager for Applied Wine in Hong Kong and a member of the HKQAA technical committee, asserts that US wines could garner higher prices if proper handling during storage and transit were assured. He stated a perception exists that wines imported from the US have not been handled carefully enough.

Survey Methodology

The second phase of the research entailed using the qualitative information gleaned from the interviews and the HKQAA criteria to design and administer a survey. The authors decided to first focus on wineries, the earliest stage in the wine supply chain, with the plan that later stages would be addressed in subsequent surveys. Focusing on wineries allowed for greater specificity in the survey instrument. The aim was to assess wineries' current internal practices as well as their knowledge and satisfaction with their supply chain partners' efforts to protect the wine from damage during transportation and storage. The survey considers distribution options relevant to supporting both domestic and foreign markets. The survey was developed to be short and anonymous, allowing for mostly radiobox or checkbox responses to reduce respondent error. Opinions were solicited via a 5-point Likert Scale with an option for "don't know" or N/A provided as relevant. In July 2014 a link to the web-based survey was emailed to addresses provided from a commercial database of US winemakers.

Limited resources and the need to reach a large number of participants restricted the survey to online implementation. The survey was implemented through Survey Monkey, a leading internet survey provider. The sampling frame consists of the 1129 California and Oregon wineries which provided email addresses in an industry contact database used in a prior study (Cholette, 2007).

Some may question why the survey focused on American producers, especially as American wines do not have the most shelf space in Chinese markets. Yet as previously mentioned, American producers represent a significant presence. Likewise, 2013 exports to China ($77 million) and Hong Kong ($78 million) comprised a solid share of California's exports, which represented 90% of all US exports, (Wine Institute, 2014). Many American winemakers are actively seeking to further expand their international presence, especially in Asian markets (McMillan, 2008), so this sampling frame represents a relevant group to study, keeping in mind results should not be assumed to apply more globally.

In July 2014 a letter was emailed to each of the wineries, requesting that the winery complete the survey by following an embedded link and guaranteeing confidentiality of individual responses. Although a contact email was included, and the survey administrator provided some clarifications by email, all communications attempted to maintain as neutral a tone as possible to minimize any response bias. A reminder email was a month later, and the survey was left open for three weeks, with the majority of responses collected within the first week. Given that the underlying database compiled more than 7 years ago, it is not surprising that 27% of the email addresses bounced due to obsolescence or other errors, reducing the actual sample population to 820. The online survey was visited 45 times (with 8 immediately opting out).

Survey Findings

A total of 37 wineries completed the survey, with four of the wineries located in Oregon and the rest located in California. Most (65%) respondents represent smaller wineries with an annual case production below 5000 cases (45 kilolitres), and only 14% represent wineries that produce more than 25,000 cases (225 kilolitres) annually. All but one of the respondents produce wines retailing for more than $15 per bottle in domestic markets. Almost half (49%) of the respondents currently export to international markets. This small number of respondents precludes formal hypothesis testing, but the following insights can be gleaned from the exploratory results.

Producers are Aware that Temperature Controls may be Inadequate

There is widespread acknowledgement among respondents that wine is a fragile good, with 90% of respondents indicating that some fraction of their products requires maintenance at a temperature between 10−16°C (50−60°F), the accepted range for fine wine according to HKQAA standards. When asked if temperatures were adequately maintained at facilities, most (73%) respondents either agree or strongly agree that controls are adequate at the winery and at independent warehouses. Confidence in storage conditions decreases the further down the supply chain wine travels, with only 32% of the respondents agreeing that distributors maintain adequate temperatures in their warehouses and a scant 11% believe so for retailers. Additionally, a fair number of respondents feel that they lack sufficient knowledge to make an assessment, indicating 'don't know' for conditions at the distributor (32%) and retailer (27%).

Transportation is perceived as more problematic than warehousing. Only 38% of respondents either agree or strongly agree that temperatures are adequately maintained during transport in their own vehicles. Respondents have slightly more confidence in the temperature controls on voyages to independent warehouses (43%) or distributors (41%), but only 16% of respondents think that adequate temperatures are maintained during the voyage to the retailer.

The varying levels of confidence respondents show with respect to the appropriate temperature range being maintained is reflected in a follow on question that asks respondents to provide estimates on the per cent of their product damaged from exposure to inappropriate temperatures. Of the 35 respondents willing to make this estimate, most (69%) expect that no wine is damaged in storage. However, the story differs for the 34 respondents willing to estimate comparable damages that occur during transit. Most (65%) estimate that 1% to 2% of their wines suffers temperature-related damages en route and only 24% estimate none of their wine is damaged in transit. This discrepancy is shown in Fig. 12.2. Overall, respondents provide lower estimates for temperature related damages than the experts previously discussed, as none of the respondents expect that more than 6% of their wines suffer damages in either storage or transport. Whether this expectation is an example of overconfidence or that

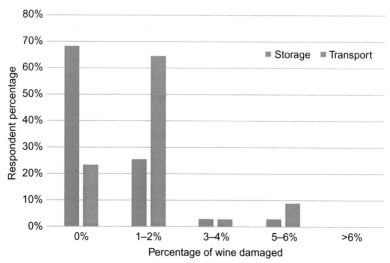

Figure 12.2 Wineries expect more temperature-related damages to their products in transport than storage.

respondents have been more active than the general winemaking population with respect to implementing protective measures is unknown.

Temperature Monitoring is Less Widespread than Control

When asked what equipment and procedures are used for temperature monitoring and control, the respondents are clearly more focused on the latter than the former. Most (73%) use refrigeration during transit. Two other respondents engage in only passive temperature control measures such as insulated trucks, pallet covers, and pallet placement, while the remainder (22%) take no measures to control temperature. Note that of the 27 respondents who use refrigeration, 17 also engage in additional passive measures.

Only one respondent uses temperature recorders. Another makes use of RFID technology but is not doing so for the purposes of temperature monitoring. Only 13% of the respondents make temperature-related requests on bills of lading. Respondents' primary concern (73%) for the movement of their goods was finding cost effective transportation services, with temperature monitoring a distant second place (16%) concern.

A Degree of Complacency Exists for Now, But Change is Expected

Despite the aforementioned lack of confidence in temperature levels being appropriately maintained and an acknowledgement that some wine is likely to be damaged in transit to the end consumer, respondents are surprisingly sanguine about the level of protection their product receives as it moves downstream through the supply chain. Nearly half (48%) of respondents report being either satisfied or very satisfied, and only 11% actively indicate any level of dissatisfaction. However, most respondents anticipate the future will be different: 75% expect more wineries will implement and track performance standards for the storage and transport of wine.

CONCLUSION

This chapter ends with the presentation of some predictions about the Chinese and Hong Kong wine markets and discussion of what implications may be for wine producers and professionals. The first point to consider is that Chinese wine demand is experiencing a long term upward trend, and consumers will continue to thirst for imports even as domestic production grows and quality improves. Imported wines already command a price premium over the locally produced wines that are currently viewed as lower quality (Bouzdine-Chameeva et al., 2014). As imports cannot compete with domestic producers on costs alone, foreign winemakers must continue to differentiate themselves from local wines through maintaining high standards of actual and perceived quality. Given the success of the HKQAA standards and the growing number of certified supply chain partners, Hong Kong will remain the most attractive destination port for fine wines earmarked for Asian consumption.

Lockshin and Spawton (2008) report that as export markets have grown, a heightened expectation of quality has become the norm. As they become more knowledgeable about Western wines, Chinese consumers' expectations will continue to rise, and they may ultimately expect assurances of quality. Wineries who take more active care to protect their wines from temperature issues may find that communicating this commitment to consumers generates additional perceived value. Lee (2009) emphasizes that the Chinese consider Western wines to be luxury products and, as such, a sign of status. Thus, such buyers are especially likely to be concerned with the risk of buying substandard goods and losing face.

Wine producers and professionals should consider the following advice. Temperature monitoring can not only provide an assurance of quality to consumers and clients, but also serves to give wineries the visibility to their downstream supply chain processes that they currently lack. While such opacity occurs everywhere, it is especially relevant for China, given their current deficit of cold chain infrastructure. The surveyed wineries clearly recognize this blind spot, given the number of respondents who either disagree that their wine is properly stored or transported or admit their ignorance about conditions. Temperature monitoring provides a window into how their wines are treated, and this information may help wineries select more reliable partners. For example, some interviewees advise wineries to ask their freight forwarders to include instructions in the bill of lading for placing containers below the water line. In actuality, freight forwarders may either ignore this request, or carriers may choose do to so. MacCawley (2014) provides evidence such requests are often ignored. Perhaps this lackadaisical approach to customer service will change in a world where more shippers possess the ability to see how their cargo is treated, but it would behove wineries not to wait passively in hope for such improvements.

While the majority of the wineries surveyed engage in active temperature control measures such as refrigerated transit, only one respondent monitors temperatures. This behaviour contradicts the very principles of TQM: measurement is necessary to drive improvement, and decisions should be data-driven (Swink et al., 2014). Given the expense of refrigerated containers as compared with monitoring equipment, it would seem a savvy and cost effective measure to invest in recording temperatures.

Just as there are not yet any universal standards for managing the storage and transport of wine through all levels of the supply chain, there is no single universal temperature control solution. An exporter of wines that retail at $10/bottle may not need to make the investment in door-to-door refrigeration that a seller of wine to be auctioned at $1000/bottle would find advisable. However, exporters of wines not destined for luxury collectors should still expect that some level of standards are appropriate. For instance, the key performance indicators defined by the HKQAA (2013) recognize that while commercial wines can be held to less stringent standards than fine wines, a base level of control is still appropriate. Even cost effective measures such as container liners and pallet covers provide some temperature protection. Not only can temperature monitoring serve as an audit trail to assure quality to buyers, but this information can be used by wine producers to determine how they may need to adjust their protective measures. Wine exporters would also be able to assess if they are being sufficiently well served by their current supply chain partners.

Certification programmes and other appropriate documentation signal a higher level of quality, and the interviewees who have adopted such standards have experienced noticeable benefits. While smaller producers may not be able to afford the cost of a full-scale solo certification, other options exist. Yiridoe and Marett (2004) document how a consortium of wineries became ISO 14001 compliant at a fraction of the cost of individual certification. Companies that cannot afford the time or expense of formal certification efforts can alternatively consider adopting appropriate standards informally. For instance, the manager of the high end Napa winery that was one of the interview subjects reported that they were able to use the HKQAA criteria to improve their warehousing processes.

It should be noted that this research was exploratory in nature and the findings have inherent limitations. The experiences of a few interviewees from mostly US-centric companies and the responses of a small number of US winemakers may not represent the experiences of all such companies worldwide. These limitations will be rectified in a more formal and inclusive survey including actors from across the entire supply chain and representing many more countries. In the meantime, these exploratory results may provide ideas and inspiration for wineries and other wine supply chain professionals to address potential quality concerns.

In conclusion, temperature monitoring can not only provide an assurance of quality to consumers and clients, but also serves to provide wineries the visibility to their downstream supply chain processes they currently lack. Monitoring and controlling for temperature is increasingly becoming an expectation in the information era where even individuals wear devices to track their daily activity level against a predefined fitness goal and broadcast this information to their support network. While no one set of quality metrics has gained universal acceptance, compliance with any reputable set of standards sends a positive signal to buyers and is currently enough to differentiate producers. Wineries and other supply chain actors looking to serve the Chinese market are advised to consider how they protect the quality, perceived and actual, of the wines they represent. Exporting to China is not smooth sailing. A firm's adoption of Total Quality Management practices will not by itself solve all of the quality problems arising from a fragmented and underdeveloped cold chain supply chain, let alone address the sea of other challenges that potential exporters face. However, the right approach may provide some aid to those looking to navigate these rough waters and bring their products to the Chinese market with a competitive advantage.

REFERENCES

Aggelogiannopoulos, D., Drosinos, E.H., Athanasopoulos, P., 2007. Implementation of a quality management system (QMS) according to the ISO 9000 family in a Greek small-sized winery: a case study. Food Control 18 (9), 1077–1085.

Atkin, T., Gurney, N., 2013. Protecting quality of wine exports to China: barriers and bridges. J. Int. Food Agribus. Market. 25 (2), 171–186.

Beaujenot, A., Lockshin, L., Quester, P., 2004. Distributor's business characteristics, buyer/seller relationship and market orientation: an empirical study of the Australian wine export industry. J. Market. Channels 12 (1), 61–79.

Bouzdine-Chameeva, T., Zhang, W., 2013. Wine distribution channel systems in mature and newly growing markets: Germany versus China. Academy of Wine Business Research Conference, Ontario, Canada.

Bouzdine-Chameeva, T., Zhang, W., Pesme, J., 2014. The evolution of wine emerging markets: the case of China. Asian J. Manag. Res. 4 (4), 683–698.

Butzke, C., 2010. Wine Storage Guidelines. Purdue Extension Commercial Winemaking Production Series.

Butzke, C., Vogt, E., Chacon-Rodriguez, L., 2012. Effects of heat exposure on wine quality during transport and storage. J. Wine Res. 23 (1), 15–25.

Canterbury, C., 2013. Moving wine: a risky business. Decanter103, February 2013.

Chandes, J., Estampe, D., 2003. Logistics performance of actors in the wine supply chain. Supply Chain Forum 4 (1), 12−27.

Chen, X., 2011. Planning a successful wine WMS for Hong Kong. Contemp. Logist. 2, 13−18.

Cholette, S., 2007. A novel problem for a vintage technique: matching wineries and distributors with mixed integer programming. Interfaces 37 (3), 231−239.

Cholette, S., 2009. Mitigating demand uncertainty across a winery's sales channels through postponement. Int. J. Prod. Res. 47 (13), 3587−3609.

eProvenance, 2010. A call to action for the provenance of fine wine, Autumn Newsletter -2010. Available at: <www.eprovenance.com> (accessed 13.01.2015).

Goedde, L., Horii, M and Sanghvi S., 2015. Pursuing the global opportunity in food and agribusiness, McKinsey & Company. Available at: <http://www.mckinsey.com/industries/chemicals/our-insights/pursuing-the-global-opportunity-in-food-and-agribusiness>.

Gunasekaran, A., Patel, C., McGaughey, R., 2004. A framework for supply chain performance measurement. Int. J. Prod. Econ. 78 (3), 333−347.

HKQAA, 2013. Wine storage management systems certification scheme handbook, Available at <http://www.hkqaa.org/en_certservice.php?catid=9> (accessed 1.06.2015).

Insel, B., 2014. The evolving global wine market. Bus. Econ. 49 (1), 46−58.

Jackson, R., 2008. Wine Science Principles and Application. Academic Press, Burlington, MA, USA.

Lam, H., Choy, K., Ho, G., Kwong, C., Lee, C., 2013. A real-time risk control and monitoring system for incident handling in wine storage. Exp. Syst. Appl. 40 (9), 3665−3678.

Lee, K., 2009. Is a glass of merlot the symbol of globalization? An examination of the impacts of globalization on wine consumption in Asia. Int. J. Wine Bus. Res. 21 (2), 258−266.

Lockshin, L., Spawton, T., 2008. Global marketing and exporting. In: Thach, L., Matz, T. (Eds.), Wine: A Global Business. Miranda Press, Elmsford, NY.

MacCawley, A., 2014. The international wine supply chain: challenges from bottling to the glass. Ph.D. Georgia Tech.

Marshall, R., Akoorie, M., Hamann, R., Sinha, P., 2010. Environmental practices in the wine industry: an empirical application of the theory of reasoned action and stakeholder theory in the United States and New Zealand. J. World Bus. 45 (4), 405−414.

McMillan, R., 2008. "2008−2009 State of the Wine Industry", Silicon Valley Bank. Available at: <http://www.svb.com/pdfs/wine/StateoftheWineIndustry1109.pdf> (Accessed 10.01.2011).

Moradian, R., 2004. The logistics of doing business in China. Inbound logistics. Available at: <http://www.inboundlogistics.com/cms/article/logistics-of-doing-business-in-china/> (accessed 21.03.2016).

Parker, R., 2008. Parker's wine buyer's guide−, 7th edition Simon & Schuster, New York, NY.

ProtekCargo, 2014. Beverage giant keeps its cool. Available at: <http://www.protekcargo.com/wp-content/uploads/2014/11/Constellation-Brands_Protek-Case-Study-final.pdf> (accessed 12.12.2014).

OIV, 2013. Statistical report on world vitiviniculture: 2013. Available at: <http://www.oiv.int/oiv/> (accessed 15.04.2015).

OIV, 2014. The wine market: evolution and trends. Available at: <http://www.oiv.int/oiv/> (accessed 30.06.2015).

Orth, U., Lockshin, L., d'Hauteville, F., 2007. The global wine business as a research field. Int. J. Wine Bus. Res. 19 (1), 5−13.

Rozelle, S., Huang J and Sumner, D., 2005. Wine in China: a report to the california association of winegrape growers. Available at: <http://iisdb.stanford.edu/pubs/21702/wine_in_china_CAWG_2005.pdf> (accessed 1.06.2015).

Supply Chain 24/7 Staff, 2014. Logistics and warehousing — China's weakest link. Supply Chain 24/7. Available at: <http://www.supplychain247.com/article/logistics_warehousing_chinas_weakest_link/ups> (accessed 21.03.2016).

Swink, M., Melnyk, S., Cooper, M., Hartley, J., 2014. Managing operations across the supply chain. McGraw-Hill/Irwin, New York, NY.

USDA, 2014. Hong Kong wine market, GAIN Report No: HK-1407, Available at: <http://gain.fas.usda.gov/> (accessed 16.04.2014).

Vogt, E., Jeannel, A., 2011. Assuring the provenance of fine wine. Academy of Wine Business Research Conference, Bordeaux, France.

Wang, X., 2014. Decomposing the growth of U.S. wine exports to China into scale, competitive, and second-order effects. M.S. Southern Illinois University Carbondale.

Wine Institute, 2014. California wine exports reach all-time high in 2013, Available at: <http://www.wineinstitute.org/resources/exports/article774> (accessed 15.04.2015).

Yiridoe, E.K., Marett, G.E., 2004. Mitigating the high cost of ISO 14001 EMS standard certification: lessons from agribusiness case research. Int. Food Agribus. Manag. Rev. 7 (2), 37−62.

PART IV

China in the Wider World of Wine

CHAPTER 13

Chinese Foreign Investment in Wine Production: A Comparative Study of the Bordeaux Region in France and Western Australia*

L. Curran[1] and M. Thorpe[2]
[1]Université de Toulouse, Toulouse Business School, Toulouse, France
[2]Curtin Business School, Curtin University, Perth, Australia

INTRODUCTION AND RESEARCH QUESTIONS

This chapter will explore the rise of Chinese foreign investment in the global wine industry, through a comparison of the level and nature of investment in two distinctive wine producing regions — Bordeaux in France and Western Australia. Although foreign interest has attracted media coverage in both these regions, there has been little academic analysis to date. Existing studies on Chinese outward Foreign Direct Investment (OFDI) in France and Australia only cover the wine sector to a limited extent (Chen, 2014; Dyan and Testard, 2014; KPMG, 2013). Furthermore, there has been no significant analysis of the link between Chinese overseas investment in wine and the Chinese domestic wine market.

This chapter seeks to address this gap. The key research questions will be:

- What is the extent of Chinese investment in the two regions in terms of total number and share of properties, as well as mode of investment (acquisition, joint venture)?
- What are the key motivations of investors and how do they differ between the two regions?
- What are the key difficulties experienced in leveraging investment?
- How has trade evolved, as investment has increased and the Chinese market has matured?

* The authors would like to acknowledge the support of Curtin University's Visiting Fellow's programme, which was vital to this research. Thanks to Wine Australia for access to their database and to all interview subjects for their valuable insights.

In taking a comparative perspective, the research also seeks to shed light on how local contexts impact on such investments, by contrasting two diverse regions. Bordeaux and Western Australia (WA) have similarities, most notably they are both known mainly for producing red wine, at the relatively high end of the market. However they also have important differences, especially in relation to their integration with the global economy. WA wine is relatively new to the Chinese market and indeed to export more generally. Bordeaux is much more integrated into the global market and has a long history of FDI in wine (Chen, 2014; Sud Ouest, 2014). We explore similarities and differences and highlight what lessons might be learnt from experience in these different contexts.

BACKGROUND LITERATURE

As China has emerged as an important wine market, research has begun to address its role in the global market. There is some limited research on the development of the Chinese wine industry (Jenster and Cheng, 2008) and domestic wine consumption (Lee et al., 2009; ABARES, 2012). Studies on the impact of emerging Chinese demand on the world market have suggested that the rapid growth of Chinese consumption is increasingly having a significant impact (Anderson and Wittwer, 2013; Thorpe, 2009). This is also because increasing demand in China has occurred against a backdrop of long term falls in wine consumption globally, especially in traditional markets. In France for example, the annual average consumption fell from 104 l per person in 1975 to 47 l in 2011. While China was still only at the level of 1 l per person in 2011, this was up from 0.3 l in 2003 (FranceAgriMer, 2013). More recent figures for 2014 suggest further falls in France (42.5 l/person) and a further slight increase in China (1.18 l/person) (Wine Institute, 2015).

Of the studies looking at Chinese wine consumers, the most pertinent to this paper are those which look at the role of country–of–origin (COO). COO is identified as the key element influencing Chinese consumers' choice of wine, particularly for gift giving, a major driver in China's overall wine market (Balestrini and Gamble, 2006; Hu et al., 2008; Yu et al., 2009). French wine has long had a considerable advantage over others in terms of consumer perception and acceptance (Liu and Murphy, 2007; Yu et al., 2009) and bordeaux in particular is the most recognized appellation (Lockshin, 2014).

The structure and distribution systems of the Chinese market have also been subject to some analysis. The distribution system was already identified as a key barrier to market entry by research in the mid-2000s (Jenster and Cheng, 2008) and this situation has not improved markedly since. While the on trade — restaurants and bars — remains a key distribution outlet for foreign wines (ABARES, 2012; Lockshin et al., 2011), this represents a relatively small segment of the market.

Increased consumption in China has fuelled growing investment in the sector (Thorpe, 2009). Several local producers produce high volumes for the local market (Ma, 2012; Lockshin, 2014) and foreign companies are also active in Chinese wine production, including the French companies Remy Martin and Castel (Jenster and Cheng, 2008). The focus in this paper, however, is on outward FDI (OFDI) from China to producing regions. Previous work on OFDI in wine has focused on the operations of large multinational companies based in traditional markets, like the US, Australia and France (Outreville and Hanni, 2013). Work on OFDI by Chinese firms is rather limited (He and Wang, 2014; Kolstad and Wiig, 2012), while the specific issue of Chinese investment in wine does not seem to have been subject to any previous academic research.

The studies by Chen (2014) and Dyan and Testard (2014) both observe that Chinese investment in Bordeaux is much more significant than elsewhere in France, although no detailed figures are provided. Published research in Australia which specifically focuses on the wine industry is even more limited. Existing research focuses on the whole agribusiness sector (KPMG, 2013).

METHODOLOGY

Our research combined analysis of quantitative data on trade and investment with qualitative data obtained from over twenty interviews with investors, local partners, institutions and support services in both regions (see Appendix for details). Several interviewees preferred to remain anonymous as they considered the information provided to be commercially sensitive. These personal interviews took place between December 2013 and September 2015. They were wide-ranging, focusing on all aspects of commercial relationships, as well as the role and impact of the policies of governments and other institutions. The objective of the interviews was to complement macro data and publicly available information, with qualitative analysis of the motivations and perceptions of key stakeholders within the markets. This enabled us to better capture the context behind observed trends in the data and the interactions between trade, investment and local institutions. In the absence of official FDI data, they also provided us with extensive information on investors and their investments.

In this study we focus our trade analysis on red wine — the key export category in both regions. Trade data covers the ten year period 2005—2014, as trade prior to that was negligible. Data for Bordeaux comes from the International Trade Centre (ITC) database[2], which is based on UN data. It reports wine trade for France by Geographic indication (GI) and category (white, red, etc.). Thus we report trade in red bordeaux wine from France. Australian GIs are not identified in the ITC database, so for Australian trade we use the database from Wine Australia[3] which does provide data by GI. The data presented is for aggregate trade in red wine for the 9 key GIs in the WA region[4]. As most world wine trade takes place in US dollars (US$), we use this currency for bordeaux trade. Wine Australia only declares trade in Australian dollars (AUS$), thus we use this measure for WA trade. Although the use of different currencies is obviously not ideal, our main focus is on trends over time within each region, rather than direct comparison between them. In addition, the period since the financial crisis has been one of high currency volatility, such that the choice of an appropriate annual exchange rate would have been very problematic. Unit prices in both cases are by litre.

THE EVOLUTION OF CHINESE INVESTMENT IN THE REGIONS STUDIED

This section explores the evolution of investments in the two regions. Official statistics on Foreign Direct Investment (FDI) flows proved to be of limited use in shedding light on the extent of investments. This was for a variety of reasons, explored in more detail in Curran and Thorpe (2015), but the key factors were the tendency for Chinese investments to

[2] http://www.trademap.org/index.aspx

[3] Downloaded from: http://www.wineaustralia.com/en/Winefacts%20Landing/Australian %20Wine%20Export%20Approvals/Export%20Approvals%20Database/Exports% 20Approvals%20Database%20incl%20GI%20regional%20label%20claim.aspx?ec_trk = followlist&ec_trk_data = Export + Approvals + Database (accessed 7.09.2015).

[4] These are Blackwood Valley, Great Southern, Geographe, Manjimup, Margaret River, Peel, Pemberton, Greater Perth and Swan District.

transit through third countries (He and Wang, 2014; Kolstad and Wiig, 2012) and the lack of disaggregation of official FDI figures by sector. We therefore developed our own database of Chinese investors (broadly defined to include Hong Kong (HK)) in both regions. This was established from press reports and interview data. Each press report was cross-checked to ensure that at least one other source confirmed the investment.

Chinese Investment in Bordeaux

The database that we developed for this research includes 86 vineyards drawn from media reports and data provided by the Bordeaux Chamber of Commerce and Industry (CCI). The latter indicated that not all sales were public knowledge and estimated that there were almost 100 vineyards in Chinese hands, out of a total of over 7000 in the region (Author interview, September 2015). This would suggest that fewer than 1.5% of Bordeaux vineyards are Chinese owned.

Although the first 'Chinese' investor — Peter Kwok — a Taiwanese businessman based in Hong Kong — made his initial investment in 1997 (Anson, 2012), it was several years before others followed. In 2012–13 the number of investments suddenly increased. It is the rapidity of this increase in acquisitions which was unprecedented. As one journalist commented: '*A movement as rapid and important as the arrival of this Chinese capital is unique in the history of wine*' (Author interview, March 2014). This rapid expansion, along with the sheer potential size of the Chinese market, fuelled concerns about its long term impacts (Chen, 2014).

However, the fact that many chateaux in Bordeaux are small, explains to some extent the number of sales. The CCI underlined that chateaux in the Bordeaux region are rarely above 100 ha (Author Interview, March 2014) and acknowledged that this is clearly a disadvantage in terms of the volumes needed for the Chinese market. Thus some Chinese groups bought several vineyards in order to secure an adequate volume of production. For example, when Goldin Group bought three chateaux in 2013 the combined size was only 15.4 ha (Le Roy, 2013a). The You brothers, whose main business is pharmaceuticals, own at least six chateaux, covering 250 ha, while the supermarket group Dashang owns at least two (Le Roy, 2013a). The largest, however, is Haichang group, a highly diversified multinational enterprise from Dalian. The company owns 23 chateaux in Bordeaux covering 500 ha (Sud Ouest, 2014).

In terms of the mode of entry chosen by the investors, until recently all investments were wholly owned. In other words, investors chose to buy out the existing owners, without recourse to any local partner. However when Bright Foods invested in Diva wine-merchants in mid-2012 they took a 70% stake (Letessier, 2012), while Peter Kwok's most recent acquisition is in partnership with two other investors (French and Belgian) (Rabiller, 2016). In addition, two of the more recent acquisitions of chateaux, in 2014, by Liaoning Energy Investment are also majority stakes (Abellan, 2014). It may be coincidence, but in both cases the investors were state owned enterprises (SOEs). Curran and Thorpe (2015) speculate that this choice for part ownership may reflect the proposition by several academics and observers that SOE investors face greater challenges to their legitimacy in foreign markets than private companies.

Our database indicates that the rate of acquisitions has reduced considerably in the last two years. In line with trends in trade, explored below, investment has been affected by negative developments in the Chinese market. The local CCI indicated that, along with this plateauing in investments, they were also witnessing a 'normalization' of existing investments. Investors increasingly see the benefit of integrating into the local institutional context, rather than relying solely on forward linkages to the home market, as some early investors had done (Author interview, September 2015).

Chinese Investment in Western Australia

As for Bordeaux, a database of Chinese investments in WA was assembled through a combination of information gathered from local institutions and press reports. The Ministry of Agriculture in WA indicated in December 2013 that there were three substantial investments in WA wineries, although it acknowledged that there may have been smaller scale investments that had not been officially recorded. Two investments were by the same company — Grand Farms Group — a private firm mainly operating in the meat sector in both China and WA. The company invested in the vineyards in partnership with a local businessman, with whom they had a long-standing business (and personal) relationship. This was a joint venture, the exact details of which are not publicly available. The third investment was in a major local winery, Ferngrove, which was 88% owned by a Chinese businessman, Mr Ma. Although his prime business was in ball bearings, Mr Ma began diversifying into agribusiness with a cattle farm in Australia before moving into wine. His interest in the beef industry was also linked to selling into the Chinese domestic market. Since Ferngrove, he has bought another vineyard in South Australia (Author interview, 17 December 2013).

Beyond these high profile investments, we found several further investments in the region. The Palandri winery was taken over by another Chinese businessman from the metal sector after it went bankrupt in 2008 (Deloitte, 2008). The company has been rebranded as 3 Oceans and is now Chinese managed and is focused primarily on the Chinese market. There is one other wine group — Palinda — which was created when both the Western Range and Woodside vineyards were bought by a Chinese businessman. Little information is available on this group and their website is only in Chinese.

Thus overall six confirmed investments have been identified. According to the Ministry of Agriculture, there are 1073 vineyards in WA covering an area of 13,225 ha (personal communication, June 2014). Chinese investors therefore own an estimated 0.5% of vineyards in the state. However at least two are large by industry standards — Ferngrove and 3 Ocean's Franklin River vineyard are 300 ha and 350 ha respectively. As a result, vineyards owned, or part-owned, by Chinese investors represent over 6% of the vineyard land area in WA. This is significantly more than in Bordeaux, where, as mentioned above, most acquisitions tend to be small. Most WA industry participants expected Chinese involvement to increase over time. The real estate agents we spoke to reported regular visits from interested Chinese investors in 2013 (Author interview, December 2013). However, new investments since then have been rare in WA, although there has been some limited investment in other regions, including a 2014 majority holding in a Coonawarra vineyard in South Australia (England, 2014). Overall, as in Bordeaux, it seems that optimism about the potential of wine investment may have dissipated in China and the focus of WA investors is more on consolidating existing investments than expanding into new vineyards.

INVESTOR MOTIVATIONS AND DIFFICULTIES

The reasons for investment in wine were various (Dyan and Testard, 2014; Le Roy, 2013b). Several respondents differentiated between those who invested mainly for the 'trophy element' and serious businesspeople. The former group invested primarily in Bordeaux and included rich individuals from the arts or industry who developed a taste for wine and for whom owning a chateau was simply a luxury. However this was a minority and most investors expected their investment to be profitable. Even those whose prime motivation was to have a 'trophy' often used their property to entertain business guests, or gave their wine as gifts to business contacts. This entertainment value also explains the preference of investors for vineyards with attractive historic buildings (Compadre, 2013), where Bordeaux has a definite advantage over the more recent properties in WA. As one estate agent in the latter acknowledged. '*We don't have the 'wow' factor they have in Bordeaux.*' However he also noted that they also didn't have the '*Hollywood prices*' (Author interview, December 2013).

Interviewees concurred that the increasing demand for wine in China was a key motivation for most investors, who were looking to boost sales volumes into their home market. However they could simply have imported wine and, indeed, many of them started their involvement in this way. A key reason for making the commitment to invest, common to both regions, was security of supply. Trust in suppliers to the Chinese market — both foreign and domestic — has been undermined by a series of scandals in the milk sector (Moore, 2013). In addition, wine is a sector where counterfeiting is widespread (The Economist, 2011; Le Roy, 2013b). It is reported that half of the wine sold in China could be fake and industry experts suggest it could be as high as 90% for the high profile bordeaux brands and premium Australian wines (Jordan, 2014). Respondents from both regions underlined that being able to reassure customers that the wine came from their own estates provided a level of confidence which was extremely important for the market.

In the case of Bordeaux, the appellation was a key factor for investors. As indicated above, research in China indicates that French wine has a large advantage on the market in terms of consumer awareness and perception (Lee et al., 2009; Liu and Murphy, 2007; Yu et al., 2009). Bordeaux epitomizes this advantage. The links to the terroir are important. As the CCI put it '*You can't offshore the terroir.*' (Author interview, February 2014). Western Australian informants accepted that their flagship 'Margaret River' appellation did not have the same brand recognition in China, but they relied on price advantage and quality consistency to gain market advantage (Author interview, 18 December 2013). Bordeaux actors acknowledged that consistency was sometimes an issue with mid-range French wine, compared to the Australian product. This difference was considered to be linked to the more flexible institutional context in Australia, which allows poor harvests to be upgraded by mixing with more quality wines. There is little flexibility in this regard under the French AOC system (Meloni and Swinnen, 2013).

The desire to cut out middlemen was identified as important in the Bordeaux context. The local wine distribution system is complex and strongly institutionalized, often involving several actors, including courtiers and wine-merchants as well as 'en primeur' sales in advance (Anson, 2007). Direct control sought to avoid this convoluted process and ensure direct supply. In Australia the market supply chain is less complex. Hence simplification of the supply chain was less of a factor in the FDI decision.

What was quite evident in the Australian experience was that investment often extended or cemented existing business relationships — *guanxi*. Most investors in the WA industry had prior business links in Australia. Personal relationships established in other sectors were the basis for the wine investment in several cases. This reflects the importance of personal contacts to doing business in China (Beverland, 2009). No such examples of leveraging established business relationships to invest in wine were found in France, where the level of Chinese investment in the broader economy is much lower than in Australia. Moreover the Australia—China bilateral trade relationship is now very significant for both countries and Australia has become an attractive destination for wealthy Chinese people seeking residency. This latter aspect is facilitated through investment commitments.

In terms of the challenges facing Chinese investors, there were issues in relation to discrimination and difficulties dealing with local regulations in the host regions. These are explored in more detail by Curran and Thorpe (2015). In terms of the specific focus of this chapter — the interaction between overseas investment and the home market — dealing with the growing complexity of the Chinese market was considered problematic by many respondents. The various actors in China added new costs, especially as the market was considered to be immature and value chains thus more extensive and expensive (Author interview, 20 February 2014). Although this was a challenge which all exporters faced (Lockshin, 2014), it nevertheless complicated attempts by the Chinese investors to leverage their investment on the home market.

One solution, which was adopted by Ferngrove's partner, was to distribute through proprietary distribution systems. In Bordeaux, the two supermarkets which invested used their own shops to distribute their wine. One key investor — Tesiro — initially distributed their wine through their chain of jewellery shops (Pedroletti, 2012), but moved to a separate distribution system (Dyan and Testard, 2014). Diva, the only bordeaux wine-merchant majority owned by a Chinese investor, distributed its wine through the latter's sales network. However it was more oriented towards tobacco sales, which limited sales (Author interview, March 2014). All informants recognized that for wine to become a widely accessible consumer product in China, distribution networks needed to be improved and consumer education assured.

It is this final element of the value chain — distribution — which was identified as most problematic by industry actors in both host regions. As indicated above, prior research underlined that wine distribution systems have been underdeveloped in the Chinese wine market for some time (Jenster and Cheng, 2008; Lee et al., 2009; Lockshin et al., 2011). Our research confirms that effective distribution in China has been a challenge, even for Chinese investors, although it is seen as vital to effectively leveraging their investment. Thus several have sought to control the whole value chain, by setting up or leveraging their own distribution systems in China. Some difficulties were experienced with Chinese owners in related, but different sectors seeking to use existing distribution systems to distribute wine. Several industry experts indicated that, given the level of maturity of the market, dedicated distribution systems which enabled wine specific education were more efficient, although they were also more challenging to establish.

TRENDS IN TRADE

This section explores trends in trade in wine over the last decade — the period prior to, and following, the observed expansion of investment. The focus is on red wine, the flagship product of both regions. We report trade for both China and Hong Kong (HK), because HK is an important hub for wine trade in the region and much wine destined for China transits through HK (Author interviews, 6 December 2013 and 20 February 2014). We note that trade has fallen over recent years in both regions. Although in our initial interviews in 2013—14, respondents were optimistic that trade would pick up once stocks were depleted, more recent interviews were less upbeat (Author interviews, June 2015, September

2015). We conclude this section with some discussion on the reasons for this change and prospects for future evolution.

Trends in Trade in Red Bordeaux Wine to China

China emerged as a market for bordeaux only in the last decade and yet it evolved very rapidly to become the second most important destination for exports by value in 2011, second only to HK, also an important entry point for trade with the rest of China. If we count HK and Chinese trade together, Greater China was already the key destination for bordeaux by 2010. This has remained the case since, although the UK was more important than both HK and China individually in 2012 and 2013. Fig. 13.1 shows the evolution of trade since 2004 in exports of red bordeaux to both China and HK, with the UK and US for comparison.

As is evident from Fig. 13.1, exports to all markets have been volatile in recent years, with China (−38%), HK (−44%) and the UK (−54%) all seeing important falls since their peak in 2011 (2012 in the UK). Exports to the US were affected by the financial crisis in 2009−10, which had a very negative impact on the wine trade, reducing both sales volumes and the premiums for quality wines (Gokcekus and Finnegan, 2013). However they have been stable in more recent years. The high level of variability in UK exports may also be linked to developments in Greater

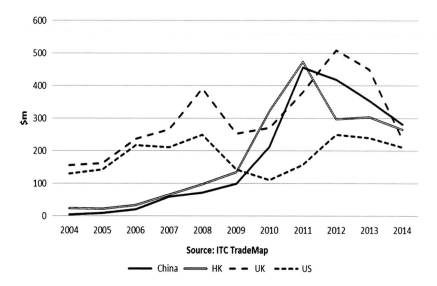

Figure 13.1 Trends in exports of bordeaux.

China. London is an important centre for world trade in quality, Grand Cru wine. Thus, in recent years the UK has been an important exporter of bordeaux to the HK market, which is in turn an important centre for quality wine sales to China. Figures from the ITC database indicate that at the height of euphoria on the Chinese market, UK exports of bordeaux to HK were the equivalent of over 78% of the UK's corresponding imports. Although that percentage fell to well under 50% in 2012—13 it rose again to 80% in 2014. Thus the volatility in sales to the UK in the later years of analysis seems, at least in part, to also be a reflection of difficulties on the Chinese market.

In terms of unit prices, Chinese export prices (US$8/l) were actually below the market average for bordeaux (US$12/l) in 2014 and, although both peaked in 2011 (US$11/l and 14/l respectively), this has consistently been the case in recent years. Consistent with its role in top end Grand Cru sales, it is HK which was the key destination for high value wines (with average prices of US$34/l in 2014, down from a peak of US$49/l in 2011). Thus the recent difficulties in the Chinese market have, as might be expected, resulted in lower unit prices. However, as some informants confirmed in interviews, mainland China has never been an 'eldorado' of wine sales, and has consistently commanded lower prices than the average export price for bordeaux (Author interviews, 20 February and 8 April 2014).

Trends in Trade from WA

As indicated in the methodology section, all trade and price data in this section is from Wine Australia's database and aggregates trade in red wine in AUS$ from the nine key appellations in WA. Fig. 13.2 reports trends in these aggregated exports for the last ten years to China and HK, as well as the US and UK for comparison. These are four of the five key markets in recent years (Singapore being the third or fourth key market depending on the year). It is clear from the figures that WA was a minor player compared to bordeaux, with a peak level of sales of AUS$7 million. However it was relatively more important in the quality wine market, with average prices of AUS$9/l in 2012 (compared to the average Australian export price to China of AUS$5.7).

The most notable feature of Fig. 13.2 is the very rapid increase, and then fall, in WA exports to China. From their peak in 2012, exports had fallen by 40% in 2014. Although the other key markets — the US and

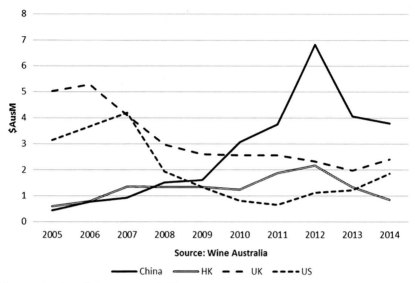

Source: Wine Australia

— China — HK ‑ ‑ UK ‑‑‑‑ US

Figure 13.2 Trends in exports of WA wines.

UK — also saw falls over the last decade, these were mostly in 2007—9 period and were thus most likely linked to the global financial crisis. HK, although an important market (fifth destination in 2014) never experienced the level of peak sales experienced in China. Given HK's specialization in the very top end of the market, this indicates that WA wine, in spite of being 'premium' compared to other Australian wines, did not compete significantly with the Grand Cru Classé from Bordeaux in this key market. Nevertheless, falls in sales to HK were even more notable than to China, with a 60% fall since their 2012 peak.

As indicated above, within Australia, WA specializes in premium wine. Wine Australia's data indicates that, in contrast to the trend evident in Bordeaux, the average unit price of its exports to China increased to AUS \$10.5/l over the three years to 2014 (compared to a fall in average Australian export wine prices to AUS\$5.8/l). This was also the case in HK, where, although exports fell significantly, unit prices in 2014 increased to AUS\$ 11.7 (compared to only AUS\$6 at market peak). Relative to the other key markets, average export prices to China were higher than for the UK (AUS\$9.5) and the US (AUS\$9.8). It is worth noting that under the recently signed China—Australia Free Trade Agreement (ChAFTA), current tariffs of between 14—20% on Australian wine will be eliminated by 2019 (DFAT, 2015), giving it a price advantage on the Chinese market compared to European wines, including bordeaux.

The reasons behind the rapid increases and the recent falls in trade in both markets are varied, but the interviewees attributed the latter in large part to the government's anticorruption drive. This policy, instigated following the accession of President Xi, targeted the ostentatious lifestyles of some state officials. Two practices that have been curtailed, dramatically impacting wine sales, are gift giving (which often included wine) and the widespread banqueting which has long been a feature of business and government interactions in China (Kynge, 2013). Official banquets were said to be '...*very, very much reduced*' (Author interview, September 2015).

All interviewees mentioned that the anticorruption campaign had impacted on the market, although initially it had been hoped that sales would pick up relatively quickly. Recent interviews indicate that this has not been the case and exporters have become resigned to a more 'normal' operating context. The export director of the Bordeaux CCI considered that China had become a more competitive market, as exporters increasingly targeted the middle market, 'ordinary' consumers, who were more price sensitive and less ostentatious than the elite buyers which made up much of the first wave of wine consumption. However he also commented: '*It is not because of this, that exporters should forget China*' (Author interview, September 2015).

Australian interviewees confirmed that the market had become more difficult. One exporter indicated that their unit prices had come down, as competition increased in the mid-market (Author interview, June 2015). In addition to the anticorruption drive, other factors explaining the fall in exports included the extensive stocks that had been built up as market euphoria peeked in 2012, the fact that 2013 was not a good vintage in Bordeaux (The Guardian, 2015) and wider trade tensions between the EU and China during a high profile antidumping conflict in 2012−13, during which the wine sector was targeted (Curran, 2015). The 2015 economic slowdown in China also undoubtedly impacted on sales of wine, as for all luxury goods (Bland, 2015).

The anticorruption drive in China also affected investment. For high net worth individuals the 'cachet' of owning a vineyard had to be balanced against the potential of attracting the attention of the Chinese authorities. This could explain the failure to convert the widespread interest reported by estate agents in WA in 2012−13 into actual transactions. Indeed, in 2015 the Australian government changed the visa rules for investors, partly to address concerns about use of illegally acquired assets, especially from China, to gain migration rights to Australia (The Australian, 2014).

Company investments have also been subject to scrutiny. The biggest investor in Bordeaux, Haichang, is being investigated by the Chinese authorities for misuse of state funds in their acquisitions (Mustacich, 2014). This follows a report of the National Audit Office in July 2014 which alleged that 13 chateaux had been illegally acquired with Chinese state funding. Although subsequent interviews suggested that this investigation didn't immediately impact on the day to day running of these chateaux (Author interview, September 2015), their long run future is in doubt and there has been speculation that these acquisitions may even become the property of the Chinese state (Mustacich, 2014).

DISCUSSION AND MANAGERIAL IMPLICATIONS

This research has analyzed the growth in Chinese investments over the past decade in the wine sector in the two regions studied, as well as a sharp increase in exports to China. Both trends have reversed in more recent years. The fall in trade has highlighted the vulnerability of this new and immature market to policy shifts by the government, particularly the recent anticorruption drive in China. Investment has also been impacted, with a marked fall in new investments in the last two years. However there has been no sign of disinvestments, suggesting that the current period is one of consolidation.

Our interviews indicated that this consolidation will likely pose managerial challenges. The institutional context in China is very different to that in the two partner regions and this has led to difficulties for investors in leveraging their assets. While many observers and partners welcomed the long term 'generational view' of their Chinese investors, others noted that ambitious initial plans for hotels and golf courses had not yet come to fruition. There have been issues with misunderstanding of local legal and regulatory systems, which tend to be extensive and quite specific in the wine sector. Institutional actors in both regions were aware of the importance of providing better support to Chinese investors to avoid such difficulties and training and information sessions have been established for the industry. In general, investors who already had experience in the country prior to investing in wine seem to have had fewer problems with their investments. This highlights the importance of experience and learning to successful operations in very different host contexts.

Another issue which emerges from the study is the need to improve wine distribution and wine appreciation in China in order to effectively exploit these investments. Several investors are actively seeking to educate Chinese consumers and have focused on improved logistics as a key to future market development. These efforts complement their moves to broaden the market beyond the first tier cities in China where sales are currently strongest. However supply chain development is a long term challenge, which requires considerable financial commitment. Some of the Chinese importers who moved into the wine trade at its peak were seen to be more interested in short term, profit maximization. A French consultant described the market at that time as 'anarchic and opportunistic' (Author interview, June 2015). However, he also noted that the fall in trade that has occurred recently has led several market participants to exit and it is now a smaller, but more professionally run sector. Interviewees concurred that the market is more efficient and also more competitive, with the emerging Chinese middle class increasingly sophisticated and cost conscious (Author interviews June 2015; and September 2015).

In terms of future research, the growth of Chinese OFDI in the wine industry is a recent phenomenon and many aspects remain underexplored. This chapter is based on a limited number of interviews in two target regions. The objective was to provide an overview of the key aspects of this emerging trend. More research is required across a wider range of contexts and over a longer period, to determine the potential long term impact of these flows on the global industry and the factors shaping them.

REFERENCES

ABARES, 2012. Economic analysis of import tariffs in the wine markets of China and the Republic of Korea. Research report 12.7. July 2012. Canberra: Australian Bureau of Agricultural and Resource Economics and Sciences (ABARES).

Abellan, A. 2014. Luc Thienpont cède le clos des Quatre Vents et le château Bonneau. Vitisphere. 19 February 2014. Available at: <http://www.vitisphere.com/breve-62860-Medoc-Luc-Thienpont-cede-le-clos-des-Quatre-Vents-et-le-chateau-Bonneau.html> (accessed 11.04.2014).

Anderson, K., Wittwer, G., 2013. Modeling global wine markets to 2018: exchange rates, taste changes, and China's import growth. J. Wine Econ. 8 (2), 131−158.

Anson, J., 2007. The Place de Bordeaux. Wine Business, 2/07 pp. 58−61.

Anson, J., 2012. Peter Kwok: the first Chinese purchaser in Bordeaux, 15 years on... Decanter China 12/12/12. Available at: <https://www.decanterchina.com/en/index.html?article = 316> (accessed 23.01.2014).

The Australian, 2014. Investor visa moves under fire. October 26th Available at: <http://www.theaustralian.com.au/business/latest/investor-visa-moves-under-fire-story-e6frg90f-1227102941685>.

Balestrini, P., Gamble, P., 2006. Country-of-origin effects on Chinese wine consumers. Br. Food J. 108 (5), 396−412.

Beverland, M., 2009. Boundary conditions to business relationships in China: the case of selling wine in China. J. Bus. Ind. Market. 24 (1), 27–34.

Bland, B., 2015. China slowdown belies consumer market health. Financial Times. 26 August. Available at: <http://www.ft.com/intl/cms/s/0/6b876934-4bd3-11e5-9b5d-89a026fda5c9.html#axzz3mk1euzBy>.

Chen, C.-Y., 2014. Investissements Chinois en France. Mythes et Réalités. Editions Pacifica, Paris.

Compadre, C., 2013. Les Chinois aiment le Bordeaux. Sud Ouest 17, 5.12.2013.

Curran, L., 2015. The impact of trade policy on global production networks: the solar panel case. Rev. Int. Polit. Econ.. Available from: http://dx.doi.org/10.1080/09692290.2015.01.1014927.

Curran, L., Thorpe, M., 2015. Chinese FDI in the French and Australian wine industries: liabilities of foreignness and country of origin effects. Front. Bus. Res. China 9 (3), 443–480.

Deloitte, 2008. Administrators Secure Palandri Buyer. Media Release. 21st April, 2008. Perth: Deloitte Australia.

DFAT, 2015. Fact Sheet ChAFTA. Agriculture and Processed Food. Department of Foreign Affairs and Trade, Canberra.

Dyan, B., Testard, H., 2014. Quand la Chine investit en France. Enquete et Portraits. Agence française pour les investissements internationaux, Paris.

Economist (The), 2011. Château Lafake. June 16th 2011.

England, C., 2014. Chinese investor buys majority stake in Coonawarra winery Hollick Wines. 10th April. Available at: <http://www.theaustralian.com.au/news/chinese-investor-buys-majority-stake-in-coonawarra-winery-hollick-wines/story-e6frg6n6-1226880125635>.

FranceAgriMer, 2013. Facteurs de compétitivité sur le marché mondial du vin. FranceAgriMer, Montreuil-sous-Bois.

Gokcekus, O., Finnegan, C., 2013. Did the Great Recession change the regional reputation premium for wine in the US? Wine Econ. Policy 2, 27–32.

Guardian, The (2015). Chinese corruption crackdown, bad harvest leads to Bordeaux wine sales fall. The Guardian, 20 March 2015. Available at: <http://www.theguardian.com/world/2015/mar/20/chinese-corruption-crackdown-bad-harvest-leads-to-bordeaux-wine-sales-fall>.

He, F., Wang, B., 2014. Chinese interests in the global investment regime. China Econ. J. 7 (1), 4–20.

Hu, X., Li, L., Xie, C., Zhou, J., 2008. The effects of country-of-origin on Chinese consumers' wine purchasing behaviour. J. Technol. Manag. China 3 (3), 292–306.

Jenster, P., Cheng, Y., 2008. Dragon wine: developments in the Chinese wine industry. Int. J. Wine Bus. Res. 20 (3), 244–259.

Jordan, R., 2014. China bottle tech checks smash fake wine market. West Aust.April 22.

Kolstad, I., Wiig, A., 2012. What determines Chinese outward FDI? J. World Bus. 47, 26–34.

KPMG, 2013. Demystifying Chinese Investment in Australian Agribusiness, Sydney: KPMG. Available at: <http://www.kpmg.com/au/en/issuesandinsights/articlespublications/china-insights/pages/demystifying-chinese-investment-australian-agribusiness-october-2013.aspx> (accessed 13.12.2013).

Kynge, J. 2013. Business of luxury: anti-corruption drive makes foreign executives take note. Financial Times, June 2nd 2013. Available at: <http://www.ft.com/intl/cms/s/0/6097a3b2-bef0-11e2-87ff-00144feab7de.html#axzz3l8ZJ9eJA>.

Lee, H., Huang, J., Rozelle, S., Sumner, D., 2009. Wine markets in china: assessing the potential with supermarket survey data. J. Wine Econ. 4 (1), 94–113.

Le Roy, L., 2013a. Asie : Liste des propriétés viticoles acquises par des investisseurs asiatiques depuis 1997. Available at: <http://loicle-roy.blogspot.fr/2013_09_22_archive.html> (accessed 4.04.2014).

Le Roy, L., 2013b. Chine: Les raisons pour lesquelles les asiatiques investissent dans les propriétés viticoles en France et à l'étranger. 18 June 2013. Available at: <http://loicle-roy.blogspot.fr/2013/06/chine-les-raisons-pour-lesquelles-les.html> (accessed 23.01.2014).

Letessier, I., 2012. Bright Food prend le contrôle du négociant bordelais Diva, Le Figaro, 22/06/12.

Liu, F., Murphy, J., 2007. A qualitative study of Chinese wine consumption and purchasing. Int. J. Wine Bus. Res. 19 (2), 98−113.

Lockshin, L. (Ed.), 2011. A letter by the Regional Editor for Oceania: China and wine: its impact on the global wine trade. Wine Econ. Policy 3, 1−2.

Lockshin, L., Cohen, E., Zhou, X., 2011. What influences five-star beijing restaurants in making wine lists?. J. Wine Res. 22 (3), 227−243.

Ma, H., 2012. A letter by the Regional Editor for Asia: The current wine production−consumption in China. Wine Econ. Policy 2, 55−56.

Meloni, G., Swinnen, J., 2013. The political economy of european wine regulations. J. Wine Econ. 8 (3), 244−284.

Moore, M., 2013. Fonterra moves to curb China baby milk scandal. The Telegraph. 5/08/13. Available at: <http://www.telegraph.co.uk/finance/newsbysector/retailandconsumer/10222807/Fonterra-moves-to-curb-China-baby-milk-scandal.html> (accessed 12.03.2014).

Mustacich, S., 2014. Chinese corruption probe targets firms that bought bordeaux wineries. Wine Spectator, July 1, 2014. Available at: <http://www.winespectator.com/webfeature/show/id/50186> (accessed 7.07.2014).

Outreville, J.F., Hanni, M., 2013. Multinational firms in the world wine industry: and investigation into the determinants of most favoured locations. J. Wine Res. 24 (2), 128−137.

Pedroletti, B., 2012. Ces Chinois qui achètent le Bordelais. Le Monde. 30th May 2012. Available at: <http://www.lemonde.fr/a-la-une/article/2012/05/30/ces-chinois-qui-achetent-le-bordelais_1709705_3208.html>.

Rabiller, P., 2016. Peter Kwok, le pionnier chinois qui collectionne les vignobles bordelais. Objectif Aquitaine. 4th March 2016. Available at: <http://objectifaquitaine.latribune.fr/business/2016-03-04/peter-kwok-le-pionnier-chinois-qui-collectionne-les-vignobles-bordelais.html#xtor=EREC-32280592-[newsletter_objectif_aquitaine]-20140604> (accessed 21.03.2016).

Sud Ouest, 2014. Les étrangers dans le vignoble : un ancrage historique. Sud Ouest, Mag 116, 15.

Thorpe, M., 2009. The globalisation of the wine industry: new world, old world and China. China Agric. Econ. Rev. 1 (3), 301−313.

Wine Institute, 2015. World per capita wine consumption. Available at: <http://www.wineinstitute.org/files/World_Per_Capita_Wine_Consumption_Revised_Nov_2015.pdf> (accessed 21.03.2016).

Yu, Y., Sun, H., Goodman, S., Chen, S., Ma, H., 2009. Chinese choices: a survey of wine consumers in Beijing. Int. J. Wine Bus. Res. 21 (2), 155−168.

APPENDIX 13.1

Overview of interviews for the research

Institution/company	Date	Means
Australia		
WA Ministry of agriculture	06/12/2013	FtF
Real Estate agent 1	13/12/2013	Phone
Real Estate agent 2	16/12/2013	Phone
Ferngrove Manager	17/12/2013, 26/06/2015	FtF
Chinese investor 1	17/12/2013	Phone
WA Wine Association	18/12/2013	FtF
Grant Farms Group, Director	28/03/2014	Phone
France		
Industry expert 1(academic)	14/01/2014	Phone
Industry expert 2(academic/consultant)	27/01/2014	Phone
Industry expert 3(consultant)	11/02/2014	Phone
Journalist expert Objectif Aquitaine	14/02/2014	Phone
Œnoloque	18/02/2014	Phone
CCI Export director	20/02/2014, 07/09/2015	Phone
CCI President	21/02/2014	Phone
Franco/Chinese œnologue/countier	21/02/2014	FtF
Former CEO of Chinese investment group	27/02/2014	FtF
Diva Manager	06/03/2014	Phone
Journalist 'Sud ouest'	13/03/2014, 21/10/2014	Phone
CEO of vineyard exporting to China	08/04/2014	Phone
Marketing Manager for Grant Crus grouping	10/04/2014	Phone
Consultant supporting wine distribution franchise in China	15/06/2015	Phone

CHAPTER 14

Wine as a Dimension of City Image: Preferences of Chinese Tourists for an Old World Wine Destination

R. Capitello[1], L. Agnoli[2], S. Charters[2] and D. Begalli[1]
[1]University of Verona, Verona, Italy
[2]ESC Dijon/Burgundy School of Business, Dijon, France

INTRODUCTION

This chapter is focused on a specific aspect of the integration of two important components of the wine industry: production and tourism. According to Zhang Qiu et al. (2013), they can be considered at the opposite ends of the industrial spectrum and, for this reason, the effectiveness of wine and tourism marketing also depends on the ability to understand how wine and tourism strategies can converge, in order to propose an integrated offering of experiences, shaping destination identity and image (Carlsen, 2004).

This study intends to analyze the relationships between wine tourism and destination marketing using a different perspective from that most applied by wine tourism researchers (Carlsen and Charters, 2006). The focus is shifted from the ability of the wine industry to generate wine tourism to the ability of an urban destination (an Old World Wine destination belonging to a traditional wine-producing region), to increase its attractiveness by bundling its cultural and entertainment aspects with the wine offering.

In particular, this research aims to understand the role of wine as a perceived component of the image of an urban tourism destination and measure the relevance of wine in shaping the destination image. Although many studies have shown that authentic local wine production is a pivotal component of tourists' experience, including for an urban destination (see, e.g., Lu et al. (2015) for the case of a historic district in China), its actual weight in tourists' choice and satisfaction is still unknown. The increase in awareness of these aspects would be of crucial importance for wineries seeking new opportunities for wine tourism and wine marketing. Many benefits can arouse: the stimulation of business networks to connect the urban destination with the wine-growing area; to channel tourist flows in these areas in patterns that are often decentralized from the main flows, which favour well-known historic cultural urban destinations or places with specific natural or entertaining attractions; the enhancement of 'memorableness' of tourist experience to trigger new business opportunities in wine export markets; obtaining new sources of differentiation and loyalty also for the tourism industry in connecting with the typical offering and the local producers (Carlsen and Boksberger, 2015).

In the light of this, the purpose of this chapter is to analyze the importance of typical wine in shaping tourism attraction of an urban destination, and in particular in an Old World Wine destination given its location in a traditional wine-producing area. The chapter aims to identify the link between wine and the other destination attributes and segment the market in relation to the different tourists' expectations.

Research objectives are met by carrying out a discrete choice experiment (DCE). The scenario is the tourism supply of an Old World Wine destination, Verona (Italy), and the target is the Chinese tourist, an emerging market for many Old World Wine destinations.

Concerning the Old World Wine destination, this case study develops new insights into the branding process of a city strongly linked to a traditional wine-producing region. It also assesses the appeal of local wine in the expectations of Chinese visitor. In this scenario, the interest of the wineries is not only in understanding the salience of the product per se or the wine region, but also their links with the tourism destinations belonging to the same geographical context (in this case study, Verona and the nearby well-known cities, like Venice and Milan for example) (Getz and Brown, 2006). This should favour the ability of wineries to take advantage of relevant tourism flows to create a new interest in the product and the wine region.

As far as demand is concerned, an increase in recognizability and distinctiveness through strategies of place management and marketing is the ambition of many cities in Western countries. They try to attract new tourism flows coming from emerging countries, arising from an increased interest in Western destinations and fuelled by economic and social development. China represents one of the most rewarding targets, given the size of the potential flows, the wish for Westernization and the willingness to pay. According to the World Tourism Organization (UNWTO, 2015), the volume of international travel by the Chinese population is increasing faster than expected: from 41 million tourists in 2007 to 117 million in 2014. According to forecasts of the China National Tourism Administration (Travel China Guide, 2015), the growth rate would have been about 12% in 2015, and more than 300 million Chinese outbound travellers will be reached in next 5 years. Since 2012, China has been the world's top spender in international tourism: in 2014, Chinese tourists spent 165 billion dollars abroad, generating 13% of global tourism receipts (UNWTO, 2015).

Italian statistics on the flow of Chinese tourists to Italy are updated to 2013 and counted about 1.8 million arrivals and 2.8 million overnight stays. The highest growth in overnight stays concerns high-level accommodation facilities. Chinese tourists spend nearly 500 million euros in Italy for tourism services. The Veneto region (where Verona and Venice lie) is the preferred destination for Chinese tourists, attracting 30% of arrivals. Veneto, Lombardy (22%), the region of Milan, and Tuscany (25%), where Florence lies, gather more than 75% of arrivals in Italy. Lazio (with Rome) follows with 8% of arrivals. China is an emerging target also for Verona. Verona is included in Italian tours as a representative city of the country, together with Florence, Rome, Venice and Milan. It has a friendship agreement with Ningbo, a city in the Zhejiang region, in the southeast of China, location of the tormented love of Liang Shanbo and Zhu Yingtai, a kind of Chinese tragedy of Romeo and Juliet. This has increased Chinese tourists' awareness of Verona.

In 2013, Verona registered 789 thousand arrivals and 1.6 million overnight stays. Foreign tourism flow plays a significant role, representing 60% of arrivals and 59% of overnight stays. Chinese visits are still marginal role, with 14,500 arrivals and 20,100 overnight stays in 2013 (Camera di Commercio Verona, 2014).

Verona entered the World Heritage list of UNESCO in 2000; its attractiveness is mainly due to its Old Town and its geographical location in northern Italy, close to Venice and Milan. It also adjoins two reasonably well-known wine-producing regions: Soave (white wine) and Valpolicella (red wine), which have traditionally added to its appeal. Verona is also the location of one of the most important wine exhibitions in the world, Vinitaly. Thus Verona can be considered as a representative destination of the Old World of Wine, given its wine industry in terms of volume and value, typicality and export propensity. China is playing a marginal role in the current wineries' market portfolios, but it is considered as one of the most promising markets.

DESTINATION BRANDING AND WINE TOURISM

The increase in recognizability and distinctiveness, and the subsequent need of a strong destination identity, is the ambition of many places. According to Kalandides (2011), place identity is a dynamic interconnection of the internal views (residents, businesses and decision makers for example) and the external views (tourists, investors, potential residents, public institutions, etc.) of a place. It is an identity-based process: place identity consistently reflects the culture and image of the place, which in turn continuously influence and are influenced by place identity (Kavaratzis and Hatch, 2013).

The literature on destination branding identifies as the primary aim to build a positive image that differentiates the destination by selecting a consistent mix of brand components (Pike, 2009; Zhang Qiu et al., 2013). Impressions of a place derive from cognitive, affective and overall image factors and many other scholars confirmed the role of these factors in influencing destination image (Baloglu and Mangaloglu, 2001; Hosany et al., 2007).

Nowadays, tourists are becoming more and more demanding: besides recreational and cultural activities, they want to live authentic experiences, to understand the customs, traditions and daily life of the host population. Further, in an urban destination they look for well-being and health not only through the environment and the atmosphere of hospitality, but also engaging with local production, particularly typical wine and food (Ritchie and Hudson, 2009). At the same time, wineries are looking for new ways to communicate their link with the territory, especially in foreign markets. The tourism experience is lived not only in a wine region, but also in the local urban destination which becomes equally important for tourists in conveying memorability and stimulating the repurchase of typical products, like wine, in their home countries (Carlsen and Charters, 2006).

This is a complex context in which communication solely of a territorial image is no longer sufficient. Rather, there is a need to manage a complex, distinctive territorial offer (composed of tangible and intangible elements); consequently, urban destinations and wine tourism destinations should collaborate to convey a consistent identity, particularly of an experiential nature, as a synthesis of a coordinated set of attributes. To understand the perceptions and the expectations of the tourist represents a fundamental advantage which can help to coordinate the efforts of the varying internal stakeholders.

An extensive literature analyzes consumer perceptions of the components of city image (Oguztimur and Akturan, 2015). However, some research limitations remain. The studies lack in terms of generalizability of city image dimensions, and statistical validation and reliability, as most use convenience samples. Further, different scales and dimensions were developed, but a set of dimensions common to many cities is still to be identified (Gilboa et al., 2015). Zenker (2011) also highlighted the prevalence of a descriptive-exploratory approach. Focusing on a heritage destination, Lu et al. (2015) emphasized the need for methods able to capture the emotional aspects of a destination image, since the analysis of cognitive aspects still prevails in past studies. Also Ritchie et al. (2011) added that the measurement of tourist's experience and its role in determining consumer utility is a prerequisite for destination branding.

In the light of these comments, this chapter represents an attempt to overcome some of the methodological limitations of past survey methods (through the application of a discrete choice experiment) and of analyzed attributes (through the inclusion of intangible and experiential aspects in the analysis of tourist utility).

THE CASE STUDY. THE IMAGE OF THE CITY OF VERONA AMONG CHINESE TOURISTS: THE ROLE OF WINE

Objectives

This section analyzes perceived city image by capturing the different sources of utility for the tourist, and the study aims to answer the following questions:

1. What awareness and expectations do Chinese visitors have regarding tourism experiences associated with an Old World Wine destination?
2. Can wine represent one of the components of the city image of an Old World Wine destination for the Chinese market?
3. How important is wine in the perception of the city image of an Old World Wine destination for Chinese tourists?
4. Can new opportunities for local wineries arise from the historical, cultural and entertainment attractiveness of the city, which could

contribute to the spread of knowledge of the territory and its wine supply in China?

5. What suggestions can local wineries gain from the segmentation of Chinese tourists according to their preferences?

Thus, the study aims at helping elucidate how Chinese wine consumers feel about well-known but not very famous European wine regions, and how that perceived image may relate to the choice of an urban destination. The segmentation process will also highlight heterogeneity in tourists' preferences in a market usually considered as a unique segment.

As mentioned, this chapter is focused on an Old World Wine tourist destination, Verona (Italy), and Chinese tourists, representing a small but promising target segment for the city.

Method

The Model

Random Utility Models (RUMs) (Train, 2009) were applied to achieve the research aims. Consumer utility is explained by the characteristics of the good (attributes) and their intensity of presence (levels). In this study, the utility concerned the satisfaction obtained by the visitor during a day spent in the tourism destination, while attributes were the main tangible and intangible features of the destination, and levels were the degree of differentiation proposed for each destination feature. RUMs can analyze information collected through 'revealed' choices, directly observed by the researcher, or 'stated' choices, resulting from hypothetical situations proposed by the researcher to the respondent. This study used a DCE to build hypothetical situations and collect stated choices.

Discrete choice models have been successfully applied to tourism economics since the 1990s (Eymann and Ronning, 1997; Wu et al., 2011). Recently, the focus of discrete choice models has shifted from destination marketing to environmental economics to evaluate the interest in the use of the natural resources for recreational purposes and provide public decision makers with environmental policy recommendations (Hearne and Salinas, 2002; Scarpa et al., 2007). Since the mid-2000s, discrete choice models have allowed researchers to segment the tourism market through the application of the latent class analysis (Beharry-Borg and Scarpa, 2010).

The attempt of the present study is to advance in the analysis of the tourism experience, building discrete choice models and segmenting the market taking into account also the intangible characteristics of a destination and the visitor experiences.

Choice Experiment

DCEs were first proposed in literature by Louviere and Woodworth (1983) and represent a more effective tool for analyzing consumers' choices than asking them directly. The choice experiment consists of a finite number of alternatives that make up hypothetical choice situations, called choice sets. Each respondent chooses the preferred alternative for each choice set. In this study, stated choices were collected for alternative tourism packages. A preliminary qualitative exploratory analysis was performed to identify attributes and levels of the experimental design (Capitello et al., 2013). Questions were open-ended and respondents were asked to express their opinions freely about Verona and Italy. The analysis of information highlighted respondents' associations of ideas for Verona and Italy, which were grouped into seven dimensions (Arena and Opera, Romeo and Juliet, Architectural and artistic features, Landscape, Atmosphere, Typical wine and food, People) described by several subdimensions. Starting from the elicited dimensions and subdimensions, the choice experiment was built by choosing the main attributes and their levels. Attribute and level choice also took into the account the need to limit the number of choice sets to avoid respondent fatigue. Five attributes, characterized by different levels, were identified: location, activity, atmosphere, experience and price. Table 14.1 illustrates the levels chosen for each attribute.

Respondents were asked to imagine deciding how to spend a day in Verona, and to choose the preferred tourism package for each of 12 different choice sets composed by four alternatives. An example of one of the four tourism packages proposed in a choice set is: "Enjoy Verona': visit the Arena of Verona, taste typical wine and food, walk on the most elegant streets of the city, for only 212 renminbi".

Data Collection and Sample

A survey by questionnaire was developed. The questionnaire included three sets of questions on tourism attitude, salience of Verona and socio-demographics, and the choice experiment.

Data were collected through an online survey hosted by a panel provider company. The questionnaire was administered online in April 2015 among panel members living in China. A quota of 1300 respondents and

Table 14.1 Attributes and levels of the experimental design

Attribute	Level
Location	Arena, the Roman amphitheatre
	Juliet's balcony
	Squares
	Churches
Activity	Tasting typical wine and food
	Guided tour to a museum or an exhibition
	Shopping card −15% for purchases in the city
	Ticket for a concert or a theatrical event
Atmosphere	Lively
	Quiet
	Elegant
Experience	Escape in Verona (Escapism, according to the four realms of experience by Pine and Gilmore, 1998)
	Verona Beauty (Aesthetics)
	Verona and culture (Education)
	Enjoy Verona (Entertainment)
Price	212, 424, or 636 renminbi (30, 60, or 90 euros)

a screening question, to ensure a basic knowledge of some Italian cities, were set. The final sample consisted of 1261 valid observations.

The main characteristics of the sample are summarized in Table 14.2.

Data Analysis

Discrete choice models were applied to explore utility of attributes and levels composing the hypothesised tourism packages (Train, 2009). The Multinomial Logit Model analyzed the overall utility of Chinese tourists, while the Latent Class Choice Model (Greene and Hensher, 2003; Kamakura and Mazzon, 1991) identified visitor segments based on stated choices. Following the criteria suggested by Scarpa and Thiene (2005), the seven-class solution was judged as the best one to represent the heterogeneity of the collected sample.

RESULTS

Respondents demonstrate a high propensity to travel. They had travelled at least once in the last year. A domestic destination is favored, in line with the trend recorded by national statistics (Table 14.3). Because of the selection method adopted to obtain the sample, including only

Table 14.2 Sociodemographic characteristics of the sample ($n = 1261$)

Characteristic	Level	n	%[a]
Gender	Male	644	51.1
	Female	615	48.8
Age	20 years old or less	42	3.3
	21–30 years old	453	35.9
	31–40 years old	475	37.7
	41–50 years old	232	18.4
	51–60 years old	40	3.2
	61 years old or more	10	0.8
Education	Primary school	2	0.2
	Secondary school	10	0.8
	High school	188	14.9
	University	1,053	83.5
Job	Worker	38	3.0
	Office worker	664	52.7
	Freelancer	176	14.0
	Manager	257	20.4
	Student	58	4.6
	Other	57	4.5
Family income	49,999 yuan[b] or less	88	7.0
	50,000–99,999 yuan	203	16.1
	100,000–149,999 yuan	294	23.3
	150,000–199,999 yuan	258	20.5
	200,000–239,999 yuan	196	15.5
	240,000–299,999 yuan	141	11.2
	300,000 yuan or more	71	5.6
Area of residence	East	497	39.4
	North	237	18.8
	South Central	237	18.8
	North East	82	6.5
	South West	79	6.3
	North West	11	0.9

[a]Given that some missing data have occurred, relative frequencies are calculated on the total sample size ($n = 1261$).
[b]When the survey was administrated, 1 euro was equal to 7.066 yuan.

respondents aware of Italy, Italy is the second preferred destination. The other main countries visited are Asian short-haul destinations.

Leisure is the main reason for travelling (Table 14.4). About 10% of respondents are attracted by the sociocultural aspects of the destination, like knowing the lifestyle of the population, wine and food tasting and attending cultural events.

Table 14.3 Last country visited by the sample

	N	%
China	403	32.0
Italy	187	14.8
Japan	100	7.9
South Korea	78	6.2
Thailand	38	3.0
Russian Federation	36	2.9
Hong Kong	34	2.7
Canada	33	2.6
Taiwan	30	2.4
United States	27	2.1
Germany	24	1.9
Singapore	23	1.8
France	19	1.5
Australia	16	1.3
Malaysia	14	1.1
Macau	13	1.0
Maldives	12	1.0
United Kingdom	12	1.0
Other	162	12.8

Table 14.4 Main motivation for the last travel

	n	%
Leisure	951	75.42
Monuments	51	4.04
Business	51	4.04
To know the lifestyle of the population	49	3.89
Wine and food	43	3.41
Cultural event	35	2.78
Artworks	26	2.06
Show or concert	16	1.27
Other	38	3.01

One-third of the sample had already visited Verona. The interest in the city is confirmed by the fact that 83% of people having never visited Verona stated that they would visit it and only 4% of former visitors had a negative experience with the city and would not recommend it to their friends.

Multinomial logistic models were applied to analyze stated choices of respondents for hypothetical tourism packages for Verona. Econometric estimates have been graphed for clarity (Fig. 14.1). The pie chart illustrates part-worth utilities for the attributes of the design, namely the importance of each attribute in driving the choice of the preferred tourism package by respondents, and the significant coefficients of the levels for each attribute are reported. Activity is the most relevant attribute of choice (42% of the obtained utility) and wine and food tasting results to be the preferred activity (with the coefficient estimate equal to $+0.373$). Conversely, Events (-0.176) and using a Shopping card (-0.222) decrease visitor utility. Price ranks second (20%), but visitors are not strictly price-sensitive, preferring a medium price level. Intangible elements, enclosed in experience and atmosphere, have the same weight as the tangible elements enclosed in the attribute Location in influencing consumer utility. The investigated sample wants to visit the symbols of Verona (Arena and Juliet's balcony in particular), and be entertained in an elegant atmosphere.

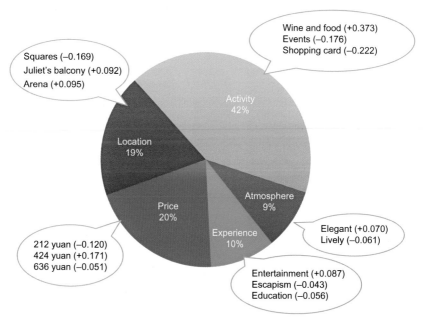

Figure 14.1 MNL part-worth utilities of attributes and coefficients estimated for each attribute level for the overall sample.
Note: Coefficients of significant attribute levels are included in parenthesis ($p < 0.05$) in descending order of importance. The symbols $+$ and $-$ respectively indicate the positive and negative effect on consumer utility.

However, it is important also to consider tourists' heterogeneity, which does not emerge by applying the Multinomial Logistic Model. Therefore Latent Class Models were applied to segment the observed population. Seven Latent Classes (LCs) emerged, representing different tourist profiles.

Part-worth utilities were estimated for each class (Fig. 14.2). A strong choice heterogeneity in the different classes emerges, highlighting different perceptions of the attributes characterising a tourism package. Some classes are price-driven (LC4, LC5 and LC2), other are mainly attracted by the activity to be practiced (LC3 and LC1). Activity is also relevant for other classes, following price in importance (LC2 and LC5). Locations represent the priority for LC6. Finally, the involvement through experience drives the tourist choice of LC7.

The coefficients of the attribute levels were estimated for the seven LCs (Table 14.5). They highlight the strong heterogeneity of preferences among Chinese tourists. The analysis of attributes levels (third column, Table 14.5) illustrates the widespread interest in typical wine and food tasting. Five classes out of seven are attracted by this activity: the levels

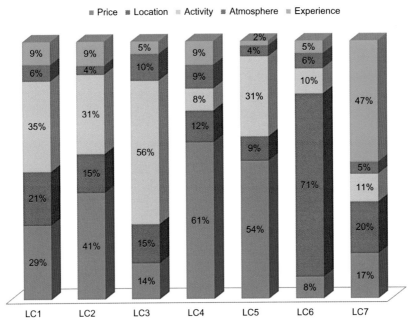

Figure 14.2 Attribute importance for the Latent Classes (part-worth utilities in percentages).

Table 14.5 Attribute and level importance for the seven latent classes

Attributes	Part-worth utilities (%)	Attribute levels*	Characteristics of individuals with the highest belonging probability	Sample share (%)
Latent Class 1: Pragmatic tourists seeking for a cultural experience				
Activity	35	Guided tour (+0.184); **Wine and food (+0.102)**; Shopping card (−0.251)	Younger	52
Price	29	Medium price (+0.196); Low price (−0.163)	Higher expenditure on travel	
Location	21	Arena (+0.181); Churches (−0.068); Juliet's balcony (−0.079)		
Experience	9	Education (+0.053); Escapism (−0.058)		
Atmosphere	6	Elegant (+0.042)		
Latent Class 2: Price-sensitive shopping lovers				
Price	41	Medium price (+0.740); High price (−0.697)	Higher educated	12
Activity	31	Shopping card (+0.541); **Wine and food (+0.367)**; Event (−0.385); Guided tour (−0.523)	Household including few underage people	
Location	15	Churches (+0.168); Squares (−0.356)		
Experience	9	Entertainment (+0.162); Education (−0.163)		
Atmosphere	4	n.s.		
Latent Class 3: Local wine and food lovers				
Activity	56	**Wine and food (+2.211)**; Guided tour (−0.621);	Male	11

Table 14.5 (Continued)

Attributes	Part-worth utilities (%)	Attribute levels*	Characteristics of individuals with the highest belonging probability	Sample share (%)
Location	15	Shopping card (−0.729); Event (−0.861) Arena (+0.284) Churches (+0.240); Squares (−0.563)	Older age Higher income	
Price	14	Medium price (+0.334); Low price (−0.437)	Small family	
Atmosphere	10	Elegant (+0.243); Quiet (+0.089); Lively (−0.333)		
Experience	5	n.s.		

Latent Class 4: Conspicuous tourists

Price	61	High price (+1.288); Medium price (+0.352); Low price (−1.640)	Higher income	9
Location	12	Arena (+0.307); Squares (−0.286)	Lower expenditure on travel	
Activity	9	**Wine and food (+0.168)**; Shopping card (−0.239)		
Atmosphere	9	Elegant (+0.263); Lively (−0.180)		
Experience	9	Aesthetics (+0.193); Education (−0.250)		

Latent Class 5: Price-sensitive tourists interested in local wine and food

Price	54	Low price (+1.285); Medium price (+0.272); High price (−1.557)	Higher educated	9
Activity	31	**Wine and food (+1.003)**; Event (−0.386);		

(Continued)

Table 14.5 (Continued)

Attributes	Part-worth utilities (%)	Attribute levels*	Characteristics of individuals with the highest belonging probability	Sample share (%)
Location	9	Shopping card (−0.636) Squares (−0.318)		
Atmosphere	4	n.s.		
Experience	2	n.s.		

Latent Class 6: Romance-driven tourists

Attributes	Part-worth utilities (%)	Attribute levels*	Characteristics of individuals with the highest belonging probability	Sample share (%)
Location	71	Juliet's balcony (+1.750); Churches (−0.323); Arena (−0.595); Squares (−0.831)	Female	5
Activity	10	n.s.	Younger Higher	
Price	8	n.s.	expenditure on travel	
Atmosphere	6	n.s.		
Experience	5	n.s.		

Latent Class 7: Fun-driven tourists

Attributes	Part-worth utilities (%)	Attribute levels*	Characteristics of individuals with the highest belonging probability	Sample share (%)
Experience	47	Entertainment (+3.984); Escapism (−1.794); Education (−2.023)	–	2
Location	20	Juliet's balcony (+1.412)		
Price	17	Medium price (+1.439); Low price (−0.794)		
Activity	11	n.s.		
Atmosphere	5	n.s.		

* Coefficients of significant attribute levels are included in parenthesis ($p < 0.05$) in descending order of importance. The symbols + and − respectively indicate the positive and negative effect on consumer utility. Low, Medium and High prices stand for 212, 424, and 636 yuan respectively; n.s. = not significant.

are statistically significant and the coefficients are positive (as highlighted in bold). The preference for local wine and food is combined with different components of the destination. This highlights that the value of the wine and food offering should assume different connotations, taking in turn advantage of links with the different destination components, depending on the target.

LC1, called 'Pragmatic tourists seeking for a cultural experience' and representing the largest cluster (52% of respondents), approaches wine via an attitude devoted to a cultural growth: (1) choice is mainly driven by the proposed activities and, in particular, guided tours and wine provide these visitors with the highest utility; (2) visits to historical monuments, such as the Roman amphitheatre, are preferred; (3) an education experience and an elegant atmosphere are required, (4) visitors are willing to pay to meet these needs. This class offers good prospects for tourism in general, and specifically for wine tourism, because it consists of a relative large segment, mainly including young people having high propensity to spend during their holidays.

LC2, 'Price-sensitive shopping lovers', are characterized by a high willingness to pay. This is highlighted by the importance attributed to the variable 'price'. As for LC1, the relationship between utility and price is not linear, and a medium price level provides these consumers with higher utility than the other price levels. A tendency to ostentation, or the consideration of price as a proxy for product quality, may be the causes of this choice. Indeed, this class obtains utility in visiting an urban destination because of the opportunity to go shopping (+0.541) and to taste typical products (+0.367). Visits to churches and an entertainment experience are two other important components of visitor satisfaction. Educated people belonging to households with few young children are more likely to belong to this class. This means that they have to an increased availability of time for their preferred activities.

LC3 is composed of people who are real 'Local wine and food lovers' and represent about one-tenth of respondents. Wine and food drive the visit (+2.211), given that the activity performed in the destination is the main source of utility from a tourism package (56%). They are more likely males, older aged, with higher income and small households. They have clear stated preferences for the other attributes of the tourism package: they prefer to visit historical monuments like the Roman amphitheatre or churches, they love an elegant and quiet atmosphere and they prefer a medium price level, as the previous classes.

LC4 comprises 'Conspicuous tourists', representing 9% of the sample and having a high household income. Price drives their choice and they get utility from upper and middle price levels. The other elements of the tourism package have overall the same weight in the choice and provide this class with satisfaction when they include: visiting historical monuments, intangible elements of elegance and aesthetics and tasting typical wine and food.

LC5, 'Price-sensitive tourists interested in local wine and food', are indeed price-sensitive, and low price is the main driver of choice contrary to LC4. Local food and wine tasting is their favourite activity, while locations and intangible elements do not influence choices. This class has a high education level.

LC6 and LC7 together represent 7% of the sample. They are not interested in local food and wine. They are interested in some specific aspects of tourism activity and especially a particular location of the city (Juliet's balcony). This location has been promoted as the symbol of the city to attract new tourists in recent years. In particular, this attribute is the main element (71% of utility) in influencing choice for LC6 called for this reason 'Romance-driven tourists'. This class is mainly composed of young females having high propensity to spend when travelling. Their interest is likely linked to an intangible aspect of the city, the romance inspired by Shakespeare's tragedy which is enhanced by tour operators with many popular initiatives (letters to Juliet, shows and events, Valentine's Day) and by international movies. These initiatives are also consistent with the needs of LC7 ('Fun-driven tourists'): the interest in Juliet's balcony contributes to achieving their main motivation of choice, namely to live an entertainment experience.

CONCLUSION

This chapter contributes to the understanding of the different components of the image of a city located in a traditional wine-producing region in Chinese tourists' eyes. These components were measured through a DCE that, compared to other studies on city image, allows for the weight of their importance in tourist choice. This study highlights the role of wine for the investigated urban tourism destination and the findings allow for the answer to the five research questions of the study.

Concerning the awareness and expectations of Chinese visitors about tourism experiences associated with an Old World Wine destination, the analysis applied to the overall sample highlighted that, despite expectations, choice is more driven by activities or experiences to be lived in the destination than by the peculiar tourism locations representing the iconographic symbols of the destination (like the Roman amphitheatre or Juliet's balcony for this case study).

This leads to a positive answer to the second research question concerning the ability of wine to represent one of the main components of the city image of an Old World Wine destination for the Chinese market. Chinese tourists are attracted by typical wine and food tasting and they positively associate it with an elegant and fun atmosphere and experience. One-fifth of the utility of a tourism package is given by the price, but the Chinese tourist does not strictly follow the law of demand and is attracted by the medium price level. Price becomes a proxy for the quality of the tourism offering, with positive implications for local wineries. On the one hand, this is generally due to the high willingness to pay of the Chinese consumer who travels, and on the other hand, by the attraction of occidental culture and the ostentation of Chinese consumer (Lin and Wang, 2010; Banks and Overton, 2010).

Concerning the fourth research question, new opportunities may arise for local wineries given the implications of Fig. 14.2 and observing the preferred city characteristics by the average Chinese tourist. The tourism package that could provide them with the highest utility should be composed by wine and food tasting at Juliet's balcony or the Arena at a medium price level in an entertaining experiential context and an elegant atmosphere. Wineries can get benefits from the synergy with these elements, in terms of communication strategies and wine tourism linked to the urban destination and the nearby tourism attraction centres. However, a network of wineries, local institutions and tour operators is required upstream.

The sample segmentation allows also for an answer to the third and fifth research questions. The seven identified classes show high heterogeneity of preferences in conducting the tourist choice. Against this heterogeneity, wine and food are a leitmotiv between segments: five of seven classes (93% of the sample) obtain utility from tasting local wine and food. This leitmotiv should in turn be combined with different components of the tourism offering, giving rise to the possibility of identifying different market trends among Chinese tourists and using a different marketing mix.

The main and interesting trend (represented by LC1) mostly involves young people and connects wine and food with a cultural approach and a self-directed tourism, favoring guided tours or the history represented by the monuments which symbolize the city. In this case, wine is linked to local culture and promotion based on historical elements impacts on customer appeal.

Another trend (mainly represented by LC2), mostly followed by well-educated people belonging to households with few young children, shows a propensity to be fashionable, preferring shopping activities, as well as wine and food tasting at the destination, and reveals high willingness to pay. In this case, wine becomes an element linked to Italian style, a souvenir to take home, to be used there to relive the tourist experience. The trend, driven by 'Local wine and food lovers', mostly followed by older men with high income and small families, places wine and food at the first position of importance in generating satisfaction when choosing a tourism package, and links them to elements of local history and the distinctiveness of the destination in an elegant and quiet atmosphere. In this case, the typicality becomes an element of interest and this can be supported by the links to the culture and history of the urban destination.

Another trend involves conspicuous tourists characterized by the search for an aesthetic experience in the tourism destination, and wine becomes part of this experience. For this segment, wine is a status symbol and can be connected to the attraction of Chinese people to western life styles, as pointed out by many studies in the literature (Li et al., 2011; Somogyi et al., 2011).

Finally, another trend (mainly represented by LC5) is price-sensitive and is mainly linked to a tourism having popular connotations. The resulting segment is able to express positive assessment only for wine, unlike for the other attributes. In this case it is better to consider the class in terms of wine involvement. A suitable wine offering for this trend could be linked to the destination in a simply way, to meet the needs of novice consumers who could be also interested in increasing their knowledge about wine.

Ultimately, this chapter has further demonstrated the need to strengthen ties between the wine and tourism industries to better meet expectations of an emerging market both for wine and tourism businesses and leverage preference heterogeneity.

REFERENCES

Baloglu, S., Mangaloglu, M., 2001. Tourism destination images of Turkey, Egypt, Greece, and Italy as perceived by US-based tour operators and travel agents. Tour. Manag. 22 (1), 1–9.

Banks, G., Overton, J., 2010. Old World, New World, Third World? Reconceptualising the Worlds of Wine. J. Wine Res. 21 (1), 57−75.

Beharry-Borg, N., Scarpa, R., 2010. Valuing quality changes in Caribbean coastal waters for heterogeneous beach visitors. Ecol. Econ. 69 (5), 1124−1139.

Camera di Commercio Verona, 2014. *Rapporto sul turismo nella provincia di Verona*. Available at: <http://www.vr.camcom.it/page.jsp?id_menu = 8405&show = view&tipo_content = GENERICO&label_content = Rapporto + sul + turismo + nella + provincia + di + Verona + -Ed. + 2014> (accessed 30.09.2015).

Capitello, R., Agnoli, L., Begalli, D., 2013. A new approach to the analysis of visitor perceptions towards a tourism destination: the role of food and wine experiences. Sci. Pap. Ser. Manag. Econ. Eng. Agric. Rural Dev. 13 (1), 57−64.

Carlsen, J., 2004. A review of global wine tourism research. J. Wine Res. 15 (1), 5−13.

Carlsen, J., Charters, S., 2006. Global Wine Tourism: Research, Management and Marketing. CABI, London, UK.

Carlsen, J., Boksberger, P., 2015. Enhancing consumer value in wine tourism. J. Hosp. Tour. Res. 39 (1), 132−144.

Eymann, A., Ronning, G., 1997. Microeconometric models of tourists' destination choice. Reg. Sci. Urban Econ. 27, 735−761.

Getz, D., Brown, G., 2006. Critical success factors for wine tourism regions: a demand analysis. Tour. Manag. 27 (1), 146−158.

Gilboa, S., Jaffe, E.D., Vianelli, D., Pastore, A., Herstein, R., 2015. A summated rating scale for measuring city image. Cities 44 (April), 50−59.

Greene, W.H., Hensher, D.A., 2003. A latent class model for discrete choice analysis: contrasts with mixed logit. Transp. Res. Part B Methodol. 37 (8), 681−698.

Hearne, R.R., Salinas, Z.M., 2002. The use of choice experiments in the analysis of tourist preferences for ecotourism development in Costa Rica'. J. Environ. Manag. 65 (2), 153−163.

Hosany, S., Ekinci, Y., Uysal, M., 2007. Destination image and destination personality. Int. J. Cul. Tour. Hosp. Res. 1 (1), 62−81.

Kalandides, A., 2011. The problem with spatial identity: revisiting the "sense of place". J. Place Manag. Dev. 4 (1), 28−39.

Kamakura, W.A., Mazzon, J.A., 1991. Value segmentation: a model for the measurement of values and value systems. J. Consum. Res. 18 (2), 208−218.

Kavaratzis, M., Hatch, M.J., 2013. The dynamics of place brands: an identity-based approach to place branding theory. Market. Theory 13 (1), 69−86.

Li, J.G., Jia, J.R., Taylor, D., Bruwer, J., Li, E., 2011. The wine drinking behaviour of young adults: an exploratory study in China. Br. Food J. 113 (10), 1305−1317.

Lin, X., Wang, C.L., 2010. The heterogeneity of Chinese consumer values: a dual structure explanation. Cross Cult. Manag. Int. J. 17 (3), 244−256.

Louviere, J.J., Woodworth, G., 1983. Design and analysis of simulated consumer choice or allocation experiments: an approach based on aggregate data. J. Market. Res. 20 (4), 350−367.

Lu, L., Chi, C.G., Liu, Y., 2015. Authenticity, involvement, and image: evaluating tourist experiences at historic districts. Tour. Manag. 50 (October), 85−96.

Oguztimur, S., Akturan, U., 2015. Synthesis of City Branding Literature (1988−2014) as a Research Domain. Int. J. Tour. Res.. Available in Early View. [accessed 28.09.2015).

Pike, S., 2009. Destination brand positions of a competitive set of near-home destinations. Tour. Manag. 30 (6), 857−866.

Pine, B.J., Gilmore, J.H., 1998. Welcome to the experience economy. Harvard Bus. Rev. 76 (July-August), 97−105.

Ritchie, J.R.B., Hudson, S., 2009. Understanding and meeting the challenges of consumer/tourist experience research. Int. J. Tour. Res. 11 (2), 111–126.

Ritchie, J.R.B., Wing Sun Tung, V., Ritchie, R.J.B., 2011. Tourism experience management research: emergence, evolution and future directions. Int. J. Contemp. Hosp. Manag. 23 (4), 419–438.

Scarpa, R., Thiene, M., 2005. Destination choice models for rock climbing in the Northeastern Alps: a latent-class approach based on intensity of preferences. Land Econ. 81 (3), 426–444.

Scarpa, R., Thiene, M., Tempesta, T., 2007. Latent class count models of total visitation demand: days out hiking in the eastern Alps. Environ. Resour. Econ. 38 (4), 447–460.

Somogyi, S., Li, E., Johnson, T., Bruwer, J., Bastian, S., 2011. The underlying motivations of Chinese wine consumer behaviour. Asia Pac. J. Market. Logistics 23 (4), 473–485.

Train, K., 2009. *Discrete Choice Methods with Simulation*. Cambridge University Press, Cambridge, UK.

Travel China Guide, 2015. China Outbound Tourism in 2015. Available at: <http://www.travelchinaguide.com/tourism/2015statistics/outbound.htm> (accessed 10.09.2015).

UNWTO, 2015. *UNWTO Tourism Highlights*, 2015 Edition. Available at: <http://www.e-unwto.org/doi/pdf/10.18111/9789284416899> (accessed 20.09.2015).

Wu, L., Zhang, J., Fujiwara, A., 2011. Representing tourist's heterogeneous choices of destination and travel party with an integrated latent class and nested logit model. Tour. Manag. 32, 1407–1413.

Zenker, S., 2011. How to catch a city? The concept and measurement of place brands. J. Place Manag. Dev. 4 (1), 40–52.

Zhang Qiu, H., Yuan, J., Haobin Ye, B., Hung, K., 2013. Wine tourism phenomena in China: an emerging market. Int. J. Contemp. Hosp. Manag. 25 (7), 1115–1134.

PART V

Final Reflections

CHAPTER 15

Practice Viewpoint: The Chinese Way

B. Mazzinghi

Journalist and consultant, Shanghai, China

INTRODUCTION

China's wine market development is going to transform the global framework for the wine industry. Some companies started to invest in the country 10−20 years ago with considerable results; some others are still waiting "to better understand the situation", maybe in vain. It is not easy to comprehend China, also because sometimes there is simply no explanation. The *Chinese way* is an attempt-and-adjustment succession, action and reaction. It is flexibility, improvization, inexperience and speed. In China everything is new, and this is true for the wine sector in particular. Wine is not a part of the Chinese diet and the first experiment with it by consumers is always for business or for fashion reasons. In these last few years, after the 2012 Government policies to reduce corruption, expensive banquets and gifts to politicians, we have often heard that the market is undergoing normalization: premium imported wines sales are no more boosted by government-related expenses and the China wine market is more 'real', which means that consumers choose and buy what they like and what they can afford. However, it is difficult to define the 'Chinese consumer': the more developed Shanghai, Beijing and Guangzhou markets (not considering Hong Kong) are a completely different world to inner China, where most people have never heard about wine.

Is it better for a winery to invest in the mature but already saturated cities, or start to penetrate the still-not-ready but promising deep China? All the importers have different strategies, with the best one maybe lying in between; but just a few can afford it. Everyone is therefore trying to create his own way and contrive alternative and new solutions.

Whoever decides to approach the Chinese market has to be aware of the difficult context, but also of the huge possibilities: The Chinese are drinkers, the local middle class is growing fast, and Shanghai− Beijing−Guangzhou can drive the market. Moreover, if the leadership one day decides that the people have to start to drink wine (maybe to support the local producers), they would start to drink wine.

In this chapter, I will tell my story with a 100% Chinese wine importer, light years away from the model of companies in the same business but with a foreign management. It is a personal, and therefore limited, experience; however, after dozens of business trips all around the country and some books on my bookcase, I can guarantee that many realities in this country are similar to my experience and Chinese companies organized along Western lines are still the exception.

It was not easy: I worked with a Chinese importer for more than two years before leaving for a more structured and international company. To work in a different cultural context is challenging but it is necessary to try to understand the reasons behind choices, in order not to leave the table and go back home with nothing to show for the time, and only to come back a few months later because the Chinese hope is too tempting.

THE OLD SYSTEM

Personal Experience(s) with a Chinese Wine Importer

"Even our leaders sometimes don't know the effects of their decisions, how could I know or plan everything in advance?" my boss once replied, after our umpteenth discussion about the 'first think and plan, than act' strategy versus the 'first act, than keep on acting on the basis of the results and consequences'. He is a typical Chinese leader, one from the 'old-school'. We discussed this approach to strategy for more than two years, with me trying to understand what appeared as unreasonable decisions and him trying to link each choice to Chinese history, tradition or eminent examples of modern local businessmen. The point is that China has a saying (and justification) for everything and its opposite.

'True meaning cannot be defined by words, it can only be perceived by intuition' (*zhike yihui buke yanchuan*) is a popular saying that effectively explains a lot of intuitional and instinct-driven Chinese behaviour, or the importance they give to the first impression (so that appearance and attire become, for example, fundamental). However, at the same time, it is widely believed that 'just time reveals a person's heart' (*rijiujian renxin*): personal instinct has to be trusted, but always with prudence, suspicion, and an appropriate sense of distance between each person. Then there was another example, used by a colleague: 'The shot hits the bird that pokes its head out' (*qiang da chu tou niao)*; but there is also: 'Who strikes first prevails' (*xian xiashou wei qiang)*. China is contradiction, ambivalence; China is a continuous experiment.

It is fundamental, as in any cultural context different to our own, but perhaps especially so in China, to have a basic knowledge of how the workplace culture functions so as not to be completely disoriented by otherwise incomprehensible behaviour. I joined the Chinese importing company in April 2013. We imported and distributed premium Italian wines. My title was brand manager but my task was also to bring an 'Italian touch' and wine knowledge in a very traditional Chinese team. Or, at least, this is what E.M., the general manager, had told me. A lot of friends, in China for years, tried to discourage me from working with a local company. Asked about the reason, they replied that I would quickly under-stand and just suggested to always remember to clarify everything. In a few days I not only realized that no one in the company had a basic knowledge of wine, but also that I seemed to know much more about finance than the Finance Department or about human resources than our HR manager. Everything seemed to be so approximate. 'It is normal,' E.M. reacted. 'In China everything is new and your colleagues have to learn too. You are the first foreigner: The HR manager doesn't know anything about your contract.' I asked a lawyer friend to help me with my *laowai* (foreigner) contract, I found myself insurance (and of course, a home), I opened a Chinese bank account, I fought for 6 months to finally see my rights written on paper: even if everything had previously been agreed with E.M. there was always an obstruction or something that appeared impossible to change. Their systems were not set up to deal with a foreigner.

Over time, I understood that even the boss was reluctant to interfere with the specific work of one department. Companies in China are strictly divided into different departments: marketing, finance, logistics, sales, HR, on the model of the communist party units of the 1960s. Each manager (the unit section head) has complete power in his unit and responds directly to the boss, who draws up the guidelines then gives freedom and autonomy to the loyal subordinates.

Every department acts as a closed community: there is no communi-cation between units and all the tasks and duties are rigidly fixed. New projects are discussed weekly during a meeting and specific responsibilities divided. Each chore has its own *fuze ren*, a 'responsible person'. If there is a new issue during the week, a meeting is necessary to decide who will be responsible for what; this contrasted with my professional experience where a single person, with spontaneous individual initiative, could have dealt with the issue in half the time of the meeting. Each worker is part of the department more than the company itself. The boss would not complain to department managers if something in the company failed because no one takes the initiative to solve even a banal and simple problem which is not clearly under his/her responsibility.

After a few months in the company, I had the unhappy idea of proposing to organize, myself, a trip to Italy for some guests, in order not to involve a tour operator and cut some expenses; this was naïve. When I asked the (really nice, not ironic) finance girl to pay for some hotel and flights, she kindly replied that I was to use my credit card and then apply for reimbursement. 'I cannot use my credit card for 20 guests because I do not have enough money and it is not legal,', I replied. 'Ah, *zenmeban?*', So, what can we do?, she asked me. In her conception, trying to find a solution was a personal favour to me, not her duty. She was not responsible for the trip. Now I know that I should have fixed a meeting with the boss and all the departments and clarified all the roles, from payment to visa or marketing promotion. At the time I made the assumption that everyone would take up their responsibilities. However, within the business the person authorized to think and make decisions within the Marketing department was the Marketing Manager, A., who had to solve everything without involving or informing E.M. When the latter was updated, he tolerated huge mistakes and treated the employees like the members of a family, as if they children who have to guarantee complete loyalty, extreme admiration and self-denial in return for this tolerance.

The Marketing department seemed to be a little bit more structured and skilled than other parts of the company. The results were not perfect but at least the six women working there had the goodwill to try their best. On my first day in the office, A. sent me hundreds of documents and pictures of wineries and wines, inviting me to check and eventually change what I wanted. In two days I completely rewrote some technical sheets and realized that all the material they had used in the past year was, by my standards, unpresentable.

I clearly remember the astonished faces of the marketing team when I said that I would need at least 3 days to prepare a pair of presentations for the weekend event. '3 hours?' they asked in English. 'No, *san tian*, 3 days,' I confirmed. The day before the dinner I gave the speeches to the marketing girl, responsible for my translation. My Chinese was not so good at the time but I could understand that she wasn't translating my version but simply repeating the original one, with the pairing of a red wine with a seafood pizza, strange aromas smelled in the glass and the suggestion of decanting a simple wine 4 hours before drinking.

I went out of my mind. 'The Chinese market does not need a high professional level; they do not know anything about wine' — the marketing manager tried to calm me down, worsening the situation — 'Do not worry: no one can understand English in here and no one noticed the differences'.

The days that followed were a continuous compromise between my standards and theirs, attention to details versus extreme speed and the *chabuduo* notion ('almost', 'more or less'). E.M. seemed to tolerate all the mistakes of his beloved children. Problems and errors are the norm in China. Working is dealing with problems. The Chinese throw themselves headlong into everything, run and do before planning, and when some obstacles arrive, try to find a way to elude them. The Western approach is usually more pondered and we normally think first, to avoid problems later. It is a huge difference.

During one of our discussions, E.M. drew a set of scales on paper; he wrote professionalism on one plate and sales on the other, the one which was up. The message was clear: most of the resources should go to marketing and sales. 'The Chinese market' became a mantra to reply to all my doubts and observations. Sometimes they were right: we cannot for example introduce a wine to China in the same way as we would in a mature market, but we must find stories, anecdotes, underline prizes and impress the public. But I did not tolerate the extreme *huyou*, the art of fudging, considered here an appreciated talent. The Chinese would say anything to gratify the clients and sell their products. 'You always have to act and say what the other wants to hear,' was another of E.M.'s mottos.

Every three months all the sales managers and the best salespeople came to Shanghai for the great meeting, three days of reports and analysis but most of all for team building practices and motivational speeches. Shouts, hugs, slogans, toasts and melodramas were carefully planned in advance by the boss, who had in these days to confirm himself as a leader and as the ingenious and magnanimous father of the family. He prepared himself for more than one week, rehearsing the speeches for several days shut in his office and writing down schemes and stories to be projected on the wall to communicate the importance of unity, loyalty to the leader, sacrifice and hard-work. As for the Chinese company, it was held together by the leader's proclamations, the cautious ability to choose what to communicate and what not to say on the company evolution and the promises of a bright future, and as for the Chinese employees, my colleagues believed in more or less everything the good leader was telling them.

The meetings were organized in a huge room in the upper floor of the building, with a long black table. From each department members took the lift all together, entered the room in teams and sat in line. Every single speech could last hours. The first day was all enthusiasm and energy, on the second and third the hangover of the night before was clearly visible on all their faces. Chinese people drink to demonstrate that they can drink a lot. 'How many bottles can you drink?' is a standard question in the sector and one of the most important in my interview. Their strength is based on the *ganbei* (ability to drink a full glass) they are able to have during the dinner, no matter if they exit the restaurant inebriated. It is expected. Countless times my boss told me, wrecked but proud, that he could not come to the office or to an important meeting because the night before he was drunk.

Distribution Channels

We used to organize two wine dinners per week all around the country, just for a single brand, without receiving a cent from the winery. My role was to speak about the wines and Italian wine in general. Sometimes I had to shout over the loud voices of the guests, not accustomed to listening in silence to someone speaking on stage. Each event was different, depending on the city: from a professional wine dinner in a 5 star hotel in Shanghai to something like a teen party in some other places in second or third tier cities, with everyone drunk in 10 minutes. The imperative was to impress: 'These people go to a lot of events,' A. told me, 'but they have to remember ours as the best one.' They also had to be impressed by the *beautiful ladies* of the team, and A. considered an attractive face and an elegant dress much more important than a good wine introduction. The strategy of my company was to invest a lot in events and create wonderful locations, especially in inner China, taking advantage of the 'unexplored land' in terms of wine and trying to establish before others a solid guanxi network, necessary to do business in this country.

Guanxi, personal relations and connections, are determinant in China, much more that the real quality of the work you can offer (I have been told this many times). If you have a friend in the wine business, you are obligated to buy wine from him, even if it is not the best on the market. The first concern of the leaders (and the workers too) is to create a strong network, and the more important the people you know, the more important (and powerful) you are. My boss was always on the plane travelling to have dinners with *friends* around the country.

It is mainly for this (fundamental) reason that foreign companies have a lot of difficulties reaching internal areas. It is necessary to find good local partners to penetrate the market. Guanxi also means corruption. The new president Xi Jinping announced in 2012 a fierce repression, but it is easy to understand that a country centred on corruption remains hard to access.

Our company divided the country into 11 big regions and the main task of the 11 area sales managers was to develop and establish strong *guanxi*. Thanks to this network sales would come. The key is to enter important closed circles, to become the reference person for the wine business in the zone. A good sales manager is a good friend of the local politicians and businessmen.

We did not sell to hotels and supermarkets, the latter a really remunerative option for companies that have the possibility of entering the market. We worked just with distributors, more than 300 all around the country, mainly in Jiangsu, Zhejiang and Guangdong provinces; helping the bigger ones to open exclusive Wine Clubs with all our wines in the spotlight. They became our partner on the ground, sometimes exclusive, and the club our representative office in the area. These kinds of clubs, also wine shops, have a fundamental role in the sector development in the second and third level cities: If the owner starts to love wine they may soon become the centre of the local wine lovers' community. The majority of distributors simply do not care about wine itself, but others turn themselves into the wine apostle of the city and start to organize educational activities and tastings.

Unfortunately, most of our partners were *just* businessmen, more passionate about money and profit than wine. They had four or five other companies in totally different businesses, from pharmaceuticals to oil, food and fashion, construction or raw materials. Most of them became rich thanks to their relationship (or their parents' relationship) with the local government. Our managers had to get close to these factotums and convince them to invest also in wine as a means to expand their circle.

During my trips, I always had to visit them and spend the afternoons drinking tea (never wine) in their clubs. Some clubs were magnificent and modern wine residences with cellars; others reminded me of something like an old bohemian coffee house full of wood and smoke. After dinner, the men often used to go back to their club, drinking whisky, eating seeds and enjoying their best Cuban cigars. My boss and the sales manager had to join in to show their respect for the distributor, who, in return, had to offer the best in the house and dedicate time to the guests until late, even if everyone was dreaming of nothing but bed. I, as a woman, had the right to go back to my room a few minutes after the event. The first few times I went with them in the hope of opening some of the wonderful wines I had seen in the afternoon, but I soon realized that no one was interested in the pleasure of a great wine and, when they had the opportunity, they went back to their tea or whisky.

A couple of years ago, especially in the less developed cities, the company's main clients were people related to government. Now their clients are principally private businesses, KTV, shops and local supermarkets. Some of them were of course hard-hit by the new measures and were forced to close. Others realized that the profit in wine is low compared to other more traditional and remunerative sectors. Except in Shanghai, Beijing and Guangzhou there is very little passion, just an interest in profit. As a consequence, there is no stability since that 'real market' is simply nonexistent.

Wineries on Trip

The funniest part of the job came along with the wineries' representatives. I was working with Chinese businesses all the year and I became used to some habits. The representatives from overseas wineries were not. The more my colleagues tried to honour the overseas guest, the less they succeeded. There was always someone with the guest, from the pick up at the airport to the departure; sometimes the visitor told me they had to pretend to go back to their room and then exit the hotel again furtively, just to enjoy some free time to visit and experience the city: I too had experience that going around alone or taking a beer unaccompanied is not in the Chinese conception.

When a winery representative came to visit the office, they were often invited to drink tea for hours with the boss, with interminable silences. E.M. and the other partners were in this way demonstrating their respect to them, while the representatives felt that they were wasting their time in a faraway country. The same with our distributors. We tried to avoid organizing dinners in the most *typical* cities but sometimes we had to gratify a particularly generous distributor. Ganbei after ganbei, the clients were rapidly drunk and the dinner became a sort of circus: tomatoes in a precious wine glass, open shirt, sweaty hugs and victory pictures with the distinguished visitor.

If there were some problems, the Chinese partners tried to avoid an open dialogue but eventually they were obliged to sit at the table and talk. The wineries always had a list of issues (payment delays, unfulfilled promises, and general misunderstandings). The marketing manager and E.M. always started with half an hour of flattery, followed by justifications and reassurances. With their kindness and good manners, they maintained the situation right on the edge, a hair's breadth before breaking point. They seemed to know perfectly how much they could dare: if they perceived they could still move the limit a little bit forward and obtain more, they continued to ask, without any sort of restraint. The negotiator needs to know when and how to say no or relaunch. Analyzing the different approach of the different wineries, I learned the importance of times and ways during negotiation with Chinese business people. Those who were able to be polite but authoritative, humble but firm, to show respect for the local partner but at the same time pride for their own history, prevailed in the talks. On the contrary, if the Chinese business man perceives that the other side is not totally sure of themselves and their strategy, often changes their mind, sometimes uses inopportune language and, even if without intention, says or does something that damages their *mianzi* (face, reputation), he will start to consider the partner a weak man, and his respect will gradually fade. He will delay and delay, never interrupting the partnership or giving clear signals but simply setting it aside.

For wineries, it is important to gain the Chinese partner's trust. The winery has to approach China with humility and determination at the same time. A brand manager based in China can better understand this subtle protocol and avoid fatal errors. Furthermore, they can often visit the partner and establish day after day the essential bond of trust and mutual respect.

SYSTEM REORGANIZATION

Importers

I am not surprised that in these last two years many wine importers and distributors have closed. Even if one of the Chinese skills is the capability to react to unexpected changes, some basic structures were too weak to resist the strong and sometimes unappreciated market alteration. It was not just small or medium importers like mine which had problems; the big giants also were strongly hit by the measures. Just to give some examples, the biggest importer had to consistently reduce teams and expenses; another survived, just, thanks to investment by an international supermarket; other formerly important players are still in serious difficulty. From the big players, with an infinite portfolio, to the smaller ones with just five to ten employees, everybody had to totally change strategy and try to find the best way to react to the cuts in significant revenue.

The change in the market means that just a few private individuals/ companies with a passion for wine can buy expensive super-premium wine; the majority of people, will prefer low priced products. Furthermore, every region of China has a different speed of development and the sector is not in the same condition in the whole country.

My previous importer added some new cheap labels to its portfolio which was formerly premium only. For some important wines, they are still taking advantage of the past strong promotion in all the regions; for others, they are having difficulties. They persist in their choice not to invest too much in the biggest cities, where a few powerful importers control most of the on-trade market: these latter can offer considerable discounts and incentives, such as the assurance of booking many rooms for the hotels or giving prizes to the waiters who sell more of a specific wine in restaurants. Some of them not only sell wine, but also promise glasses, training for staff, events or educational activities and other equipment.

To compete with these big players, others have to find their particular path, such as products with a super convenient balance of quality and price or specializing the offer in a very specific area. Some of them are also investing in education (which boosts some private sales), with more and more WSET schools and courses emerging everywhere. The winery has to carefully analyze the best solution on the basis of its own nature. A lot of owners are, for example, unsatisfied with big importers, with a wide portfolio and less attention on the single brand. Some of them may benefit more from cooperation with new and dynamic companies, with lots of energy and fresh investments. There are indeed still people who hope to find the 'once in a lifetime' opportunity and rely on unclear figures, who may place one, perhaps two significant orders, make many promises and disappear a few weeks later.

E-commerce is growing fast, with 16 million online wine buyers in 2014, almost half of the drinking population. Ninety per cent of these sales were of bottles priced below RMB100. Neither the big players nor the new startups ignore the fact that the future of the market is here.

Educators

The first tasting is usually at nine in the morning. After the compulsory post on WeChat with the picture of the sleepy face or the promising bottles, they start looking, smelling, drinking and writing. Then, they move quickly to another place, another event. In the main cities in China there maybe a tasting at every hour and the new wine connoisseur runs all around the city not to lose a single occasion to practice with new products. For some young specialists, wine is the most important part of their life (a friend of mine left her boyfriend, a well-known Shanghai wine expert, because 'all his life was nothing but wine'). They constantly study, taste and travel, always posting pictures on WeChat to promote themselves or their schools. Some of them are really professional, but no more than 20–30 in the whole country I would estimate; the majority are low-medium level, sufficient to be considered an expert in Mainland China.

People are crazy about blind tastings and more and more restaurants satisfy their desires at least once a week. Sometimes it is a challenge with themselves, sometimes a competition between teams with complex rules, points and schemes. The main one in the city is organized from 5 to 7 pm, so there is still time for dinner, often a themed competition, in which each participant has to bring a bottle from a specific area or a selected grape.

The aim is to practice, since most of them are studying to get the WSET Diploma, become a Master of Wine or Master Sommelier, and at the same time reinforce the personal circle of influence. When they are well recognized in the business, they start to work as educators or journalists, with more and more loyal disciples. Each student chooses his mentor, his supreme *laoshi* (to be followed with the same devotion the Chinese pay to the leader authority); each expert cultivates his personal student groups with dinners, special lessons and immediate replies, on the dedicated WeChat group, to any doubts they may have on the argument.

The best foreign journalists are idolized and, at least in this field, their supremacy and prestige, based on long experience, is well recognized. Jancis Robinson, Bertrand Boutschy, Ian d'Agata, Robert Parker, Debra

Meiburg and Jeannie Cho Lee are some of the most admired and sought-after for tastings and lessons. Others are starting to explore this market, trying to understand the best way to impose their name.

The different wine regions of the world are investing a lot in promotion and education (with some shortsighted exceptions) and compete to gain the favour of the most followed journalists and sommeliers, with the latter envying the former who have more time to travel the world. The competent ones are still not many and they can actually influence a considerable portion of the market. The main thing is to choose the right ones.

In education, WSET at the moment does not have any rivals and it is the undisputed leader of the market. Its quite schematic teaching process perfectly matches with the Chinese learning mechanisms, offering tasting notes like the following.

Herbaceous — green pepper — high acidity — medium body — medium alcohol → Sauvignon Blanc

Medium ruby colour — sour red cherries — tea leaves — high acidity — high tannins — medium body → Sangiovese

When I travel with passionate wine tasters, they always open the laptop and write notes on the WSET standards based form, rarely (perhaps never?) enjoying a bottle of wine just for pure pleasure.

Consumers

In 2014 China became the world's largest consumer of red wine. According to the French IWSR research centre, in 2013, China (including Hong Kong) consumed about 1.865 billion bottles of red wine, the greatest number in the world. Official data indicates nearly 35 million real (but not regular) consumers of imported wine out of a total population of 1.357 billion people. However, the market is still at an early stage. The number of Chinese *regular* consumers of wine is less than 1% of the total population. The possibilities are immense.

After the anticorruption drive of the previous two years, 2015 was considered an intermediate recovery year. According to China Customs, in the first half of the year imported wine increased by 41.65% for bulk wines (to 46,321,417 L, more than half of which arrived in the Shandong province) and 7.65% for bottled (142,762,210 L), with average price-per-litre reduced by 5% to 4.59 USD. For bulk wine Chile is the unchallenged leader; France still accounts for 40% of the total of bottled wine. Nearly

60% of the imported bottled wine goes to Guangdong and Shanghai and this maybe explains how important it is to be, at this stage, present and powerful in those markets. The remaining 40% is concentrated in the coastal cities.

In the first tier cities more and more young people are starting to enjoy wine. The most requested bottles in 2014 had a final price between 45 and 125 RMB and the trend that benefits wines under 200RMB will continue in 2015. Of course the countries which take advantage of this situation are the ones with low importation taxes, such as Australia, South Africa and in particular Chile. France (and partially Italy) was heavily affected by the decrease in premium and super-premium consumption.

Usually the typical Chinese consumer is a beginner drinker, who prefers fruity and round wines, with a powerful aroma, soft tannins and low acidity. In some cases, it is better if the wine is not too alcoholic to allow the demonstration of a greater drinking capacity. Red accounts for about 90% of the total consumption (50−60% in mature markets); the market for sparkling grew 60% in 2014 but decreased by 14.09% in the first half of 2015, with the Italian Prosecco leading the market and Shanghai accounting for more than half of the total sparkling market share.

Supermarkets have an important role in direct sales to consumers, with cheap wines chosen for gifts or easy dinners at home with friends. E-commerce sales are growing and the main operators are investing a lot to find innovative and dynamic ways to reach the consumers. Some small French importers in Shanghai guarantee 30 minutes delivery to the door after an online purchase. Tmall.com, JD.com and also Amazon are fiercely competing to control the market through mobile phone access to online purchasing.

China will remain a developing market for a long time and it is essential to build up a strong, competent and dependable marketing department, taking into consideration that young consumers are just beginners, constantly connected on WeChat and highly inclined to be influenced by external intermediaries. Chinese people are travelling more and come back with a better knowledge of wine. With time, their palates will change and also wines that are not appreciated now will have their possibilities.

CONCLUSION: OPERATING IN THE CHINESE MARKET

What is the future of imported wine in China? Which partner should be selected in order to succeed in this difficult market?

A first suggestion would be to hire someone who can easily respond to these questions, with a deep knowledge of the market: three or four visits per year are not sufficient to have a significant return but may, on the contrary, generate a misleading idea of the country. After that, it is important to be clear that the period of great and easy opportunities is finished and now there is only one way to be successful in a short period of time — find a good partner and invest together.

The first step (it seems banal but it is not necessarily obvious to every producer) is to carefully analyze the winery and its expectations and possibilities. Do I need my wines in hotels or I am a small/medium quality producer so that a massive exposure with low money return is not necessary? Do I want to sell the most that I can now, or are other markets going well so that I can afford a slower process to have some benefits in three or four years? How many bottles do I produce? What styles and which quality level? Do I have a strong reputation in a more developed country and can I take the liberty of waiting for the natural development of the market? Do I want my wines (and my work) to be understood or just sold? What kind of person am I and philosophy do I have?

This last question may seem a little naive but it is fundamental to choose the right partner, in a country that, simplifying, is not Germany or the USA or New Zealand. It is the same when you open a fund and the banker starts to ask you questions to evaluate your risk tolerance.

With a clear picture of who I am and what I want, I can go to look for an intermediary, a Chinese person with international experience or a foreigner with a strong knowledge of China and the Chinese language. S/he will help me to understand the market, the new trends and to establish essential trust with my future partner. After some meetings with major players, I can have an idea of the ones more suitable for my strategy in China. At this point another important question has to be answered: why should they add my wines to their portfolio? Something similar to: why do Chinese consumers have to drink my wine in a world with millions of labels?

If I can reply to these questions and the wines are good, characterful, or at least with an honest price, there are some possibilities of being accepted and I can start to plan with my new partner. A good solution can be to share half each the cost of promotional events, or at least support the importer in some other ways. In any case, from this moment a lot of the success of the wines depends on marketing and promotion. The local partner will suggest the best channels and, in the meantime, the brand manager resident in China can organize some tastings in clubs with local experts, promote the products in some restaurants, and, of course, work with the importer and act as a reliable but physically present partner. With a solid partnership, based on trust, mutual respect and willingness to cooperate it is now possible to have long lasting results.

But it is fundamental to know the context. Too many people are losing their money because they trust cheats who pretend to be renowned China experts while they cannot speak a word of Chinese. Always be suspicious when the solution seems too easy. It no longer is.

Obviously, institutions have a fundamental role in the success of national wines and the countries with the best results are the ones with more government support.

To summarize, China needs time, money and dedication, but it is worth the effort now. Some wineries may decide to wait for the market to mature but with time the sector will become bigger, more difficult to manage, and the opinion leaders more expensive. For the moment it is still quite small and open. Wineries that have some money to invest, or just good sense, shouldn't wait any longer.

CHAPTER 16

Development Process, Current Status and Future Trends of Chinese Grape and Wine Industry

Y. Fang, H. Yang and X. Zhang
Northwest A&F University, Yangling, China

INTRODUCTION

The grape and wine industry is a traditional and universal industry in the world today. However, this industry is still emerging in China. The wine industry was included in the First Five-Year Plan upon the founding of the People's Republic of China (namely the 'new' China). Over the years, policy makers at the national level have put forward developmental goals for the production of alcoholic products. It has been targeted that wine production should move from high alcoholic volume to low alcoholic volume, from distilled to fermented drinks, from grain based to fruit based, and from low-quality to high quality. Furthermore, in 2002, the former State Economy and Trade Commission proposed to prioritize the production of grape wine and fruit wine, followed by yellow rice wine and beer, and at the same time to curtail the production of traditional liquor and spirit (*baijiu*). China has spared no effort in guiding its nongrain wine production to a much more extensive scale. Based on the facts gathered from the development of China's wine industry, this chapter analyzes the development process, current status and future trends of the Chinese grape and wine industry.

THE DEVELOPMENT PROCESS OF CHINESE WINE INDUSTRY

Viticulture and the production of wine boast thousands of years' history in China. For example, in the Tang Dynasty (AD 618—AD 907), the popularity of wine-drinking stimulated famous verses such as *from cups of jade glows the wine of grapes at night.* However, following the industrial revolution in the world, wine production in modern China lagged substantially behind the world's more advanced level of quality and productivity. There have been several ups and downs in the development of wine production in the new China. In the past 30 years, wine production standards systems and management regulations have experienced three major changes in China. The promulgation and implementation of each new standard played an enormous role in motivating wine industry development at each stage.

The first stage marked the development from no standard to half-juice wine production. There were only five wineries before the founding of the new China in 1949, and wine production nationwide had only reached merely 200 tonnes. Nonetheless, the wine industry was listed as one of the core industries to be developed in China's First Five-Year Plan. Ever since the 1980s, the Chinese wine market has experienced a period of rapid development. Until then, there were still no unified standards in terms of wine production with each manufacturer implementing its own operation standard. In 1984, the former Ministry of Light Industry created the QB921-84 Standard: 'Wine and Its Experimental Method', marking China's first wine production standard. The implementation of this standard put an end to the history of China's wine production operated with no industry controls. China's wine production began to normalize and experienced a rapid development. Wine production skyrocketed from 16 kilo tonnes in 1984 to 30.80 kilo tonnes in 1988. However, due to the low requirements of this Standard, which were far below the international wine production expectations, its power to regulate the industry faded with time. Many profit-oriented business operators seized the opportunity and entered the market with low-quality wine and even 'forged wine' (i.e., wine made of artificial flavour, saccharin, and alcohol which were then blended with water). The practice not only ruined the reputation of the wine industry but also corroded the trust of consumers on domestic wine. The industry suffered a great loss as a result. Wine production dropped from 24.20 kilo tonnes in 1991 to 18 kilo tonnes in 1994.

The second stage, from 1994 to June 30, 2004, featured the coexistence of full-juice wine and half-juice wine. In 1994, based on the QB921-84 issued by the former Ministry of Light Industry, three standards concerning wine products were promulgated. These three standards were the National Standard GB/T15037-1994 'Wine', the Industry

Standard QB/T1980-1994 'Half-juice Wine', and the Standard QB/T1982-1994 'Wild Grape Wine'. In the meantime, the previous Wine Standard QB921-84 'Wine and Its Experimental Method' was rescinded. GB/T15037-1994 was a National Standard, with definitions of wine products and requirements which were consistent with international standards. However, this was a recommended rather than a mandatory requirement. The international standards stipulate that wine must be made from pure grape juice through fermentation of the juice.

Half-juice wine products existed in China during that period of time. Half-juice wine was a product that emerged under specific circumstances during the early developmental stage of China's wine industry. The issuance of such a standard as the Industry Standard QB/T1980-1994 'Half-juice Wine' gave opportunities for the emergence of forged wine blended with chemical substances. This occurred particularly in the late 1990s, when China's wine industry moved into a new era of rapid development, with mass production and forged wine in such regions as Tonghua, Jilin Province and Minquan and Henan Province, creating huge negative effects for the whole industry. On March 17 2003, the former State Economy and Trade Commission announced the repeal of the Industry Standard QB/T1980-1994 'Half-juice Wine', setting the deadline for the end of all half-juice wine production to be on June 30 2004. Starting from July 11 2004, half-juice wine disappeared completely from the market, marking the new 'full-juice' era of wine production in China. Meanwhile, the relevant state departments worked diligently to develop new wine production standards in order to solve problems such as the low requirements of the 1994-version standards and disagreements or even contradictions existing between different standards.

In the third stage, which occurred from July 2004 to the present, the Chinese wine industry has been transitioning from pursuing quantity to enhancing quality. Ever since the end of half-juice wine, the Chinese government has been reinforcing the revisions and formulations of relevant standards and regulations. As a result, the development of the Chinese wine industry has secured standardization and switched the production focus on to quality. A great leap took place when wine production changed from 367 million litres of half-juice and dry wine in 2004 to 498 million litres of full-juice wine in 2005. The capacity of the Chinese wine market kept on expanding and consumer demands grew constantly as well. The wine market environment and the organization of competition were gradually regulated. In 2012, China's wine production amounted to 1.382 billion litres and was ranked fifth in the world. However, between the years of 2013 and 2015, both wine production and wine consumption in China decreased, to a great extent attributing to the government's efforts to crackdown on corruption which led to the reduced government consumption using public funds. Nevertheless, the Chinese government has been undertaking great efforts in order to rationalize consumption and to improve the quality of domestic wine and enhance its competitiveness in the global market.

CURRENT STATUS OF CHINESE GRAPE AND WINE INDUSTRY

Varieties of 'vinifera' and Planting Conditions

After nearly three decades of rapid development, China's wine industry has made significant progress. The total grape-growing area specifically functioning as vineyards reached 214,000 ha in 2014 (Table 16.1). Meanwhile, the production of Chinese vinifera has acquired the characteristics of development by regions, production using grape wine, and focusing on quality breeding of the vines.

Ten major wine-producing regions (i.e., geographic segments) in China have been fully formed. These ten regions are (1) Changli Region (including Changli, Lulong, Funing and Qinglong Counties in Hebei Province), (2) Shacheng Region (including Xuanhua, Zhuolu, Huailai Counties in Hebei Province), (3) Tianjin Region (including Jixian County and Hangu District in Tianjin), (4) East Helan Mountain Region in Ningxia (including the cities of Yinchuan, Qingtongxia, Shizuishan and the Hongsibao District in Ningxia), (5) Shandong Peninsula Region (including the cities of Yantai, Pingdu, Penglai and Longkou in Shandong Province), (6) the Yellow River Old Course Region (including Lankao and Minquan Counties in Henan Province, Xiaoxian County in Anhui Province and the Northern Jiangsu Province), (7) Yunnan Region (including Mile, Mengzi, Dongchuan and Chenggong Counties in Yunnan Province), (8) Hexi Corridor Region (including Wuwei, Minqin, Gulang and Zhangye Counties in Gansu Province), (9) Northeast Region (including the foothills of Changbai Mountain and Northeast Plain) and (10) Xinjiang Region (including Shanshan in the Turpan Basin, Manasi Plain, Shihezi Region and Yanqi Basin). The climate and soil conditions vary greatly between these 10 regions and the terroir differs substantially from one region to the other.

Table 16.1 shows the varietal product of the major vinifera varieties planted in China. The cultivation of red grape varieties covers

Table 16.1 Variety structure of major Vinifera planted in China (2014)

Grape varieties		Planting area (000 hectares)	Regional distribution	Production (kilo tonnes)
Red	Cabernet Sauvignon	82	Major wine regions such as Hebei, Xinjiang, Ningxia, Shandong, Gansu, Yunnan	733
	Cabernet Gernischt	17	Mainly distributed in Shandong, Hebei; with few planting in Beijing, Tianjin and Henan	146
	Cabernet Franc	13	Cultivated in Hebei, Shandong, Gansu	107
	Merlot	23	Major wine regions such as Shandong, Hebei, Xinjiang, Shanxi, Ningxia and Gansu	192
	Pinot Noir	9	Mainly distributed in Gansu, Ningxia, Shandong, Xinjiang, Yunnan, some distributed in Heibei, Shanxi, Neimeng	73
	Shiraz/Syrah	7	Planted mainly in Shandong, Xinjiang, Ningxia	61
White Grape	Chardonnay	22	Major wine regions such as Heibei, Xinjiang, Ningxia, Shandong, Gansu and Yunnan	181
	Riesling	10	Mainly distributed in Heibei, Shandong, Xinjiang, Tianjin, Gansu	82
	Italian Riesling	3	Mainly distributed in Tianjin, Shandong and Yellow River old course	22
	Sauvignon Blanc	2	Cultivated in Shandong, Hebei, Beijing	15
	Muscat Hamburg	3	Mainly distributed in Tianjin, Shandong and Yellow River old course	23
	Ugni Blanc	20	Mainly distributed in Heibei, Shandong, Tianjin, Gansu and Shaanxi	15

Note: Grape varieties with less than 1000 ha of acreage are not included.

151,000 ha, accounting for 71% of the total acreage, while the remaining 60,000 ha (i.e., 28%) go to the plantation of white grape varieties. The total grape production has reached 1650 kilo tonnes, of which 79.5% are red grape varieties, amounting to 1312 kilo tonnes, and 20.5% are white grape varieties with a production volume of 338 kilo tonnes. According to this current variety structure, Cabernet Sauvignon still dominates the list as the primary vinifera (wine grape) planted in China, occupying nearly half (38.3% and 82,000 ha) of the total vinifera acreage. The 733 kilo tonnes production of Cabernet Sauvignon captures 44% of the total wine production in China. The next primary red grape variety is Merlot, with an acreage of 23,000 ha, which occupies 10.7% of the total vinifera planting area. Together these two grape varieties, namely Cabernet Sauvignon and Merlot, account for nearly 70% of the red grape planting area. Other red grape varieties of which the acreage exceeds one thousand hectares include Cabernet Gernischt[1] (17,000 ha), Cabernet Franc (13,000 ha), Pinot Noir (9000 ha) and Shiraz/Syrah (7000 ha). The total planting area of other red grape varieties (such as Marselan, Yan 73, Gamay, Zinfandel, Malbec and Carignan) falls below two thousand hectares. In addition, these varieties have very limited number of plants, most of which are of Eurasia origins.

When it comes to the white grape varieties, Chardonnay captures the leading position. The planting of this grape variety covered 22,000 ha in 2014, which accounted for 10.3% of the total vinifera acreage and 36.7% of the white grape variety planting area in China. The second position goes to Riesling, with 10,000 ha acreage and 16.7% of the total white grape variety planting area. Taken together, Chardonnay and Riesling boast 53% of total acreage of the white grape variety. Other white grape varieties that are cultivated by more than 1000 ha include Italian Riesling (3000 ha), Sauvignon Blanc (2000 ha), Muscat Hamburg (3000 ha) and Ugni Blanc (2000 ha). The total growing area of other white grape varieties (such as Chenin Blanc, Semillon, Gewurztraminer, Pinot Blanc and Pinot Gris) covers less than 1000 ha. Again, these varieties have very limited number of plants, most of which are still of Eurasia origins.

The rather narrow scope of cultivation of grape varieties in China has caused the issue of homogenization of wine production and potentially hindered the diversified development of wine products. Wine produced by every wine region tends to be the same and therefore loses its regional

---

[1] Known as Carmenere in the rest of the world.

characteristics and traits. Consequently, the quality and style of wine made in China reveals no exciting variations. This issue will not only severely obstruct the development and progress of China's wine industry, but also seriously challenge the competence and reputation of Chinese wine in the international market.

China's Wine Production and Wine Consumption

Wine Production in China

Since the year 2000, the production of wine industry in China has continued to increase with an average growth rate of 17.7% (see Table 16.2). In 2012, wine production in China reached its highest point with an unprecedented volume number of 1.382 billion litres, rising by 19.45% compared to the previous year. In 2013, however, wine production in China was at 1.178 billion litres, declining by 14.76%. In 2014, wine production in China reached 1.161 billion litres, decreasing by 1.44%. In 2015, wine production reached 1.11 billion litres. Although the figure indicated a decline from the previous year, the whole industry maintains its stability in terms of operation and production. It is forecasted that the wine industry in China will restore its ever-accelerating growth pattern in 2016.

Table 16.2 China's wine production and growth rate between 2000 and 2015

Year	Annual production: billion litres	Growth rate (%)
2000	0.202	− 19.24
2001	0.251	24.26
2002	0.288	14.74
2003	0.343	19.10
2004	0.367	7.00
2005	0.498	35.70
2006	0.495	− 0.60
2007	0.665	34.34
2008	0.698	4.96
2009	0.960	37.54
2010	1.089	13.44
2011	1.157	6.24
2012	1.382	19.45
2013	1.178	− 14.76
2014	1.161	− 1.44
2015	1.110	− 4.39

Table 16.3 Wine production and growth rate by provinces in 2014

Province	Annual cumulative production (10,000,000 litres)	Annual growth rate (%)
Total	116.10	2.11
Beijing	0.70	− 15.85
Tianjin	2.02	− 3.55
Hebei	6.67	2.50
Shaanxi	0.63	61.66
Neimenggu	0.66	74.34
Liaoning	4.00	3.94
Jilin	16.55	− 13.27
Heilongjiang	3.82	− 22.29
Shanghai	0.03	− 48.61
Jiangsu	NA	NA
Anhui	NA	NA
Fujian	0.01	− 68.69
Jiangxi	0.85	52.21
Shandong	39.23	− 2.40
Henan	16.78	21.00
Hubei	0.16	2.88
Hunan	0.89	19.84
Guangxi	0.26	11.21
Sichuan	0.12	40.17
Guizhou	NA	NA
Yunnan	2.45	12.81
Shaanxi	5.41	30.96
Gansu	7.34	6.79
Ningxia	2.02	18.83
Xinjiang	5.43	20.13

Major wine-producing provinces and/or regions such as Beijing, Tianjin, Shandong, Jilin and Heilongjiang experienced decline in their wine production whereas Jiangxi, Shaanxi, Gansu, Ningxia and Xinjiang displayed exceptional upsurge of wine production (see Table 16.3). Evidently, wine production in China has steadily shifted from the traditional wine-producing regions such as Shandong Peninsular to the emerging regions (e.g., Shaanxi) and the western regions (e.g., Gansu, Ningxia and Xinjiang).

Wine Consumption in China

According to a report released by the China Net of Commerce Intelligence (www.askci.com), China's per capita wine consumption grew markedly from 0.25 L in 2002 to 1.31 L in 2012. However, new policies approved by the 18th National Congress of the Communist Party, such as 'Controlling the three types of public expenses (chauffeured vehicles, overseas trips, and official receptions)', 'Eight Prohibitions' and 'Prohibition of Alcoholic Drinking in Military', severely impacted the business consumption of high-end wine by government officials. The accelerating trend of high-end wine consumption was therefore disrupted. The Liv-ex50 red wine index, which indicates the trend of the global high-end wine market, has recently rebounded after hitting the bottom. China is forming a more rational and mature consumption pattern of wine featuring a combination of government consumption on more reasonably-priced wines, personal consumption and business consumption.

The major wine markets are Beijing, Shanghai, Hangzhou, Guangzhou, Shenzhen and other coastal cities in southeastern China. However, these markets are increasingly getting saturated and very little market expansion opportunities can be uncovered. It is anticipated that second- and third-tier cities as well as Midwestern cities will become the major markets for domestic wine consumption in China in the near future.

Wine-Producing Companies

China's wine-growing regions are mostly located within the wine-growing "golden zone" spreading from 38 to 53 degrees latitude north. From east to west, the regions tend to go lower and lower on the latitude. By the end of 2014, the number of wine-producing companies of national scale (with annual sales revenue over 20 million yuan) reached 217. There are also small scale wineries, bottle filling factories, companies under construction and enterprises without production certificate. Taken together, the total number of wine production-related companies is estimated to be nearly 800 in China. Table 16.4 indicates that wine-producing companies mainly operate in Eastern China, which contributes 62.2% of the total wine sales within the country. Northeast China and Central China provided 15.1% and 12.5% of the total wine sales, respectively. The total wine sales in South and Northwest China are relatively small.

Table 16.4 Key economic indicators of wine industry in 2014

Region	Number of companies	Product sales (thousand billion yuan)	Growth rate (%)	Total profit (hundred million yuan)	Growth rate (%)	Geographic segment
Total	217	420.57	3.91	43.87	0.16	
Beijing	4	2.04	3.17	− 0.15	− 51.41	Eastern
Tianjin	3	4.48	− 3.30	− 1.02	56.64	Eastern
Heibei	17	10.26	− 2.37	0.18	− 72.48	Eastern
Shanxi	4	3.04	3.77	0.44	− 7.70	Central
Neimenggu	4	7.16	19.66	0.60	− 22.41	Central
Liaoning	18	16.37	− 25.87	1.77	− 15.34	Northeast
Jilin	24	44.43	9.12	2.83	5.35	Northeast
Heilongjiang	1	2.70	19.12	0.21	11.15	Northeast
Shanghai	1	0.20	− 47.98	0.02	512.18	South
Jiangsu	1	0.21	− 25.96	0.03	− 16.45	South
Anhui	4	0.68	45.94	0.77	362.21	South
Fujian	1	0.14	− 73.20	0.00	− 30.20	South
Jiangxi	1	3.94	48.74	0.20	96.55	Central
Shandong	56	244.78	0.11	30.29	− 5.11	Eastern
Henan	23	23.69	9.92	3.11	7.77	Central
Hubei	6	4.59	11.19	0.30	62.60	Central
Hunan	3	2.28	62.42	0.27	39.55	Central
Guangdong	1	0.35	······	0.00	······	South
Guangxi	2	0.49	0.63	0.02	− 1280.69	South
Chongqing	1	2.52	65.92	0.10	90.04	Northwest
Sichuan	2	0.55	18.23	0.07	− 38.21	Northwest
Yunnan	4	8.30	9.20	0.21	− 54.38	South
Shaanxi	3	7.88	45.17	0.73	109.99	Central
Gansu	7	3.63	− 24.11	− 0.25	− 320.33	Northwest
Ningxia	7	4.27	20.35	0.34	− 8.85	Northwest
Xinjiang	20	16.60	57.83	2.83	204.43	Northwest

The Imported Wine Market
Status of the Imported Wine
In 2014, the amount of imported wine in China reached 383 million litres, increasing by 1.59% compared to 2013. The sales value reached 1.517 billion US dollars, declining by 2.51% from the previous year. The top ten wine exporting countries to China in 2014 were France, Australia, Chile, Spain, Italy, the US, New Zealand, South Africa, Germany and Argentina. France has firmly kept the status of being the largest source of wine imports to China, by both volume and value. The volume and value of French imported wine both accounted for nearly 40% of the total figures (see Table 16.5). The average price of the imported wines in 2014 was 3.96 US dollars per litre, declining by 4.1% from last year. From January to November 2015, the total volume of imported bottled wine surpassed 346 million litres, rising by 37.17% compared with that of last year. The total value exceeded 1.6 billion US dollars, marking an increase by 22.18%. The average price of the imported wine was 4.9 US dollars per litre, dropping by 10.77% over the same period of the previous year. In general, the total volume and value of imported bottled wine rose slightly while the average price declined to some extent.

Domestic Market Distribution of Imported Wine
Considered by the trading area of the imported bottled wine, the value of imports in Guangdong Province surpassed that of Shanghai. However, the volume of imports in Guangdong was slightly beneath that of Shanghai. Guangdong and Shanghai have kept their status as the major trading areas of imported bottled wine in China, accounting for nearly 60% of the total volume and value. Table 16.6 illustrates the domestic market distribution of imported wine. Most trading provinces and cities of imported bottled wine are primarily located in the coastal areas.

FUTURE TRENDS OF CHINESE GRAPE AND WINE INDUSTRY

Since the beginning of this century, the grape and wine industry in China has generally been demonstrating a positive and healthy development trend. The pattern is mainly manifested in three aspects:

Firstly, China is gradually enhancing its voice and gaining a say in today's global wine industry and wine market. Statistics have ascertained that China became a superpower of wine in 2014. During that year, the

Table 16.5 Sources of imported bottled wine from January to November 2015

Country	Imported volume (L)	Imported value (US$)	Average price (US$/L)	Volume year-on-year (%)	Value year-on-year (%)	Average price year-on-year (%)	Market share (%)
France	148,083,325	761,759,303	5.14	32.74	37.41	3.52	45.80
Australia	50,253,107	390,790,796	7.78	58.02	77.20	12.14	23.50
Chile	43,299,845	151,378,435	3.50	39.33	33.58	− 4.13	9.10
Spain	48,151,153	98,696,447	2.05	54.16	13.14	− 26.61	5.90
Italy	20,383,876	74,881,504	3.67	23.11	2.80	− 16.49	4.50
US	9,040,756	45,938,913	5.08	− 21.22	− 22.72	− 1.90	2.80
South Africa	8,551,947	36,746,279	4.30	88.47	94.08	2.97	2.20
Argentina	4,574,934	18,396,842	4.02	23.08	18.40	− 3.81	1.10
New Zealand	1,593,426	16,400,521	10.29	− 4.53	− 16.64	− 12.69	1.00
Germany	3,528,439	15,712,577	4.45	6.00	− 9.66	− 14.77	0.90
Portugal	5,087,814	14,052,025	2.76	54.49	12.50	− 27.18	0.80
Canada	1,108,087	9,130,207	8.24	27.64	1.13	− 20.77	0.50
Georgia	1,161,261	5,248,170	4.52	67.45	37.90	− 17.65	0.30
Moldova	1,754,773	4,934,609	2.81	71.63	31.36	− 23.46	0.30

Table 16.6 Top 10 trading areas of imported bottled wine from January to June in 2015

Ranking	Province/City	Volume (L)	Value (Dollar)
1	Guangdong	38,401,294	269,232,717
2	Shanghai	43,628,133	175,797,906
3	Beijing	8,418,613	38,160,877
4	Zhejiang	12,247,734	37,518,886
5	Fujian	12,945,145	32,201,457
6	Shandong	7,222,974	24,027,970
7	Tianjin	6,470,142	23,980,725
8	Jiangsu	5,843,899	19,199,611
9	Liaoning	1,288,183	7,020,319
10	Sichuan	1,135,166	5,268,502

nation was ranked as the second largest grape-growing country in the world, the 8th largest wine-producing country (6th in 2012), the 5th largest wine consuming country and the 6th largest wine importing country. The traditional classification of the world's wine-producing regions may need a revisit.

Secondly, major wine-producing regions in China have been gradually shifting from the east to the west. Wine-producing regions in Western China and emerging wine-producing regions featuring unique characteristics of wine made in China have demonstrated immense developmental potential. How to capitalize on the momentum and regulate the rapid growth have presented new challenges to the government and all other stakeholders involved.

Thirdly, the government's efforts to reduce corruption are expected to expand in the next one to three years. The market for luxury and high-end wine will diminish enormously whereas the market for low and medium-priced wine are seizing the dominant role. Imported wine of low- and medium-price is considered to have better value-for-money compared to domestic wine. Such a wine, featuring enhanced value-for-money is favoured by consumers and will definitely capture more market share in the short term. Both the marketing techniques and the distribution channels (i.e., wholesalers, distributors, direct sales and E-commerce) of wine products have undergone innovative changes. Integration of online and offline wine sales has gradually secured more popularity.

CHAPTER 17

Conclusion

R. Capitello[1], S. Charters[2], J. Yuan[3] and D. Menival[2]
[1]University of Verona, Verona, Italy
[2]ESC Dijon/Burgundy School of Business, Dijon, France
[3]Texas Tech University, Lubbock, TX, United States

As editors, the most evident conclusion which we would like to write for this book is that it has been able to consolidate the understanding of the Chinese wine market; our hope is that readers have received such insights and stimuli that they start new projects, whether academic or practitioners, to analyse and seize the new research and professional opportunities in this country.

The chapters in this book have focused on providing both the evolution of the Chinese wine market and several snapshots of different individual aspects suggesting that in many cases knowledge is still at the beginning and deserves further investigations. This would mean not only to further explore China's wine industry, but also reflect on how the world wine industry is evolving.

The world wine market can be seen as a mosaic that, both on the demand and supply side, is composed of a multiplicity of tiles whose boundaries are not just of a geographical nature. China is a part of this overall mosaic and is in turn itself becoming a mosaic of diversities and opportunities, characterized by novelty, originality and strong impact on other 'tiles'. The chapters here have contributed to underlining (recalling the Introduction to this book) that the Chinese wine market should not be necessarily be viewed in the eyes of Western expectations and the 'otherness' of China can be simply considered as a new tile of world wine industry's mosaic which is becoming increasingly rich in content, nuances, models and interpretations.

The key points that this book has explored, albeit in some cases only partially (and therefore calling for further investigations), are: the changing link between public choices, social practices and individual attitudes; the wave of Millennials; the rise of interest in wine knowledge; the regionalization of the Chinese market; relationships in the supply chain; the driving force of e-commerce and social media; the potential of domestic wine production; Chinese movement into the wider world as tourists or as investors.

Thus, in the book and in this final analysis, findings and unexplored issues permeate each other, as managerial implications are clearly connected with academic implications; some contributions have an exploratory nature or stem from direct professional experiences. In the same way, considerations on demand and supply are closely interrelated.

THE CHANGING LINK BETWEEN PUBLIC CHOICES, SOCIAL PRACTICES AND INDIVIDUAL ATTITUDES

From the demand side, one of the most relevant points in the Chinese wine market is the link between public choices, social practices and individual attitudes and how these have contributed to market development during the recent years. The grape wine industry has benefited from the support of national strategies since the second half of the 1980s aimed at improving food security and safety, public health and the consistency of the wine standards with international ones, as confirmed by Fang et al. and Zeng and Szolnoki. Moreover, according to Genand, China's accession to the WTO in 2001 began the process of convergence with the international standards of law. Regulation of the market, trade agreements and technical innovation have accelerated the development of the wine market in China, the competitive power of domestic wine production with imported wines (Fang et al.), and product variety and accessibility for the consumer. Further, the recent efforts promoted by the Chinese government to make the country a global e-commerce leader are positively impacting on the Chinese wine market (Genand). Meanwhile Mazzinghi showed the importance of social dynamics and the role of leader in influencing individual choice from a practical viewpoint. Against this background, the presidential anti-corruption campaign and the subsequent mood against ostentation are acting as a disruptive factor (Bouzdine-Chameeva et al.; Seidemann et al.; Zeng and Szolnoki), although this may in turn stimulate growth in other ways as Fang et al. note.

According to Seidemann et al., the Chinese wine market is facing a 'changing Chinese consumer sentiment'. This is demonstrated through much evidence throughout the book. Sales in on-trade channels fell (Zeng and Szolnoki) and many wine importers and distributors have closed during the recent years (Mazzinghi). The role of wine, the typologies of consumers involved with wine and the associated meanings ascribed to the product are changing; meanwhile the thirst for knowledge is increasing (Fountain and Zhu; Liu and McCarthy; Mazzinghi; Menival and Han; Seidemann et al.).

Before the anticorruption measures, wine was mainly seen as a status symbol or a way to embrace Western culture. According to Wine Intelligence (2016)[1], wine consumption is no longer driven by the 'government wealth' but by the 'private wealth'. Income growth makes quality wine accessible also to the middle class and it is perceived as a way to express lifestyles and education choices, multiple interests, professional achievements and life aspirations (Liu and McCarty). On the supply side according to Seidemann et al., business practices are also changing; the cultural emphasis on *guanxi* may be decreasing due to regulatory procedures and western influences. 'The Chinese consumers' dilemma is: How to maintain face without using the established instruments? And how to be frugal while being ostentatious?' (Seidemann et al.). Thus, new marketing approaches are suggested: new product lines and sub-brands, sober brands and new packaging styles, combination between local styles and global trends, development of consumer's knowledge and experience (Seidemann et al.).

Wine consumption is no longer only a social practice, which raises individual or professional reputation and authority in relationships with other people, but also an individual behaviour to express in one's own private context, in which product knowledge, evaluation of intrinsic characteristics and experience are new behavioural attitudes (Fountain and Zhu; Liu and McCarthy; Menival and Han).

Future research should focus on analyzing the consumer in the sphere of individual choice, aiming to answer questions such as: What are the social and psychological antecedents of behaviour in the Chinese wine consumer? What is the relevance of social pressure and individual attitudes towards the product? How are social practices changing and impacting on consumption? Are these changes resulting in short-term trends or in an evolution in the long-term?

THE WAVE OF MILLENNIALS

Young people form a wave which is influencing the wine supply chain from different viewpoints.

---

[1] http://www.wineintelligence.com/from-ganbei-to-gamay/ [Accessed 2 Aug. 2016].

Most Chinese belonging to the upper-middle class are young, under 40, open to Western practices, and love fine wines for private consumption (Seidemann et al.). Fountain and Zhu found that the perceptions of young people are different from those expressed by elder cohorts of the population in previous studies. They are developing a new relationship with the product: they seek wine experiences in different and external contexts (such as tourism or education courses) rather than those within the family; they feel ambivalent about the 'weight' of the traditional view of red wine as a status symbol (even if they may aspire to this for their future) or as beneficial for their health; they want to enjoy wine, promote new trends in the private sphere or with friends, explore new wines and match them with food. Young women express their own wine perceptions. They are prone to use the Internet to seek information, use social media and buy wine online.[2]

Future research should therefore focus on analysing how businesses could develop their marketing mix to reach this market target. Experiments with external validity should be preferred to yet more exploratory studies and convenience samples mostly used by researchers so far. Future research questions could be: What are Chinese Millennials' attitudes toward wine? How can brands engage with them? How does wine education influence involvement with products and brands in new consumers? How does social media impact on their product satisfaction, brand engagement and consumer loyalty? How does electronic word of mouth impact on these relationships?

THE RISE OF INTEREST IN WINE KNOWLEDGE

The educational organisation, the Wine & Spirit Education Trust (WSET)[3] recently reported an increase of overall candidates worldwide (up 17% to 72,171) in the last year. Mainland China accounts for 12.5% of WSET candidates; they were up 38%, the biggest national increase for the WSET. The rise of interest in wine education demonstrates the dynamic nature of the Chinese wine industry. This aspect has not been

[2] https://jingdaily.com/chinas-millennials-up-their-wine-consumption-as-they-buy-more-online/ [Accessed 2 Aug. 2016]

[3] https://www.wsetglobal.com/news-events/news/2016/august/02/demand-for-wset-qualifications-continues-to-accelerate/ [Accessed 3 Aug. 2016]

directly developed by the book, however many contributions highlighted that as individual attitudes develop, there is a greater interest in wine education; in China wine educators and foreign journalists are idolized (Fountain and Zhu; Mazzinghi; Seidemann et al.; Zeng and Szolnoki).

Future research should explore the role of objective and subjective knowledge in the Chinese market. According to Mazzinghi, the consumer seems to be mainly driven by a thirst for objective knowledge and the wish to become an expert and reduce purchase risk, rather than to be subjectively involved and experience the product from an affective point of view. The study of proposed types of wine education, educators and learning models could help to understand the future developments that this market will experience. It should also contribute to understanding the role of wineries and their associations in wine education; information asymmetry between producers, intermediaries and consumers is one of the main constraints in the development of some products and territorial brands in China (Loureiro and Cunha).

REGIONALIZATION OF THE CHINESE MARKET

Some contributions (Mazzinghi; Menival and Han; Zeng and Szolnoki) demonstrated how it is hard to define the 'Chinese consumer': huge differences can be found between consumers living in coastal cities compared with those living in the inner China, or between consumers living in big cities and those in small cities or in rural areas and even among consumers living in the three tiers of cities. In the case study by Menival and Han, consumers of two big cities, Beijing and Shanghai, associated different attributes and meanings to wine: more relied on cultural and social aspects in the former, more focused on intrinsic quality and brand promotion in the latter.

China is not one whole; it is rather a grouping of multiple heterogeneous regional markets which retain their own market structure in terms of history, climate, economic development, education, income and technology. Mazzinghi focused her attention on some implications for business related to the regional differences in the structure and management of the distribution channels.

Therefore, when researchers or practitioners want to approach China, they should take into account the multiple regional differences in distribution channels, intermediaries, culture and preferences.

Future research should focus on the effect of regionalization, globalization, or indigenization in Chinese wine markets again preferring an analytical approach rather than an exploratory one.

RELATIONSHIPS IN THE SUPPLY CHAIN

The effective management of the wine supply chain in the Chinese market is closely connected to the quality of business relationships, resulting from both professional and personal factors. The cultural context suggests the definition of a 'Chinese way' in relationship management characterized by a mix of 'flexibility, improvization, inexperience and speed' (Mazzinghi).

In winery-intermediary relationships, Loureiro and Cunha pointed out some key factors involving personal bonds between the counterparties: trust; direct and frequent contacts and physical participation in meetings; interdependence and cooperation; understanding of the Chinese business culture; patience and resilience. The chapter by Atkin and Cholette, through a case study, analyzed the importance of personal relationships in ensuring the quality of the product through temperature monitoring. Interviewed wineries recognized the problem, mainly from a technological viewpoint, but little is being done to face this issue from a relational viewpoint. Personal engagement and coordination in the compliance of the cold-chain would promote exchange of information and new solutions which could be perceived as positive signals by buyers, turning this problem into a competitive advantage.

According to Bouzdine-Chameeva et al., French producers are benefiting from high reputation due to origin brands and product quality in the Chinese market, but these key arguments for selling their wine will not be sufficient in future. The successful case study by Hanf and Winter demonstrated indeed that an entrepreneur's market knowledge, personal involvement and experience are pivotal in order to enter and develop a new market, even for a small business proposing wines almost unknown to the average Chinese consumer. Some suggested key factors for successful penetration of the Chinese market are: knowledge of local culture and customs; compliance with Chinese etiquette during negotiation; finding a product as a 'door opener' and sub-brands and private labels for trade intermediaries; carefully selecting importers and getting information about their trade networks; building strong, personal, trustworthy relationships with a long-term vision (Bouzdine-Chameeva; Hanf and Winter; Mazzinghi).

Future research should contribute to improve knowledge on the characteristics of a quality relationship and how it can be evaluated. Significant financial efforts are made by wineries and their associations, and also by government (e.g., the national programs supporting promotion in 'third countries' within the European wine CMO) in order to penetrate new business networks or to promote product and territorial brands. Future research should offer criteria for allocating investments and assessing the effectiveness of private and public investments taking into account the individual characteristics of the country and the audience.

THE DRIVING FORCE OF E-COMMERCE AND SOCIAL MEDIA

Corsi et al.'s chapter investigated an aspect of the Chinese wine market that is still little explored. Retailer reputation has many implications for the supply chain: downstream towards the consumers to better understand their decision-making process, and upstream towards the wine producers to develop their relational skills.

In consumer—retailer relationships, competition in China is developing on different levels: between offline and online retailing; within offline retailers, between large stores (with competitive advantages in wine selection and product assortment) and local stores (preferred because of their better customer service); and within online retailers characterized by different price strategies, reliability and services. Corsi et al's study found out that there is no one, single retailer distinctively capturing the market and consumers potentially use all store image dimensions to choose the point of sale.

Therefore, in the winery—retailer relationship, the presence of the product in the market becomes a complex decision, because the winery should consider many commercial networks simultaneously and at the same time ensure consistency of supply and prices (Boudzine-Chameeva et al.). The competitive power of a local store in terms of service and relational ability with buyers can be beneficial for small producers. In this case, the key factor is the careful evaluation of achievable market targets and the establishment of a good relationship with the local partner. Conversely, wineries already investing in marketing and promotion should definitely consider the major retail channels (Corsi et al.). For these businesses, an online store also ensures a wide audience. E-commerce is driving China's wine sales: according to Wine Intelligence[4] one consumer out of two buys wine online. With more than 21 million online wine buyers China is the largest and fastest growing e-commerce market in the world. Online retailers are working on pricing strategies and website navigability and this will further impact the development of this channel (Corsi et al.).

The current governmental efforts to make China a global e-commerce leader will generate a great potential for e-commerce and social media communication both in tier-three cities and inland areas.

Consequently, future research should focus on the development of online wine marketing and communication. Types of information and activities, relationships between the several tools and platforms (websites, blogs, social media; e-commerce, online databases and apps, online advertising and so on), and their impact on consumer engagement and buying decisions, are still under-investigated issues. Collaborations between Western and Chinese researchers could overcome the language barrier and foster a beneficial exchange of knowledge with both academic and professional implications.

THE POTENTIAL OF THE DOMESTIC WINE PRODUCTION

China is deploying its production and economic potential also in the global wine industry as one of the main wine-producing countries in the world: this trend is foreseen to be positive also in the future even if the anticorruption measures are still negatively affecting its development (Fang et al.; Zeng and Szolnoki). Production is gradually shifting from the eastern to western wine-producing regions. The favourable characteristics of these areas for grape cultivation will further help the quality improvement of domestic wines, which are increasingly meeting the quality-driven demand of the upper-middle class. The domestic wine industry is also benefiting from an increased consumer attention on value-for-money, fuelled by the anticorruption measures on one hand, and by

---

[4] http://www.drinksint.com/news/fullstory.php/aid/6425/Nearly_half_Chinese_imported_wine_drinkers_purchase_online.html [Accessed 3 Aug. 2016]; https://www.thedrinksbusiness.com/2016/08/e-commerce-driving-chinas-wine-sales/; the drinks business [Accessed 3 Aug. 2016]

the interest in wine knowledge on the other hand. For foreign wines, the decreasing sales of luxury and high-end wines are implying an increasing level of competition, not only in price, with domestic production. The latter have also a higher competitive power in inland areas of the country which are more difficult to reach for foreign producers.

The greater the Chinese consumer involvement with wine, the greater is the growth of the domestic wine industry, and therefore its relevance on the global wine sector. Technological as well as know-how and qualitative gaps are gradually reducing. It seems that the full participation of the Chinese wine industry in the global wine market is only a matter of time.

CHINESE MOVEMENT INTO THE WIDER WORLD AS TOURISTS OR AS INVESTORS

The development of the wine market in China is in turn generating a growing attention on this sector as an attractor of investments, and as a generator of value-added products and prestigious images, enlarging interest beyond the domestic supply chain in the global wine scenario.

Two contributions of this book have investigated these issues. They focused on very different contexts: Chinese outward foreign direct investment in vineyards and wineries (Curran and Thorpe) and Chinese tourism in a western urban destination (Capitello et al.). Both studies analyzed the specific nature, challenges and opportunities of these phenomena, and found that the interest in the product and its image is the main driving factor for both tourists and investors.

Since the beginning of the Millennium, Chinese companies have initiated a stage of overseas investment and in recent years this trend has also affected the wine industry. There is increasing pressure towards the production of value-added goods in driving Chinese investments abroad[5], and this is confirmed also by Curran and Thorpe. They found that the main motivating factors in investing overseas are: to better seize business opportunities in the domestic wine markets; to achieve reliability and security of wine supply; and to leverage the prestige associated with this industry. In Bordeaux the 'appellation' reputation is the main purpose of Chinese investment; in Australia cementing existing business relationships and access to residency prevail. The impact of anticorruption measures

[5] Taylor, R. (2014). *The Globalization of Chinese Business*. Oxford: Chandos Publishing.

revealed the vulnerability of these investments; however there has been no sign of disinvestments and increasingly companies are more professionally run (Curran and Thorpe).

The chapter by Capitello et al. investigated the different components of the image of a city located in a traditional wine-producing region in the eyes of Chinese tourists. The Chinese tourist is an emerging and already promising target for many western destinations, but his/her expectations as a visitor to an urban destination as well as his/her interest in wine tourism activities in Western countries are still almost unknown. The case study highlighted that the wine supply is perceived as an essential tourism component of the city which is able to affect the choice of the tourist. The intrinsic link to place characterizing the wine and tourism industries can be the key argument in bonding territorial wine brands and urban destination brands in the Chinese tourist's imagery and experience. This argument can use on-site to activate interactions between the multiple interests of visitors (local wine, historical landmarks, cultural attractions, entertainment events, experiential and emotional activities, etc.). It can also use in the target market to promote a bundling of products and services with a higher potential value in terms of reputation and salience than its single components.

Finally, the analysis of all these key points addressed throughout the book allows us to identify the factors that could influence, to a greater extent than others, the development of the Chinese wine market and enrich the mosaic of world wine industry in the future: consumer engagement with different wines, brands and territories, diversification of Chinese wine markets, penetration of e-commerce, the role of social media for consumers, online marketing strategies adopted by the wineries, and a steady increase of the quality of the domestic wine. These issues must, above all, form the focus of both wine business practitioners in their future dealings with the country and academics in the further research which they will pursue.

INDEX

Printed in the United States
By Bookmasters